Further praise for *The Chair*

"[A] lively, acerbic survey of the history, physiology, and sociology of that object in which most of us spend too much time."
—Peter Hellman, *Metropolitan Home*

"Galen Cranz illuminates the inexplicable in the obvious, making the word 'furniture' seem somehow inadequate."
—*Flaunt*

"An inexhaustible subject deserves an indispensable book. At last the chair has one that brings together the insights of design history, social science, medicine, and ergonomics for us, the sedentary masses. Galen Cranz's own body-mind approach is an important new perspective sure to provoke discussion and research. Don't sit at home—or work—without it."
—Edward Tenner, author of *Why Things Bite Back: Technology and the Revenge of Unintended Consequences*

"A concise, multidisciplinary gem. . . . Cranz's clear book—half survey, half polemic—may successively delight, instruct and alarm professors in their endowed chairs, designers at their slanted tables, drivers in drivers' seats, parents with carseats and, of course, the armchair intellectual."
—*Publishers Weekly*

"[A] lively social-historical study and body-based design critique of the chair. . . . Bit by bit, [Cranz] provocatively advances . . . her thesis."
—Diana Scott, *San Francisco Bay Guardian*

"The success of Cranz's case can be measured in direct proportion to your discomfort as you read."
—Philip Nobel, *Metropolis*

"*The Chair* is important in that it takes a ubiquitous artifact and gears a meditation and a discourse around it. The book is thoughtfully organized, easily accessible, yet weaves in much complexity."
—Mike Brill, professor of architecture, State University of New York at Buffalo

"Cranz continues to occupy an unusual and valuable position at the forefront of our field, owing to the creative connections she establishes between architecture and related disciplines: environmental sustainability and human physiology. She makes the connections with grace and dexterity, maneuvering agilely between areas of thought not usually linked."

—Denise Scott Brown, principal,
Venturi Scott Brown and Associates

"Galen Cranz's work on the culture of chairs is unique, creative, scholarly, and has the potential for being a landmark piece of work."

—Irwin Altman, Distinguished Professor of Psychology,
University of Utah

"A soundly intellectual perspective on the chair. . . . Provocative yet thoughtful, with more than a kernel of truth." —*Booklist*

"*The Chair* is uncommonly exciting work. The way in which Dr. Cranz has creatively and successfully combined ideas and facts from sociology, history, biology, Alexander Technique, art history, and carpentry is simply breathtaking."

—Donald N. Levine, Peter B. Ritzma Professor of Sociology,
University of Chicago

"Galen Cranz probably knows more about the complexities of chair design and has a better grasp of the literature and theory than any other person in the United States."

—Robert Gutman, professor emeritus of sociology,
Rutgers University

ALSO BY GALEN CRANZ

The Politics of Park Design: A History of Urban Parks in America

RETHINKING CULTURE, BODY, AND DESIGN

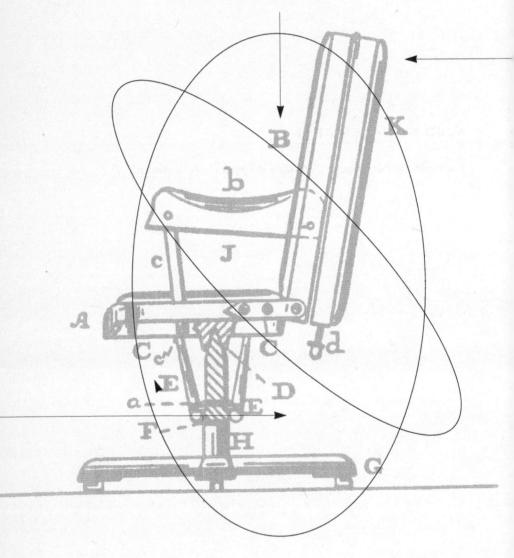

The Chair

GALEN CRANZ, PH.D.

w. w. norton & company

new york • london

First published as a Norton paperback 2000

For information about permission to reproduce selections from this book, write to Permissions, W. W. Norton & Company, Inc., 500 Fifth Avenue, New York, NY 10110.

The text of this book is composed in Garamond #3
with the display set in Banque and Frutiger Black
Composition and manufacturing by The Haddon Craftsmen, Inc.
Book design by Judith Stagnitto Abbate/ABBATE DESIGN

Library of Congress Cataloging-in-Publication Data

Cranz, Galen.
     The chair : rethinking culture, body, and design / Galen Cranz.
         p. cm.
     Includes bibliographical references and index.
     ISBN 0-393-04655-9
     ISBN 0-393-31955-5pbk.
     1. Chairs. 2. Chair design. I. Title.
TS886.5.C45C73 1998
749'.32—dc21   97-43898
                                                         CIP

W. W. Norton & Company, Inc.
500 Fifth Avenue, New York, N.Y. 10110
www.wwnorton.com

W. W. Norton & Company Ltd.
Castle House, 75/76 Wells Street, London W1T 3QT

5 6 7 8 9 0

ontents

List of Illustrations

Acknowledgments

The Notes and Bibliography for this work offer insight into its intellectual roots, but they cannot describe all the sources and influences of a study that draws on as many realms of experience as this one does. Here I would like to acknowledge and honor those institutions and individuals who have assisted me in both diffuse and specific ways.

In general, teaching sociology to architecture students has helped me move between theory and practice, between idea and form, and for this opportunity I am grateful to the Department of Architecture at the University of California at Berkeley, where I have been teaching since 1975. One year later, a search for ways to keep my body working led me to acupuncture, tai chi, the Alexander Technique, and the world of integrated body-mind philosophy. My deep appreciation to healers and teachers Lam Kong, Thomas Lemens, Rivka Cohen, Howard Moscow, Sally Dan, Mitchell Corwin, Laura Bertele, Patrik Rousselot, Bill Weintraub, Martha Eddy, and my two Alexander peers, Elaine Belle and Claire Creese.

Students in architecture provided the context in which the work of synthesizing social-cultural studies, body-based experiential education, and design could be nurtured. I would particularly like to acknowledge and thank all of those, numbering around fifty, who have taken my seminar, "Designing for the Near-Environment," since 1989. I feel special sentiment for those who worked with me in the early versions of this course, but later students helped me in more focused ways by reading first drafts of every chapter.

The Committee on Research and Humanities Research Grants at UC Berkeley have made it possible for me to hire conscientious research assistants at different stages: Amita Sinha, Canna Patel, David Robinson, Jessica Sewell, Marie-Alice l'Heureux, Denise Hall. A Sabbatical Supplement Grant in 1991 helped me while I was developing the structure for this project. My fellow Kellogg Fellow, Bruce Swain, had enough faith in me and my project to offer useful advice on getting my ideas onto paper.

Several colleagues have made helpful readings of my first drafts: Mel Weber, Clare Marcus, Russ Ellis, Mike Brill, and Karen Franck. Theresa Park, agent and whippersnapper, guided me through the process of shedding the protective covering of academic jargon (and various forms of moral indignation). The Fernwood Community Group in Oakland, unbeknownst to them, helped me find my voice; a memo I wrote to this group of people I had never met set my new standard for balance between information and passion. Colleagues Kathleen James, Mirjana Stevanovic, Leora Auslander, Harvey Molotch, and mentor John Pock commented on Chapters 1 and 2 on social and cultural history; Pamela Lewis, Claire Creese, Michael Ostrow, Michael Salveson, and Martha Eddy helped refine Chapter 4 on an integrated body-mind perspective. Peter Opsvik and Dr. A. C. Mandal were generous in sharing their knowledge about seating reform with me. Twelve anonymous reviewers representing specializations in furniture history, furniture design, architectural design, and ergonomics stimulated me to clarify my reasoning at various points. Finally, at W. W. Norton, Amy Cherry—the editor who championed this project—helped me discriminate between the essential and the extraneous; Ann Adelman polished the manuscript through rigorous and thoughtful copyediting. Thanks to Gail Sher, Jane Heirich, Gary Brown, Mark Kmicikiewicz, Albert Pfeiffer, and Thea Cranz, I have made several grammatical, factual, and typographic corrections in the paperback version.

Friends and family have accommodated and encouraged my devotion to this project for many years. Personal thanks to Susan Green, Don Jacot, Ken Cole, "Toes," and Phyllis Cole.

A funny thing about a Chair:
You hardly ever think it's *there*.

—from "The Chair," by Theodore Roethke[1]

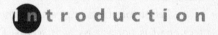ntroduction

We spend much of our waking lives in a chair. In our sedentary culture, we each have a choice of over two dozen seats throughout the routine of a day—in our dining rooms and kitchens, living rooms and bedrooms, studies and sewing rooms, patios and decks, cars, subways, and buses, offices and schools, waiting rooms, movies, and restaurants. We touch chairs not just with our hands but with our whole bodies. Yet despite their intimate place in our lives, we know little about them and their effects on us, physically and mentally.

Without a doubt, their effects are profound. What is true of the chair is true of all the artifacts we create. We design them; but once built, they shape us. As sitting in chairs spread to the common person over the centuries, it left its mark on the human body and human consciousness. The chair offers a glimpse into our collective ideas about status and honor, comfort and order, beauty and efficiency, discipline and relaxation. As our ideas change, so do our chairs.

Because our current ideas about seating originated in the past, understanding contemporary chairs requires an appreciation of their social history, ancient and modern. Their development as objects of art also deserves attention since part of our emotional relationship with them derives from the way they mix style and status. By comparing the use of chairs in

Western culture to practices in cultures without chairs, we will find that chairs are true cultural artifacts, not, as we often imagine, mere extensions of our bodies.

This book is part cultural criticism, part design study, and part celebration of the human body. It offers a new paradigm for thinking about chairs. It is a freewheeling effort to pull together insights from a variety of sources—the humanities, the arts, the physical and social sciences—for the purpose of thinking creatively and imaginatively about how we might want to live. Looking at the chair this way contributes to our understanding of the near environment, that ubiquitous realm that we touch with our bodies. New ideas from the field of ergonomics are changing chair design. Even newer ideas come from holistic health approaches, which insist that mind and body are one. This study will discuss both.

People often ask me, what is the perfect chair? But defining the perfect chair is not as easy as it seems. Despite the wide range of specialties involved in seating design—human engineering and ergonomic research, rehabilitative medicine and market research—basic concepts of beauty and comfort elude definition. In part, this is because both beauty and comfort are mixed up with status.

The chair a person sits in often reveals his or her social status, which then takes priority over beauty or comfort. The chair comes to represent a role, so that people are careful not to sit in others' chairs. Vice President Bush was always careful not to sit in President Reagan's chair when Reagan was out of the country. When we hear the tale of Goldilocks and the Three Bears as children, part of the sense of excitement and danger lies in our response to the keen observation and disapproval implicit in "Who's been sitting in my chair?"

A chair can also come to stand for a whole person or to express that person's individuality. Photographers sometimes compose a man's portrait by seating him in his special chair; decorators and moviemakers choose chairs to convey information about their power. Journalists use chairs to paint pictures of people—telling us, for example, that Steve McQueen was "sockless and in sandals, sitting in a wicker chair with the cuffs of his khakis rolled up," while Laurie Anderson's voice intoning a chilling little text was accompanied by a hard chair and a bare light.[2] Poets have been known to build on our association between a chair and a particular person; over a century ago, Eliza Cook evoked the memory of her mother by cherishing the old armchair in which her mother used to sit. Painters often use the image of a chair to stand for a person, or to show something about the person's life.[3] By the same token, when a visitors center gives us a chance to sit in or at least stand near a celebrity's chair—Eleanor Roosevelt's or Andy Warhol's—we feel that it allows us to imagine the world from their perspective.

Professional image consultants advise that the "wrong" chair, just like the wrong clothes, could be perceived as too lowbrow or too feminine. Some people, for this very reason, experience "chair anxiety" and delay making any choice at all, even after they have designed and built their own homes![4] But for every person who seeks the right chair for the right social message, or even for the perfect ergonomic fit, we can probably find another who clings to his or her old chair purely for the mood of retreat and psychological ease. Oblivious to professionals and the Joneses, they might join Eliza Cook when she wrote: "I love it, I love it; and who shall dare to chide me for loving that old armchair?"

Chairs can express other moods, as well—even anger and rage. Sports coaches—and players—have been known to vent their frustration by hurling chairs. In prisons, high school cafeterias, and action films, good guys and bad use chairs as weapons.

The mere provision of a chair traditionally communicates compassion, just as its absence communicates disrespect and lack of empathy. Many executions in the United States are performed in a chair. Technically speaking, a deadly shock or lethal injection could work as easily on a person strapped to a table. Since even somebody condemned to death is granted the dignity of a chair, those who have a right to expect appreciation and respect are understandably miffed when someone fails to offer them one. Missing chairs were one of several signs of disrespect experienced by the Royal Ballet visiting Monte Carlo some years ago. A troupe of twelve dancers, after being ushered into a back room, found only nine chairs and insufficient food and drink, which caused embarrassment all around— enough to make the news.[5]

Certainly, manipulating the number of chairs at a gathering is one way to regulate what happens socially. In his life at Walden Pond, Thoreau chose only three chairs—one for solitude, two for company, and three for society. In an interview with busy women about how they save time, Gloria Steinem said that she might deliberately run a meeting without any chairs whatsoever. Social scientists have proved that arranging seats in rows facing one direction has very different consequences for social interaction and the flow of information than arranging them in a circle. Lining up two chairs side by side, face to face, or at right angles to one another produces three different kinds of communication. At airports, we might be grateful that the chairs are lined up so that we do not have to interact with strangers. In contrast, if we want to interrogate someone or look deeply into his or her eyes, we would be more likely to sit directly in front. And when we want the sociable option of looking at someone directly and also being able to look away, we prefer sitting at right angles, which is why the maître d's of most restaurants seat couples at the corner of a table.

Teachers, restaurant designers, and office managers act on this kind of social information every day without relying on any codified social policy. But the health implications of seating might require the formulation of public policy, because lower back pain is second only to the common cold as a reason for absenteeism from work, which has been estimated to cost $70 billion yearly.[6] While sedentary work is the obvious culprit, more specifically the apparatus th-- ------- +h- ------ted body is to blame. Those who set policies for selecti   hey pay lip service to comfort, often choose chairs tha   cheap but not adjustable to the individual. But where i   ,,airs that cost money in lost time, repetitive stress inju   ?

Let's face the conside   ill chair sitting is, actually, harmful. Experts report an   blems over the last century that correlates directly w   umber of hours we spend seated. We may be out of touch with this reality; psychologically, we may feel a chair is comfortable even as it is harming us physiologically. So, rather than face the possibility that chairs as such may be harming us, we spend more and more time and money trying to find or create ideal ones.

Certainly those businesses that design, manufacture, and sell office furniture perpetuate the cultural myth that a better chair could solve our back problems—many of which were induced by the practice of chair sitting in the first place. They promote the chair as the prime weapon against the "dangers lurking in today's high-tech office." The substantial investment in ergonomic office furniture could possibly be better directed toward inventing an entirely new system to promote movement at work and at schools.

This perspective might tempt us to conclude that chairs are a lost cause, a wrong turn humankind took millennia ago. But the fact is that sitting in chairs is now deeply ingrained in Western culture, and even prized as a symbol of modernization around the world. So even if chairs should—from a purist point of view—be abandoned because they create so many problems, from a pragmatic point of view we need to explore how they can be fixed, or at least improved. Doing so will require a fundamental rethinking of the concept of comfort.

Since this book talks about both old ideas and new ones, history and advocacy are intrinsically connected. Mine is a selective view—of history and the science of ergonomics—based on my many years of experience with the Alexander Technique and other body-mind disciplines.[7] My direct experience and my observations of others set me off on a fascinating quest: Where did chairs come from? What is a comfortable chair? Why are so many chairs *un*comfortable? What concerns shape chair design? Eventually, a hypothesis emerged that I never expected. At the same time, examining other cultures and our own past helped me to understand and appreciate how Westerners got themselves so attached to chairs. That understanding may enable us to envision better ways of living, ultimately affecting the design of everything from car seats and baby strollers to dining-room chairs and tables, offices and schools.

I invite you to take a seat and start reading. But be warned that you might find your chair getting less comfortable as you progress through this book. Certainly I hope that your "position" will have changed.

PART I

hy Do We Use Chairs?

Why do we have chairs, where did they come from, and why do we continue to sit on them? How have they become so fundamental that we take their presence for granted? They did not originate as a straightforward response to the bends at our ankles, knees, and hips. Biology, physiology, and anatomy have less to do with our chairs than do pharaohs, kings, and executives. Part I shows how the chair has become a way of displaying hierarchy in complex societies.

Chapter 1 turns to history and sociology for an understanding of the origins of chairs and their evolving social purposes. Ancient chairs reflected the relationship of power between rulers and ruled; chairs in today's homes, offices, and schools also elaborate differences between men and women, bosses and employees, young and old.

Why do chairs look the way they do? Chapter 2 explores the idea that chairs are carriers of style, through which we differentiate ourselves from others. Sculptors and architects have always been interested in the chair as a sculptural object. With artistic license, they treat chairs as a sculptural problem of intersecting planes and forms. Chair design poses teething problems for students, presents an opportunity for seasoned architects to take advantage of lulls in their practice, and forms part of the fashion for designing all the details of an environment to be consistent with its larger architectural ideas. Chairs are the favorite of contemporary Western architects, who love them because they are both anthropomorphic and architectonic. Nearly all of the big names in twentieth-century architecture—Breuer, Mies van der Rohe, Bertoia, Wright, Corbusier, Aalto—have designed famous chairs that we live with today.

Chapter 1

How Chairs Evolved

LIFE WITHOUT CHAIRS

In 1852, an English colonialist working in India voiced his complaints about the local workmen. He was particularly irritated and offended that blacksmiths, carpenters, and masons squatted to work, complaining indignantly, "All work with their knees nearly on a level with their chin: the left hand—when not used as the kangaroo uses his tail to form a tripod—grasps the left knee and binds the trunk to the doubled limbs." This man was not the first or last to liken people who sit on floors to animals. He was more explicit than many about why he found the posture inferior: it suggested "indolence and inefficiency . . . especially irritating to an Englishman," but even more so to one who hires and pays such workmen.

The colonialist tried to force these men to work his way, but they ignored him; so he ordered the anvils on which they worked to be bolted to surfaces at table height. The next day, he was pleased to see them working off the floor. But not for long. He returned the following day to find the men squatting on top of stools in order to reach the anvils. He gave up, reasoning that he could not get workmen to stand while working because of "a deficiency of muscular power in the lower limbs," which he attributed to their not using chairs. Our amateur sociologist speculated that chairs or raised seats were "one of those natural steps toward a higher civilization."[1] He was wrong about that, but right in observing that we are apt to overlook the function of such artifacts until we imagine or experience life without them. Chairs have become second nature to us, virtually indivisible from us—and therefore invisible to us.

In the past century we have come to appreciate, rather than condemn, the way people in other cultures do things. The attitude of a nineteenth-century English colonialist toward Indian workers now strikes us as stuffy and disrespectful. Nevertheless, our lingering ideas about "progress" still tempt us to look down on or misunderstand the habits of others, including how they sit. Take an extreme example: the excitement and disgust Western tourists experience on having to use a squat toilet, even a clean one, for the first time. Though it is an anatomically efficient position for elimination, most visitors feel revulsion, superiority, or some combination of both. Northern Europeans call such toilets "Italian" and Italians call them "Turkish." Either way, this artifact comes from a more "primitive," less developed place.

In the United States, an example of our confused feelings about cultural differences is as near as your local Japanese restaurant. Such restaurants may have tatami mats where diners sit on the floor, but this touch of authenticity can only go so far. Westerners do not generally sit cross-legged or kneeling, so many of these floors have hidden wells under the tables for diners to sit in the classic right-angled posture we are used to. But do we accept this as a cultural difference, created by lifetimes of sitting one way versus another? No, we kid ourselves otherwise, with vague references to some imagined anatomical difference.

We still need anthropologists to remind us that almost everything—including how we hold our bodies—should be understood in its cultural context. The American anthropologist Gordon Hewes has done that for posture. He documented the tremendous variety of recognized postures—over one thousand steady postures—that human beings assume all over the world.[2] The right-angle seated posture is just one example, utilized by only a third to a half of the people in the world. But, you might ask, how can a person rest, eat, or write a letter without a chair? A Chinese might squat to wait for the bus; a Japanese woman might kneel to eat; and an Arab might sit cross-legged to write a letter. Are they forced to sit without chairs simply because they are too poor to own one? People who can afford chairs throughout the Middle East, Asia, Africa, and Polynesia do not necessarily buy them; a common posture in Africa and Australia is what anthropologists call the "Neolithic" stance: the person stands on one leg and plants the sole of the other foot near the knee of the standing leg. As you will see, the reasons for sitting on the floor, on mats, on carpets, platforms, Chinese *k'ang,* or stools stem from cultural traditions rather than economic development.

Hewes emphasized that postural variations are culturally, not anatomically, determined. Sitting, like other postures, is regulated all around the world according to gender, age, and social status. Sitting on the floor with both legs straight out in front is generally a woman's posture, wherever it is found. The cowboy squat—the one used by Indian workmen to the annoyance of British colonists—is mostly a man's, with one knee up.

A particularly common alternative posture is sitting Turkish-style, what Westerners call cross-legged, or sometimes tailor-fashion. In Turkish homes, traditional "divans," from which we get one of our terms for couches, are deep, wide, and firm enough to permit sitting in this way. The divans are low wooden platforms with pads and bolsters, built into a room called a "sofa" for receiving visitors and enjoying oneself with family. From this we have derived another of our terms for couches.

In mosques, Turks sit and kneel on richly carpeted floors. Carpets are butted one against the other, even overlapping—but never displayed in a sea of gleaming hardwood. Muslim religious practices are refreshingly sensitive to bodily experience. Carpets do more than protect the knees; all who enter a mosque (or home) take off their shoes, ostensibly so that no dirt is brought onto the carpets where people will put their hands and faces. But going barefoot stimulates the nerves of the soles, in turn refreshing the whole body. The bending and stretching ritually required five times a day is also good for the spine, a useful counterpoint to constant upright posture. The ritual use of water inside the mosque to cleanse the nose, neck, forearms, and ankles was initially practical in dry, sandy climates, but refreshes the skin in any climate.

In India today, especially rural India, many of the activities Westerners would pursue in chairs, from sewing to university physics seminars, Indians perform while seated on the floor.[3] Ergonomics researchers have attempted to measure the physiological effects of performing tasks this way; for example, the impact on the heart rate of making chapatis while squatting on the floor. Surprisingly, the effect is aerobic—so I no longer worry so much about lack of exercise for those women confined to family courtyards.[4]

Posture is regulated symbolically worldwide, whether on the floor, on a stool, or in a chair. *(Fig. 1)* In Africa, initiates use stools in special ceremonies to rest, eat, or watch dances. Stools are viewed as extremely personal, so that one would not even use a relative's in the same household. They were associated with leadership; when a king died, his stool was preserved in order to preserve the prosperity of the kingdom. When the European-style chair was first introduced to Africa by the Portuguese in 1481, the Africans quickly recognized it as a signifier of prestige and power.[5]

All around the world, the chair and chair sitting has become a symbol—and sometimes direct evidence—of Westernization. An American traveler gave this account of his visit to a remote mountain valley in Afghanistan in the late 1960s:

Figure 1. Contemporary Tibetans live comfortably on the floor with carpets and low furniture.

I had a good look at my first Kafiristani as he passed. He was fair-skinned with grey or blue eyes, very Western looking in-deed. "Looks like a farangi," I said to Sarkal, forgetting that I was a "Frank" myself. "Yes, many of them do. People say that they are descended from the people of Alexander, but I don't know. They sit on chairs, like the Franks, though."[6]

In turn, Westernization has become a symbol of modernization and progress. Hence, journalists equate Japan's economic miracle with its rise from the floor to chairs.[7] Chrome kitchenette sets crowd Japanese apart-ments—sometimes unused by the inhabitants, who continue to sit on the floor, but powerful symbols nonetheless. Conversely, when Gandhi wanted to make a point about the importance of retaining traditional culture, he chose to sit cross-legged on the floor, self-consciously rejecting a chair and the modernism that goes with it.

In cultures outside the West, then, the specific connotations of chairs are different, but the chair is still used to communicate status dif-ferences. When it was introduced to China in the second century A.D., the Chinese called it the "barbarian [their word for anything foreign] bed." It connoted informal use because of its years of association with military camps, temporary travel furniture, and garden use. It was more like a cot, and for years was never used indoors. People sat on it tailor-fashion, show-ing contempt, indifference, or extreme confidence. Nine hundred years later, a new seating type evolved: a folding chair with a back. This chair then became acceptable and was used by all, but the language of dignity and honor retained the use of the term "mat" rather than "chair."[8] The Chinese are noteworthy for having integrated the chair into their lives without letting it dominate. In contemporary mainland China, people sit mostly on backless stools in schools, most workplaces, and the home—including when dining.[9] *(Fig. 2)* One interesting exception is that on a parent's sixtieth birthday, he or she is accorded the special honor of being asked to dine in a chair.[10]

By and large Westerners, scientists and humanists alike, have gen-erated few alternatives to the chair-and-table culture. We are, in a sense, locked into it. After all, even our architecture is shaped by chairs. The height of window openings, for example, is determined by our sitting about 18 inches off the floor. Furthermore, chair imagery pervades our sym-

Figure 2. Often Chinese schoolchildren sit on stools or benches, like the ones lined up against the wall in this photo, rather than on chairs with back support.

bolic life. University professors hold "chairs"—positions funded especially for research and teaching in a designated subject. Departments everywhere have "chairmen," "chairwomen," or better yet, "chairpersons." When a person has to choose between two jobs—say, acting and dancing—we sometimes say he cannot sit between two chairs. County seats, district seats, embassy seats, a private seat, seats on the stock exchange are all metaphors for position, social role, and power, but the concrete object from which the metaphors have evolved is a chair. A hot seat is never a sofa, might possibly be a stool, but is most likely a chair. Sigmund Freud was famous for his couch; but today the reflection and conversation of therapy is more closely associated with chairs.[11] In Christian religious communities, an empty chair represents Christ, who may be understood to be present in the person of an unexpected guest; this convention has dual purposes, one symbolic and the other practical, if an unexpected guest arrives.

CHAIRS THROUGH THE AGES

Since not all peoples sit in chairs, why do we? The answer to that question may never be known, but historians do know a fair amount about the early history of chair use in the West. One thing is certain: our chair habit was created, modified and nurtured, reformed and democratized in response to social—not genetic, anatomical, or even physiological—forces.

The purposes of designed objects change over time, just as the meanings of words do. Etymology always offers insight into contemporary usage, just as history helps us understand why things are the way they are today. The word "chair" comes from the Greek language, a contraction of *cathedra*—in turn a compound of *kata,* meaning "down," and *hedra,* from "to sit." A chair is a piece of furniture with a back, and usually four legs, on which one person sits. But so is a throne.

However, the word "throne" has a different origin. It comes from the Indo-European base *dher,* meaning "to hold or support." The throne supports, while the chair is a place to sit down. A throne suggests the palanquins on which a potentate might be carried, while the underlying meaning of a chair is quite different. Physically, almost anyone can sit down, whereas only a very privileged few can be carried. Thus, a chair is more common and ordinary than a throne. From the beginning of recorded history, two types of chairs developed: the upright throne, and the more relaxed *clismos,* a chair with a modestly inclined back. Today, we mock the lowliest chair of all, the toilet, by giving it the term of greater privilege, "the throne." President Lyndon Johnson held early morning audiences seated on such a throne.

Neither thrones nor chairs originated in classical Greece; they are far older. Chair sitting was already a widespread practice in the ancient Egypt of 2850 B.C. The oldest physical chairs we have come from the tomb of the young pharaoh Tutankhamen, who died in about 1352 B.C. Ancient Egyptian furniture lasted because of the dry climate and because the wood was encased in gold. But paintings, carvings, and hieroglyphs on temples and papyrus all show that chairs were used by many people, not only royalty, with rank determining who could sit in whose presence. Whether royal or common, ancient Egyptians did not use chairs as much as we do. For example, scribes sat on the floor to do much of the accounting and record keeping. Chair sitting continued into Islamic, medieval Egypt; by A.D. 650, Egyptians were routinely using chairs and stools in their homes.[12]

What about that other great river valley, the Euphrates? These two highly developed civilizations flourished at roughly the same time, and they had interchanges with one another. Mesopotamian civilization arose in a more humid climate, where wood and rush rot easily, so no actual examples of its chairs have survived. But carvings on stone funerary monuments (called stelae) show frequent chair use by kings and in domestic scenes with attention to rank. The Assyrian language has two different words for *generic seats* (stools and benches) and *chairs* (seat with a back). So chairs were significant in Mesopotamia as well as in Egypt.[13]

Did these early civilizations invent the chair or were chairs in use before the societies flourished? Just how far back do chairs go? According to experts on Paleolithic times (the Old Stone Age), no existing cave paintings anywhere in the world include chairs.[14] Before the last ice age, humans lived in caves or tents as nomadic hunters and gatherers who are thought to have revered the animals they hunted. The animals in their paintings are colorful, animated, dimensional. The human beings are few and far between; when they do appear, they are sticklike. Occasionally human tools are included, and they are even more sketchy and feeble in comparison to the vivid animals. But no chairs, or even stools, have been identified. Cave paintings depict actions and movement, possibly rituals, which might explain the absence of chairs in these pictures. So, we will probably never know if chairs existed in 40,000 B.C. before the last ice age.

But after the ice age, during the New Stone (Neolithic) Age around 10,000–4000 B.C., chairs did leave their mark. That was the age of flint tools and permanent stone houses, part of a settled way of life, with furniture. The archeological digs of building interiors and drawings of their reconstruction show benches and ledges for sleeping and sitting. Most intriguing of all, archeologists of southeastern Europe, the former Yugoslavia and Bulgaria, have found a large number of pottery models about two inches high of human figures, all of them female, some of them seated on chairs.[15] Their relaxed, reclining posture communicates without doubt that they are not giving birth. *(Fig. 3)*

Besides providing the earliest evidence of use, these models are also the first example of the chair as a symbol of elevated status. But why only women? And why are they seated on chairs? One school of thought speculates that

Figure 3. Clay models of full-figured females seated on four-legged chairs with backs indicate that chair sitting was a part of Neolithic culture.

Neolithic societies may have been matrifocal—even though Fred played a bigger role than Wilma in *The Flintstones.* A settled way of life focused on women because managing crops in relation to water and seasons was primarily their work. Women were doubly fertile, the producers of babies and agricultural products. Hence, female fertility symbols dominate the representations of this period. In some Neolithic cultures, women's graves have ritual objects placed within them, while men's graves do not. Depicting women on chairs was probably yet another way to heighten or reinforce their status.

Because of its importance in both matrifocal and patriarchal cultures, we can conclude that the chair—the seat with a back for a single person—is a powerful symbol, potent enough to be appropriated by the most influential group or groups in a society as a way to communicate their significance. Yet, what was it about the chair that gave its sitter status? Or, put another way, what was it about the floor, a stump, stool, or bed that made those things inadequate for the purposes served by chairs?

Chairs are an improvement over what came before them—if Henry Petroski, the historian of engineering design at Duke University, is right that form follows failure.[16] Being off the ground makes chair sitting different from floor sitting but not different from stools or benches. The chair generally holds only one person at a time, so it acknowledges the individual, unlike raised benches, sofas, beds, or platforms, which can accommodate two or more. Finally, chairs differ from stools because the chairback can display decoration and, if large enough, frame the sitter from the front view as a throne does. Thus, most chairs have directionality, while most stools do not.

Thinking about the differences between stools and chairs, early experiments with communication in small groups come to mind. An American sociologist named Alex Bavelas examined what happened to information when it was passed directly from one group member to another versus when it first had to be passed to a group leader.[17] He set up boards between individuals to block communication by sight or sound to anyone but the leader in the center, and this experimental apparatus was named after him. One can imagine chairs as stools with Bavelas boards attached. From this perspective, chairbacks are like the individual windowpanes in jalousie windows, which allow us to direct incoming breezes; we can direct people's attention by turning chairs in one direction or another. Stools, without directing backs, promote a star or network pattern of communication, whereas chairs promote a centralized or pyramidal pattern of communication. Obviously, stools lend themselves to more democratic, egalitarian social life and chairs to more hierarchical social structures. The back also can serve as a rest, which tells the lucky occupant he or she deserves to relax. The form of the chair literally expresses high status; it separates, and elaborates the separation, providing distinction, while it legitimizes support of the occupant's whole physical and psychological being.

We may never know when or where the first chairs originated, but we know that they are older than the period of recorded history when most furniture histories begin. The existence of chairs in Neolithic times raises new questions about the origin of chairs in classical antiquity—Egypt, Greece, and Rome. Egyptian thrones were of two types. The most common in depictions of royalty was planar and right-angled; the second type, with curved seat and back, came later and was probably the precursor to the Greek *clismos.* Does the *clismos* represent recumbent ease and the throne upright authority? Western civilization may have both because our classical culture embodies the fusion of two cultures—matrifocal agriculturalists and patriarchal nomadic invaders.

Yet another possible interpretation is that the throne has more to do with the sacred function of kings and pharaohs as links to the gods than with patriarchal social order. Sculptors may have depicted pharaohs upright in thrones because erectness was recognized as a necessary part of the path of connecting with a higher plane. Pharaohs were supposed to perfect themselves as evidence that it is humanly possible to connect with the forces (which Egyptians called "neters") that make up the universe. Accordingly, their posture could indicate not only social rank but also the cultivation of self-awareness. Transhuman consciousness has been recognized in all meditation traditions from China, India, and the Middle East. Keeping the spine erect and self-supporting, with the head lifted on the tip of the spine, is an essential means to this end. Thus, the pharaohs' uprightness is not unlike the uprightness of the Buddha's posture. The sculpted pharaohs do not lean back on their chairbacks; this is not because their stoneworkers were not skilled enough to depict flowing ease and movement, but rather because autonomous seating has physical, psychological, and ultimately spiritual significance. According to this interpretation, thrones represent not so much patriarchy as spiritual aspiration. By the same token, the *clismos* would not represent matriarchy as much as it represents earthly comfort and ease.

The problem with this interpretation is that one pharaoh slumped! He is the heretic pharaoh Akhenaton, a controversial and mysterious figure in Egyptian history because he tried to convert the country to monotheism before his death in 1362 B.C. His likenesses look inexplicably different from other pharaohs' in that his features are irregular, his face narrow, his nose huge, and his thighs fleshy as a full-figured woman's. But to me he stands out for other reasons. He sits with a rounded pelvis in chairs with curved seats. *(Fig. 4)* Some people think the intent was to show reality, as opposed to the ideal; while others suggest satire. One thing we know for certain: sitting upright without leaning back, without letting the pelvis slide forward as the lower back rolls backward into a C-shaped slump, takes discipline. So, was he telling us that even monks and pharaohs do not live up to the demands of their role every day? Or was he simply more relaxed, more ordinary, or more feminine than any of his predecessors?

No matter how this mystery is ultimately resolved, I venture to say that the Greek *clismos* is an elegant expression of the age-old behavior of slumping. Typically, furniture connoisseurs single out and praise the *clismos,* with its curved back and curved legs, for its grace, ease, and domestic use. *(Fig. 5a and b)* Drawings on pottery art of Greeks sitting in these chairs show people—usually women—reclining on their chairbacks. This relaxed posture—leaning backward while seated—is one that we use today, and maybe one we have used since prehistory. Contemporary scholars view this Greek posture as superior to the upright, unassisted position of the pharaohs, but I

Figure 4. Pharaoh Akhenaton was the first pharaoh to be depicted with a rounded pelvis and lower back.

Figure 5. The clismos *(a)* and the throne *(b)* represent two different types of postures—recumbent ease and upright alertness.

think they fail to appreciate both the long-term stability and the spiritual aspiration associated with uprightness. Mies van der Rohe obviously preferred the elegant slump of the *clismos;* his famous Barcelona chair of 1925 distilled the X-shape in its profile. Advertisers draped flappers into them and these chairs still prohibit upright posture to this day. *(Fig. 6)*

One certainty amid these speculations is that the Greeks adopted a good deal of science and culture from Egypt, including their furniture. Roman furniture, in turn, followed Greek types: a high-backed upright throne for occasions of state, the *clismos* of lighter build with arms for general domestic use, along with stools, footstools, tables, couches, and chests.

In Rome, furniture was sparse by contemporary standards. Even in wealthy homes, people showed their wealth not in the number but in the quality of items, including the precious materials used to make them and special shapes that would express their owner's sensibilities. For all classes

Figure 6. Mies van der Rohe designed this chair for the German pavilion at the 1929 World's Fair in Barcelona, introducing one of Modernism's enduring incongruities between formal purpose and informality of posture.

the bed was the all-purpose piece of furniture, far more important than the chair. Besides sleeping there at night, a Roman would eat, read, write, and socialize on a bed bolstered with matting, cushions, and fabrics. For the poor, such a surface might be as simple as a pallet on a built-in masonry shelf; for the rich, it could be as elaborate as cast bronze or carved wood, local or exotic.[18]

Banquets and dinner parties were organized around couches, called *triclinia,* configured as a U-shape with one side open for the server. More than nine guests required a second configuration. Jesus' Last Supper was a Roman-style banquet, meaning that he too lay down with his disciples "Oriental-style," each person propped up by pillows on one side, and each with a personal napkin. The napkin was primarily used to protect the pillow coverings, but also to take home special tidbits—an ancient version of the doggy bag. Over time the Last Supper has been converted to a table-and-chair event in order to seem more familiar to Western eyes.[19] Passover, by contrast, symbolically expresses Jewish freedom by eating while reclining. A couch and pillows are part of the Seder, a direct legacy from the time when pharaohs reclined while eating and the chair symbolized the oppressed position of the Jews. Part of the ritual is to ask: "Why on this night do we eat reclining?" The answer is, To symbolize freedom, because in Moses' time only free men had the honor of reclining to eat. (*Fig. 7a and b*)

Roman chairs were rare, decorative items of luxury,[20] but even so, the two chair types were maintained. The chair with an upright back, the

Figure 7. Upper-class Romans throughout the Empire ate while reclining, which means that the Last Supper was not a table-and-chair event. *(a)* Outdoor dining room in the House of Caro at Pompeii. *(b)* The earliest surviving image of the Last Supper, a sixth-century mosaic in Ravenna.

thronus, was used for governmental, religious, and scholarly functions. The *cathedra* had a sloping back and was reputed to be especially popular with women. Literature of the day described the indolence of high-class ladies, who reposed in them languidly.[21] (Are there two competing ideas about comfort—one about alertness, the other about rest?)

Within the Roman family itself, these two extremes of posture were tied to status. A family in republican Rome would dine together in the following hierarchy: the father would be served recumbent on a couch, the mother would sit nearby on a chair, while the children would sit on stools (as they did at school), and servants would sit at a separate table with stools.[22] This pattern shows a differentiation of status between male and female, young and old, master and servant. Later, the arrangement changed to include both man and wife on the bed, but children and servants continued to sit. One nobleman, in order to protest the tyrannical rule of Julius Caesar, vowed to eat seated rather than reclined, a vow he kept until he chose the even more drastic protest of suicide.[23]

After the fall of Rome, furniture and its development atrophied for a millennium. The Visigoths and Germanic nomads who sacked Rome had no interest in what the architectural historian Siegfried Giedion, who was a professor at Harvard University in the middle of the twentieth century, called the "instruments of a differentiated culture"—the chairs, statues, baths, inlaid furniture. Instead, he wrote, "Their habit was to squat on the ground, and so it remained."[24] All through the medieval period, people sat in improvised and informal ways, often squatting more than sitting, on the bare floor or on cushions. Individuals sat crowded together, with their bodies touching. Sometimes they sat on storage chests pushed up against the walls of a castle, or took meals on benches, with their backs to the wall. Thus, the few chairs of the time were modeled on other types of furniture: storage chests and possibly choir stalls in churches.[25] The chairs with backs from this period looked literally like storage chests with pieces of wall attached at right angles. *(Fig. 8)* A table was a trestle frame across which boards were laid for meals—hence the phrase "setting the table." Many people sat on three-legged stools. Even the wealthy owned little furniture except a trestle table, a few benches and stools.

The scantiness of the medieval household is usually attributed to the need to move frequently. The feudal household, which included both the

rich and their poorer servants, moved often because of political insecurity and the need to seek protection elsewhere or because landowners had to travel continually to supervise their scattered holdings. Their houses stood virtually empty when the owner was away. In order to avoid theft, furniture was either heavy, immovable, and built into the walls, or freestanding and easy to take apart and move to another place.[26] (The significance of the word for furniture in many European languages, usually a variation on the Latin *mobilis* for "movable," comes from this distinction between built-in and movable pieces.) Finally, classicists remind us that until the Renaissance all people lived with simple furniture because they went to bed at dark and lived outdoors as much as weather permitted.

In any case, folding X-chairs or foldstools were used long before chairs, which remained a rarity. Even the richest houses seldom boasted more than one, reserved exclusively for the master of the household. Massive and stately, it was too heavy to move.[27] No ordinary person would have dared use it.[28] So the trestle and board were set up in front of the chair, rather than vice versa. When we use the title "chairman of the board" today, we are casting a linguistic line back to the time when the leader was important enough to get the stationary chair in front of which a table would be assembled. The relative scarcity of chairs gave them significance in church life as well as in secular life. The highest religious authorities of this era announced their decisions seated in their special chairs—hence the term *ex cathedra*, "from the chair."

The social functions of medieval chairs reflected patriarchal style, power, and authority. Historians concur that throughout the Middle Ages all chairs were "rigid, upright symbols of power and rank."[29] Those entitled to use them sat up; no one sat back. Reclining, warmth, and texture were clearly found elsewhere, probably in the beds where people lived and entertained.

As social conditions changed, chairs changed with them. By the fifteenth century, peace had gradually been restored in Europe, and trade centers and governments had become more centralized. Noblemen, therefore, were not forced to move as often and could concentrate their wealth in their homes. Furniture no longer had to be anchored to the wall. Now chairs moved out into the room, which gave them a freer status.

Around this time, the medieval foldstool evolved into a chair. Light, and easily transported, the new chair was a descendant of the Roman *curule,* a folding campstool used by magistrates. Still endowed with official dignity, it became the seat of kings, important laymen, and ecclesiastics. Additional honor was achieved by placing it on a dais with a footstool and cushions, probably with a canopy above.[30] A more common type of chair, a three-legged stool—with peg legs set directly into the seat and a narrow, slablike back, sometimes curved—evolved around 1490.[31] Several preserved from the Strozzi Palace in Florence look alike, meaning that, at least in that part of Europe, the chair lost its rare, honorific value since it was used in series.

By the 1600s, decoration had become part of the design of ordinary chairs, chiefly in imitation of clothing fashion. Throughout this century, furniture in Holland, France, England, and Germany became more stylish. In England, the change took place during the Restoration period from 1660 to 1770, when carving and inlaid decoration began to appear on chairs. Foreign influences on the decoration of chairs came from India via Portuguese, Dutch, and British colonists, and from Japan, where lacquering captured the attention of European furniture makers.[32]

The term "armchair" was first adopted during the seventeenth century to distinguish chairs with arms from backstools, also known as side chairs or single chairs.[33] During this period, chairs became more common as life became more sociable. Padded armchairs with high backs and decorative knobs at the tops of the uprights began to appear in the wealthier homes. The folding X-shaped chair survived from the Middle Ages in an elegant and balanced form called, in Italy, a Savanarola or Dante chair, and in Germany, a Luther chair.[34] The upper classes had time for social life—conversation, card games, and music—so they needed more easily movable chairs. Thus, chairs on the average were becoming lighter even as tables were becoming heavier. During this time, chairs were specifically designed for women by widening the arms or lowering the back to accommodate women's dresses—a step that some historians have interpreted as a sign of women's rising status in society.

In England, the Renaissance changed the layout of the house. The hall became a reception area rather than the main meeting place. The family ate in a smaller dining room, with the dining table in a permanent position in the middle of the room. Since the table was no longer placed against the wall, benches were discarded in favor of chairs. The main reception room moved to the second floor, creating plenty of space for entertaining and relaxing, so that furniture did not have to be put against the wall. This in turn created a demand for a wider variety of furniture. The Baroque style was introduced, and the search for ease became linked to a desire for lavish display. Furniture in general, including chairs, became ostentatious and sumptuous.

The eighteenth century is widely viewed as an apex in chair history because of the new attention paid to comfort and artistic unity. Historians do not fret about the meaning of comfort, assuming that any response to the body represents a move in the direction of comfort. For example, Siegfried Giedion judged that eighteenth-century France took up seating comfort where it had been left during the fifth century B.C. by the Greeks.[35] Although the sociological contexts were radically different, in terms of topography he viewed the eighteenth-century chair as the return of a forgotten standard: support for the body that would allow it to enjoy a highly relaxed posture. (Giedion didn't realize just how "forgotten" this standard is. From what we now know about prehistoric Europe, Giedion was attributing to the Greeks a seating posture seen millennia before, in Neolithic times.) In any case, whether ultimately comfortable or not, ease, luxury, and flexibility in posture became fashionable in the eighteenth century, and chair styles adapted.

Historians have drawn seemingly different pictures of this Neoclassical European furniture. Some focus on architectural, rather than physiological, conformity, noting that in the eighteenth-century reception rooms, the shapes of sofa- and chair-backs fitted into similar shapes in the wall paneling, and seating was upholstered to create a uniform band of color around the room. Even at the height of the Rococo period, with its flowing asymmetrical forms, furniture was still placed symmetrically. What was important was matching decor, not matching the human body. Sofas and chairs were richly upholstered in fabrics that matched, or at least blended with, the hangings in the room. The upholstery was the most expensive and prized part of the seating.[36] When chairs were derived from the classical orders of architecture, the unyielding, vertical back was retained. Some judge that this strategy produced uncomfortable furniture. However, for the purpose of maintaining alertness, uprightness has proved the most comfortable position over time. For the kinds of social and political functions staged in such rooms, alertness was undoubtedly appropriate and desired, and this chair style supported that purpose.

In eighteenth-century England, the old terms "cabinetmaker" and "enjoiner" had been dropped. These had stood for *parts* of the process of producing chairs. What is important about this change in terminology is that chairmaking now became a distinct craft, combining the skills of turner, carver, joiner, and upholsterer. This new occupation is credited with integrating, refining, and codifying the best rules for chair design—through craftsmen's pattern books—from both the physiological and the aesthetic point of view. For example, the cabriole leg "gracefully united opposing curves—converse above, concave below," and this leg "became part of a curvilinear composition, instead of an isolated support," since the back, too, was curvilinear.[37]

Whether or not chairs succeeded in uniting comfort with beauty, they continued to play a part in social differentiation. Furniture for people with discretionary income elaborated themes derived from the Greeks, Romans, Egyptians, and Syrians.[38] In the meantime, the cramped conditions of working-class Londoners who lived near their work, since the city lacked any sort of mass transportation system, stimulated the production of ingenious, space-saving, dual-purpose furniture, such as an armchair that converted into a bed, or even a piano that converted into a bed.[39] *(Fig. 9a and b)*

Not surprisingly, the American social history of the chair roughly recapitulates that of Europe. Again, status, not comfort, was the main issue. Most people in precolonial times sat on benches and stools, and chairs were special items denoting status. In fact, chairs were used to denote status from the 1700s through the nineteenth century in North America.[40] Only people of means could afford chairs in those days. By the 1800s, most households had enough chairs for family members to sit down to meals or to offer seats to guests, which meant that the average existing inventories in Massachusetts or Pennsylvania farmhouses show six to nine chairs or more. But prosperous households treated chairs as items for display, lining them up along the walls of parlors and sitting rooms.[41] By the mid-1820s, there was a revolution in the marketing of factory-made "fancy chairs," a democratizing process that made it possible for more families to display matching sets of chairs in their sitting rooms and parlors. The average number of chairs per household in central Massachusetts almost doubled between 1800 and the 1830s. (Inexpensive fancy chairs from Sears, Roebuck still show up in country auctions and antique stores today.) The urban poor,

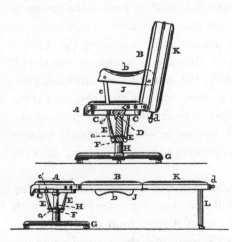

by contrast, sat on their beds or made do with a broken barrel or two.

By the nineteenth century, the Industrial Revolution made a great deal of difference to how much time Americans, Europeans, and sitters everywhere spent in chairs. One reason is that the factory manufacture of chairs made them cheaper, so that more people could afford them. The more important reason is that the nature of work itself had changed. Industrial work was more likely to be seated

Figure 9. This armchair *(a)* becomes a daybed (1875) and this piano *(b)* becomes a bedroom suite (1866).

than agricultural work. Work at assembly lines and in the offices where accounting and record keeping took place was usually done seated, usually on chairs with backs, and only occasionally on stools. English clerks used to work standing, but that practice was never as common in the United States, and today office workers almost everywhere work seated at desks in chairs.

Most furniture historians overlook the significance of this watershed event. Instead of evaluating the social significance of people spending so much time in chairs, they merely focus on the object itself, appreciating the formal beauty of the eighteenth-century chair and lamenting the artistic decline in nineteenth-century ones. Their list of complaints is long. Originality played second fiddle to stylistic conventionality. Concern for comfort (as ease) overwhelmed structural expression and visual integration. To be viewed as luxurious, a chair had to be padded, upholstered in silk or brocade, and tasseled.[42] In Victorian England, the new demand for comfort stimulated the use of spring upholstery, which in turn changed the easy chair's proportions,[43] causing it to grow "heavy and bloated."[44] The legs became shorter, while deep seats and inclined backs encouraged lounging—which quickly degenerated into sprawling and slumping. The woman's easy chair has been sneeringly called "well-upholstered rather than well-designed." Its low seat, with either tiny arms or none at all, made this easy chair look "squat."

Historians have criticized nineteenth-century taste in furniture decoration as eclectic, using the pejorative phrase "cult of antiquity" to refer to the Greek, Roman, and Egyptian motifs that had been so fashionable, and condemning the other traditional Gothic, Renaissance, Elizabethan, and Rococo themes as well. At the time, two movements did react against this decorative eclecticism. The first, William Morris's Arts and Crafts movement, opposed the new "obsession with comfort" (i.e., padding) and the "low standards of design and production." The second, known as Art Nouveau, promoted a non-historical style, despite its roots in the Rococo, in order to protest against the imitation of traditional types that critics felt "commanded and wasted so much skill."[45]

Historians may have downplayed the significance of more people sitting for longer periods of time, but some have at least been alert to the contrast between the conservatism of chair design and the rapidity of social change during the nineteenth century. Despite the fast pace of social and technological change throughout Europe and America, one American furniture historian, Phyllis Oates, concludes that "style rather than technology still dominated furniture design."[46] In addition to the strictly visual concerns for pattern, balance, rhythm, and the like, the ideas associated with a motif were important. Gothic was considered sound and sober for solemn masculine rooms, like the library, hall, and dining room, while the drawing room, boudoir, and ladies' rooms were settings for the more frivolous Rococo style. The so-called Elizabethan style represented sturdy national traits. Light-colored wood was believed to create a happy, friendly atmosphere, whereas oak and mahogany were considered quiet and restful.

Of course, such ideas about decoration are also ideas about social relations—usually connected with power and wealth. In America, as earlier in England, furniture type often matched social class. Specifically, elite markets concentrated on revival furniture; popular markets concentrated on the adjustable, mechanical furniture known as patent furniture; and folk markets concentrated on vernacular styles such as the Windsor chair or the rocking chair.[47]

The sharpest critic of nineteenth-century furniture was undoubtedly the architectural historian Siegfried Giedion. He dismissed a good deal of nineteenth-century furniture because so much of its style was copied from previous eras. He felt that such copying was an opportunity lost to create more original designs based on physical comfort and convenience. He thought patent furniture was genuinely inventive, because it was adjustable, could perform multiple functions, and could respond to any desired position of the human body. Thus, he cared literally about the body, and presumably hoped that new designs based on its comfort and convenience would generate new tastes and preferences in style. He reported that Americans were proud of the patent furniture exhibited at the Paris International Exposition of 1878, with its emphasis on comfort and on functional problem solving. So he could not understand why patent furniture did not get the attention it deserved. Actually, the emphasis on body-based design rather than status probably guaranteed that such furniture would sink into oblivion. Patent furniture of the nineteenth century may have what Giedion calls its "distinct place in the history of comfort," but I would say that it lost its place in the history of style precisely because it did not

Figure 10. Why isn't this chair (ca. 1853) stylish?

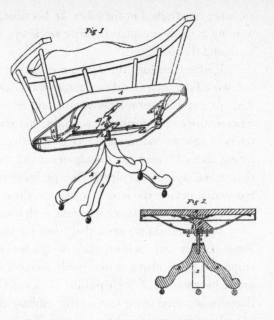

make claims to exclusivity, allowing an office worker to be as comfortable as the office boss. *(Fig. 10)*

Giedion thought that the turning point in taste from American inventiveness to European ruling taste came at the Chicago World's Fair of 1893. This event glorified neoclassical architecture and elaborate embellishments, so that people began to be ashamed of the "flat, machine-made surfaces of American equipment—and patent furniture . . ." This furniture was relegated to special technical purposes and work environments—factories, dental offices, and business offices—but banished from homes. Giedion accuses the nineteenth century of the rule of pseudo-monumentality, responsible not only for architecture but also for the "furniture of the ruling taste, with its excess of decoration and ornamentation." He blamed the wealthy for their assumption that traditional European styling would elevate their taste and prestige. Emulating their betters, the middle class could now purchase machine-made furniture created in the style of handmade furniture, and this gave them the illusion of being able to live at a higher-class level: "the insignia of wealth and panoply wield a fascination that . . . may inhibit healthier instincts."

According to Giedion, the posture that was distinctive to the nineteenth century—involving both movement and relaxation—could only be permitted in the work environment because "ruling taste" dominated the domestic scene. In their parlors, people comported themselves somewhat formally, the reverse of our practice today, when we relax in the home and are more constrained in the office. In his time, movement and relaxation were more easily accepted in office work and in dentists' offices, railway seats, and the like.[48]

If adjustable furniture had come into our living rooms a century earlier, would our increasingly sedentary ways have caused so much trouble? Perhaps our back problems would not be so severe. Maybe critics of nineteenth-century furniture *are* right that style is the problem. If style refers to how we communicate social identity, then, insofar as communicating status blinded our grandparents and their parents to the value of movement, style is the culprit. They probably took movement for granted, but prized having the leisure to sit upright and still as an achievement. Why not elaborate that achievement with brocade and tassels?

Social realism suggests that until the social elite adopts new ideas about posture and comfort, chair design for the general market will not emphasize physical or practical needs. Remember that changes in women's dress, for example, from painfully corseted Gibson girls to uncorseted flappers, occurred when a social elite embraced the new physical freedom as high style. Similarly, chair design will express first and foremost claims to superiority—in art, education, money, and power.

And the home is the place where people communicate their social identity.[49] This is connected not just to income but to what work one does for a living, how one chooses to spend money, one's educational level, travel experience, family and religious affiliations. Such status was once revealed in public by one's dress and accent; but increasingly over the last two centuries, starting with the Dutch, it has been expressed by how one furnishes the home—how much and what kind of furniture, the quality and symbolism of fabrics (draperies and upholstery), carpets, paintings, sculpture and other art work, sporting trophies, travel mementos, musical equipment (including stereos and CDs), books, and now TV, video, and computers.

All these things are arranged with some regard for practical movement and purpose; but even more important are unwritten codes about how to unify and order all this material. The rules for what should be in a nineteenth-century parlor and how it should be arranged were different from the rules we follow today. So we can appreciate that nineteenth-century Americans might not be able to incorporate mechanical patent furniture into a Victorian tableau that consisted of richly upholstered furniture, swagged drapery, fringed tablecloths, and such newly affordable luxuries as carpet, along with keepsakes, travel knickknacks, Romantic statues, and nature paintings. Critics like Giedion hoped that the body's needs might come first; but higher-status groups have to be convinced of the social superiority of this approach, not just the physical benefits. This is where designers can be most persuasive. Body-conscious design has to be aesthetic, fashionable, or very, very familiar.

The rocker is a good case in point. It is responsive to the body first and status second, but it fared far better than patent furniture. Rockers—curved pieces of wood, allowing a rocking motion—were first attached to babies' cradles in Europe, but the rocking chair is an American invention. An ingenious inventor, or perhaps more than one, attached rockers to chair legs around 1760.[50] Regular Windsor chairs fitted with rockers on their legs came to be known as Boston rockers. Platform rockers were patented sporadically until the late 1760s,[51] but no Hepplewhite, Chippendale, or Sheraton chairs were converted into rockers, so we must assume that rocking chairs were a vernacular taste, not an elite one.[52] Yet the rocker became acceptable to those who could afford parlors, probably because of its familiar materials and home-grown connotations. Visually and symbolically, it could fit into Victorian parlors, despite being good for the body.

Moving into the twentieth century, the Modernists made no claims to comfort but to moral and aesthetic superiority. Architects like Mart Stam, Marcel Breuer, Ludwig Mies van der Rohe, Le Corbusier, and Charles Eames took up the challenge of designing overtly with industrial materials and production processes. As chair designers, these architects valued sculptural originality rather than recognizable tradition. Their reaction against nineteenth-century imitation was even more severe than either the Arts and Crafts or Art Nouveau. They emphatically rejected the use of coiled upholstery, a nineteenth-century trademark in both comfort and the illusion of comfort.

The Modernists experimented with new manufacturing processes—lamination and steel production—and new construction materials like steel and plastic. European theoreticians wanted to embrace the reality of industrial processes while at the same time suffusing them with intelligence and harmony in proportions. They believed that the discovery of new principles would yield rational new designs—hence their emphasis on originality. Not surprisingly, hopes for standardization were stalled by an "endless series of new starts."[53] Twentieth-century furniture designers were more interested in novelty than in improvement of form or function. Their designs have become high-art classics, often seen in the lobbies of corporate headquarters today.

The split that Giedion noticed between the home environment and the office environment was to widen throughout the twentieth century, even yielding two different design fields—one for status furniture and the other for technical work settings. Thus, on the one hand, the chairs of early twentieth-century Modernist architects are revered as pure sculptural statements, and newcomers seek novel and surprising twists in appearance; on the other, computer chairs have become fairly sophisticated, physiologically speaking. Will the twain ever meet?

CHAIRS AND GENDER

Today, as in the past, chairs are differentiated by age, gender, and class. They still remain embedded in power relations. Rarely is the power literal; it is usually more subtly interwoven into ideas and emotions about social order that we unconsciously tolerate or support. The modern office separates the furniture of men from that of women, of manager from that of employee. In schools, children learn to regulate their bodies first and foremost by the chairs they are given to sit on. Even at home, furniture continues to reflect age and gender distinctions.

In the hierarchy between men and women, posture has always played its part. *(Fig. 11)* Today, even the most quintessentially female activity of giving birth has been regulated by males. Various midwives and birthing specialists have argued that giving birth in a crouching, sitting, or squatting position is anatomically easier than giving birth while lying on the back; nevertheless, starting in the seventeenth century,[54] for the convenience of the male doctor, women were placed supine on a bed for delivery. Only today are reformers trying to change this situation.

Since the chair is one of the chief regulators of posture, it has played a major part in maintaining hierarchical and power differences between the sexes. Royalty in different cultures might extend the privilege of sitting in a chair to the women in their immediate family or court, but in that case usually some kind of distinction would be made between the

Figure 11. Spaniards in the thirteenth century differentiated themselves from Muslims, animals, and women by sitting on chairs rather than on the floor.

throne or the chair of the male rulers and the seating for their female entourage. Early in Rome, wives could not recline to eat with their husbands, but later this rule changed so that they could. In Roman Britain, men sat on wooden chairs while women used wicker and basket chairs.[55] The Chinese considered it indecorous for women to sit in chairs, long after men had gotten used to them.[56]

By the nineteenth century, in capitalist economies women of the ruling class were supposed to spend in the private realm what their men had earned in the public realm. Many historians have documented this division of spheres—with the home becoming the female domain, including the supervision of servants, the planning of meals, entertainment, supervision of children, provision of moral uplift for the family, and the comforting of the male. As manager of the home, women also spent money to buy things, including furniture.[57] For example, women chose feminine styles for their bedrooms and other private areas, but they selected masculine styles for the more public rooms of their homes.[58]

In the late twentieth century, feminists began to criticize the fact that women's posture and use of furniture were different from men's and that women's conventional posture was contrived to emphasize vulnerability, weakness, and debility.[59] One British ergonomics researcher, E. F. Le Carpentier, agrees that women sit differently from men: with their lower legs close to the vertical and their trunk erect, whereas men lean back and stretch out their legs. However, he accepts rather than criticizes this gender difference, which could have to do with dress codes or underlying differences in feelings of authority and self-confidence or both. In any case, he recommends that chairs for use by the general public should be available in at least two models, differing in size as well as shape.[60] A less convoluted reason for his otherwise perfectly sound proposal is that men and women vary in size.

Accordingly, even the most stereotypical male chair, the recliner, now comes in two sizes. In mainstream America, the recliner, made by La-Z-Boy, Barca, and others, has traditionally been the male chair for relaxing and watching television. In 1991, *The New York Times* commented: "Perhaps no piece of furniture in modern times is more gender-specific than the one that has cradled, rocked, pivoted and massaged the American man. While women have not been moved by motion furniture, as the industry calls it, until recent years, men have attached themselves like barnacles to mechanized chairs almost from the day they got off the ground . . . in 1927." Twenty-five percent of U.S. homes have this male reclining chair, according to industry figures. The *Times* article continued: "Historically, of course, women's relation to the recliner was to dust under it or to decorate around it. Women also carried food and beverages to the chairs, some of which were fitted with snack trays."[61]

In the nineties, some manufacturers and retailers attempted to expand their market by restyling recliners to create a female version. A new scaled-down ladies' style for those five feet five and under, in "feminine" fabrics like velvet and "feminine" colors like red, with details like skirts, hit the market. Some couples are now buying matching loungers in two different sizes. More likely, the woman's chair is flowered in velvet or damask or "sweet rose velvet" in contrast to his "mahogany-colored leather with studs." The women's styles also have different names: cashmere, champagne, sterling, chablis, opulence, first lady. Women want the reduced scale, not only because of their smaller size but also because it is more fashionable, and the chair has a different rocking mechanism so that it can fit closer to a wall than the standard size.[62]

Clearly, women's concern with expressing the correct image for the whole family and for managing the interior environment endures. According to the furniture industry, seating is becoming feminized because women buy the seating.[63] Sheila de Bretteville, a graphic designer and feminist critic, contends that the couch is essentially feminine because it accommodates more than one person, which allows people to sit touching each other. She may be right that the couch is less individualistic and more group-oriented than the chair, which we associate with masculinity.[64] However, men seem to do a good job of stretching out on the living-room sofa. One wonders if buying more couches or a more feminine look in chairs can truly undermine the hierarchical differences between men and women that have been part of domestic politics.

What about women as designers rather than consumers? Is male-female hierarchy still an issue for them? Women have only recently entered the arena as chair designers, in any number. Charlotte Perriand did design the famous 1928 chaise longue with Le Corbusier and his brother Jeanneret, but she is seldom acknowledged for this achievement.[65] The architect Eileen Gray also designed several early modern chairs that few people remember.[66]

Women designers do not want to be classified by gender, and their work varies considerably. Journalists, however, prefer generalization, and thus ignore these variations. A contemporary British journalist's coverage of "Sit," an American exhibit on chairs, emphasized soft, organic shapes; humor, elegance, oceanic scenes; thoughtful practicality; refinement and comfort: "Some of the stereotypes do . . . hold. . . . Comfort and practicality are definite priorities. Very few chair designs by women lose sight of their use, as objects that should be both pleasant to sit in and able to fit in the broader design of a room. This, rather than . . . the womb, is probably why so many women . . . use curving organic forms in their work. The human bottom, whether male or female, is rounded." (The female journalist here fell into the trap of thinking that mimicking the human shape is the best way to support it. More on this in later chapters.)

Perhaps women designers are less interested in the chair as an agent of hierarchy and power than as a medium for relatedness and physical ease, *à la* Neolithic goddess. The same journalist notes, "Even among the few women who work in metal, there is a delicacy and a concern for comfort that is not present to the same degree in men's work."[67] Women designers may in fact epitomize traits shared broadly with women consumers; market researchers report that men are likely to buy something solely for its image and status, whereas women will always be juggling a second equal concern for what it will be like to sit in.

The relationship between comfort and status for women's predilections in furniture appears tangled, because women certainly do not ignore status, especially in light of their role in communicating the family image. One male journalist, who loves his La-Z-Boy no matter what his wife says, exaggerates and simplifies women's concern with status, saying that women "see furniture the same way [they] see shoes: comfort's irrelevant, all that matters is whether it looks good."[68] Certainly, women desire what they anticipate others will admire. The apparent contradiction over status versus comfort may be resolved by the work of the Harvard psychologist Carol Gilligan, who has made the point in the context of ethics and moral development that females often refuse to prioritize two competing values, but instead seek a way to have both.[69] Perhaps as both designers and consumers, women really are juggling two values, status *and* comfort.

These are not the only two relevant values. We have already discussed others like relatedness and sensuality, which have long been considered feminine strengths—or weaknesses, depending on your point of view. What happens to all these qualities in the workplace, especially the office, where women today are so numerous?

THE MODERN OFFICE

In the modern office, hierarchy rules, and chairs play their part in expressing and creating rank. A recent novel by Po Bronson, *Bombardiers,* satirizes bond trading, the information economy, and the workplace of the 1990s for exactly this reason. Bronson creates a bureaucratic creep, Kalinov, who berates the fearless new kid on the salesfloor, Eggs Igino, for standing rather than sitting in his corporate padded chair to make telephone calls. Eggs Igino insists that he can stand up to work if he wants to. Kalinov asks, What would happen if everyone got rid of their chairs just to be more comfortable? What if they did? Eggs rejoins. Kalinov explains that it's a slippery slope: jogging shoes, blue jeans, individual desk lamps. These would destroy corporate image. Chairs are embedded in a network of symbols.

In this novel, the national corporate office is lavish but nevertheless as much like its branch offices as motel chains; corporate culture tolerates no variation in carpeting, wallboard, chairs, lights, telephones, or desks. Ergonomically correct pretzel chairs are prescribed to stop the further degeneration of wrists and backs by the corporate physical therapist Dr. Perkova, but the young stud explains to the hero, Sid Geeder, that standing up would protect his back by making it easier to move around and avoid holding one position all the time. "Our bodies are not made to stand still. Our bodies are made to move. . . . Stand up! They want you to sit down all day," he cries, confirming Sid's lament that the firm has got him locked in, "chained to his seat."[70]

Obviously this is a novel based on close observation of real life. A journalist told me about a colleague of hers who after many hours at a computer terminal wanted to rest his back by lying down. The office was cramped, so he lay down under his work table, out of sight of visitors. But the boss came by, saw him on the floor, and made him get up, yelling, "I can't believe you're doing this! It is *not* professional to lie down!"

Researchers in ergonomics have studied many aspects of office function, including status, and have concluded that the workstation *should* be an indication of the worker's status in the office hierarchy. In open-plan offices, with their overtly democratic intentions, distinguishing between managers and ordinary workers became difficult, and dissatisfaction on both sides has resulted from this incongruence.[71] Managers had assumed that workers would like a more egalitarian-looking environment and might consequently be more productive; but that did not turn out to be the case.

Which type of office do you work in? Can anyone visiting for the first time guess who the boss is without being told? You can probably tell by looking at differences in partition height, amount and location of work space, lighting, color, as well as such intangibles as privacy, ability to control access to others, and the opportunity for personalization. You might also consider very tangible traits—quality of furniture, upholstery, number of chairs, thickness of carpet.[72] Researchers report that idiosyncratic status markers like the color of telephones or wastepaper baskets developed in the absence of the opportunity to display conventional markers.

Since appropriate markers contribute to satisfaction, and worker satisfaction is essential to productivity, status differences have to be maintained, ergonomicists say. One textbook on office planning emphasizes the need for a clearly defined status understood by all users: "It is not so much a question of *what* they are, as *that* they are." Practically speaking, the trick is to get people to assign value to easily transported objects, such as telephone color, ashtray size, nameplate type or location, which can "denote status without impairing flexibility and without resulting in wasted space and dollars."[73] One could speculate that since clear expression of status is directly related to worker satisfaction, it might indirectly be related to productivity. This conclusion would be disappointing in the context of our democratic ideals generally, and especially in the context of rhetoric about stimulating productivity in the workplace by tapping people's creative potential without regard to rank. I wonder if they feel that as long as pay and authority differences exist, the environmental messages should be consistent. Alternatively, perhaps people need the ethical guidance implicit in such rankings; the practice of creating distinctions and then matching them to notches along a moral dimension from inferior to superior may serve the cause of moral development. A simpler explanation is that people like to know where they stand, and the physical environment helps to communicate this.

In any case, as status markers in the office, chairs are important. After surveying 529 office workers in three government and three business offices, psychologists at Buffalo, New York, confirmed the expert opinion of industry consultant Fred Steele that the number of chairs in a personal office (wooden chairs were preferred to metal) was a crucial indicator of the inhabitant's supervisory status. Other indicators were large desks, multiple work surfaces, greater storage capacity, and privacy.[74]

Most of the research done to date on office environments stems from an interest in worker productivity. But which is more important to worker satisfaction—physical comfort or status symbols? When interviewed by the American pollster Louis Harris in a survey sponsored by Steelcase, the world's largest manufacturer of office furniture, 80 percent of those who complained (70% of the total) said that discomfort reduced their productivity a great deal or somewhat.[75] They defined "comfort" in rank order as: good lighting, a comfortable chair, a place to concentrate, quiet. Chairs have become so important that finally organizations recognize that individuals' chairs should be adjusted to fit them instead of being assigned to them on the basis of their place in the organizational hierarchy. Concern for productivity, more than concern for democratic fairness, is responsible for the trend to push for physical comfort for each worker.

But concern for productivity may eventually do something for equity. Here is where numerous research and popular magazine articles remind us that "creativity is not, after all, a reflection of rank or title; the potential is everywhere. To tap that potential, companies will have to change their static and status-ridden ways."[76] In other words, to be more productive, status differences may have to go. From this point of view those scientific studies that do not acknowledge status issues are correct, if naive, in reporting only their findings, for instance, that desks should be lower and adjustable in height for women office workers.[77]

These two contradictory conclusions about productivity—the need for status and the need to be free from status—create a riptide, indicating perhaps a sea change in office culture. Until recently, all U.S. commercial furniture lines still carried "executive" and "secretary" chair models. More progressive firms now use the terms "managerial" and "task," although in that language I still hear managers being distinguished from workers. I suspect that the effort to overcome the use of seating to symbolize hierarchy in the office will be a back-and-forth struggle. As Linda Brown and Deyan Sudjic, organizers of a British exhibition on the modern chair in the 1980s, put it:

> The issue that most manufacturers only coyly hint at in their sales brochures is that of status. In the supposedly democratic open plan office, with its characteristic low partitions and screens replacing full-height walls, the rhetoric is all of teamwork, and non-hierarchical working methods. In fact, however, office furniture, and in particular the chair, conveys the status of the occupant. Considerable ingenuity is used to suggest the status of the owner. There are ironies here. The most costly chairs are generally those that offer the most movement, but these have come to be associated in many organizations with clerical workers, which can provide undesirable connotations

for the more insecure of managers. So, paradoxically, the executive chair in a range may actually be the cheapest to produce. And, rather than add directly useful or comfort-providing extra features, the high status chairs simply use a more costly covering, or are, with unsubtle obviousness, made flatteringly larger. As a result, the pricing policy for the standard chairs is affected by the possibility of making better returns on the supposed luxury, top-of-the-line models. Of course this is simply the modern manifestation of a very old tradition in furniture, realized for once in injection-molded plastics and cast alloys, rather than wood.[78]

Their observations reminds me of a 1980 survey of ten thousand office workers by the Buffalo Organization for Social and Technical Innovation, in which researchers discovered that those whose work actually required the best lighting were the least likely to have it, while managers usually had the best.[79]

An important distinction in the office, still clearly maintained, is the one between bosses and secretaries, which is still mostly a difference between men and women. Not surprising, then, that marketers of the Norwegian balance chair have had to confront the unwritten law of office status symbols, because their chair does not differentiate between the boss and the secretary. In the United States they were especially handicapped because their chair does not have a back, and the height of a chair's back is one of the "essential indicators of high social status." In response, a leading manufacturer of balance chairs brought out a line with high backs. The brochure of another company marketing conventional chairs with a tilting seat deals with the issue by using double entendre, calling theirs a chair "for any position."[80]

Over and over, we will see status locked in a life-and-death struggle with other values, such as equity and worker health, the two current contenders. The modern office relies increasingly on the use of computers and video display terminals (VDTs), and numerous physiological problems have come to be associated with that fact: eyestrain, back pain, and repetitive strain injury are only the most prevalent. For all three problems, the underlying condition is the static posture held by workers in front of VDT screens. Insofar as the chair stabilizes posture, it contributes actively and directly to disorders of the eye, back, and wrist. People cannot take advantage of ergonomic chairs, with some capacity for movement built in, because their eyes and hands become entrained with the keyboard and screen they are working on. In this case we cannot really blame the chair; it is simply a part of an integrated complex of chair, keyboard, person, and screen, which together forms a new machine. Ergonomics was once defined as the interaction between man and machine. Now, there is no longer interaction. It is exaggerating only a little to say that man has now become *part* of the machine and no longer disengages from the keyboard and terminal.[81]

The physical consequences of this entraining with machines is of course infamous: already carpal tunnel syndrome is a household phrase. While some people might accept the demands of an electronic workplace as requiring high degrees of hand-eye coordination with mouse, keyboard, and display screens for prolonged periods of time, I want to challenge the wisdom of accepting such a work environment. If stable support is necessary for tasks requiring hand-eye coordination, then the people who perform those tasks also should be assigned other tasks in the course of the day in order to vary their posture.

One would think that the advent of the home office would subvert the rhythm of machines and the power of status in office furniture. Surely here, of all places, one could develop a way of working based on personal physiological patterns and rhythms. Advertisements for equipment for home offices show wood grain rather than metal shelving, and desk systems, potted plants, Oriental rugs, family photos, and views out of residential-scale windows. The chairs, however, are the same ergonomic computer chairs being used to promote increased productivity in offices. Ironically, many furniture companies targeting those with home offices offer an executive high-back chair, as well as a leather ergonomic chair, so you can, presumably, continue to feel like a big shot even while working at home!

SCHOOLS

So how do people learn distinction by rank, or that leather is better, or that wider is more powerful? The process begins early in life. It is well known that schools prepare children to reproduce the workforce, with appropriate habits—both physical and mental.

A contemporary German philosopher and historian, Hajo Eickhoff, has argued that the chair is a sedative to create a docile population not inclined to criticize or become politically active. (Note that the verb *sedate,* meaning "to calm," comes from the Latin "to sit.") This process of socialization to passivity starts early in schools, where the first task is not to teach children content, but to teach them orderly behavior—specifically, the ability to sit still for long periods of time.[82] Don Johnson, an American philosopher and head of the department of somatic studies at the California Institute of Integral Studies in San Francisco, also fears that the way in which children sit at school is evidence of a disturbing educational philosophy.[83] He sees the practice of sitting quietly in rows of seats as primarily a way for teachers to maintain authority and keep radical ideas safely contained. He would like both students and teachers to have the freedom to move around energetically.

Montessori and Steiner schools offer two examples of how education can incorporate activity with learning. Dr. Maria Montessori wrote *The Montessori Method* in 1912, describing how children were reduced to immobility in the Italian classroom, "not disciplined, but annihilated." She recommended simple tasks and spontaneous work rather than enforced, seated effort.[84] In the United Kingdom, state primary schools have adopted the Montessori model, and in the United States Montessori theory has made a resurgence, mostly in private schools, but also in some public school systems. Recently, American brain researchers have also come to believe that learning increases with physical activity.[85] More public schools have been experimenting with allowing kids to sit without chairs and in clusters rather than rows. But for generations American schoolteachers have struggled to get children to sit still.

Thanks to a detailed study of what a seven-year-old boy did at school and at home over the course of one day in a small midwestern town, we can scroll back in time to see, minute by minute, how a teacher in 1949 regulated students' posture.[86] This early study by two psychologists, Roger G. Barker and Herbert F. Wright, is still respected for its attention to behavior in natural settings, as opposed to laboratories or clinics. I recently reread it with an eye to how, when, and where the boy named Raymond used chairs. One of the more striking points is that the teacher continuously monitored the first and second graders' posture, frequently telling them to "sit up straight," "settle down," and "get in position." Another striking pattern is that on his own, Raymond *never* sat. All play—at home, on the courthouse grounds, school, and a vacant lot—involved running, skipping, hopping, jumping, twisting, dipping, and generally cavorting to entertain himself kinesthetically. In fact, the only times Raymond ever sat in a chair were at the dining table at home and at his desk at school. Children have little natural inclination to sit in chairs, so it's little wonder schoolteachers have to invest so much time and effort to get them to stay still there.

Adults certainly have become fully devoted to chair sitting. One of the psychologists who recorded Raymond's behavior inadvertently projected adult feelings. After an exactingly detailed description of the young boy sitting at his desk slouching, sliding, jiggling, shuffling, turning, slumping in boredom, she concluded with the nonsequitur: "I had the feeling that although the story wasn't especially interesting, he liked this restful part of the day when he could just sit." Other observers had recorded that keeping up with Raymond on the playground or on his way to school was challenging. The observer who got to record during one of the thirty-minute shifts when Raymond is in one place must have been pleased that *she* could just sit.

Children know by an early age that adults want to sit in chairs, and Raymond knew this well before age seven. How do children learn? Raymond would have picked up this information from scenes like the following. A female observer explained to Raymond, "I'll pretend these steps are a chair and I'll sit here while you play." Raymond's mother was surprised that the observer was sitting on the back stoop; so she asked, "Wouldn't you like to have a chair?" The observer had to explain: "No, I'm very comfortable. I often just sit on steps because I like to." The expectation shared by Raymond, his mother, and the recorder is that adults sit in chairs; deviation from the norm requires justification. Part of the definition of being an adult is sitting in a chair—a primary lesson in the unspoken curriculum of schools. How refreshing then that Pee-Wee Herman's television character "Chairy" from the eighties was capable of creative ideas and was very animated. Chairy may be subversive, subliminally suggesting that chairs and the children in them should be interactive and creative.

The most common explanation for children avoiding sitting is that they prefer active play. However, that obvious reason obscures another very important one. Having to sit at tables and chairs is the most common source of physical stress for children, and probably for adults too, for that matter. But children, being young, are particularly deformed by stressful postures. As early as 1743, a French orthopedic physician, Dr. Nicolas Andry de Bois-Regard warned against the deformities caused by improper school furniture: "It is usual to give Children, when they are taken from the Nurse, small Elbow-Chairs, made of straw or Rushes, which have all a hollow in the Bottom, because they cannot be made otherwise. Thus they place the Children upon these little Chairs, by which means their Bodies begin to grow deformed, by little and little, in their tender Years."

We no longer have a problem with rush seats today, although we still have overly contoured seats that are scooped in the bottom. Dr. Andry de Bois-Regard enumerated other such problems in the design of furniture for children, including the relationship between chairs and tables: "Most part of Children have their Bodies made crooked in learning to write, because People are not at the pains to give them a Table high enough for the purpose." But the tables could also be too high: "Those Masters and Mistresses who teach Children to read or write upon too high a Table, which rises above their Elbows (for it ought to be two Inches lower) expose them to the same Deformity."[87] He thought this problem especially acute in schools for young children where there was only one table for all the children. Imagine how surprised he would be by our situation today: the luxury of individual desks, but all at the same height! Despite having spent more money on education, we have not taken advantage of the opportunity to adjust each desk to each child.

A contemporary Danish physician, A. C. Mandal, continues to worry about these issues. The best place to begin effective prevention of crippling back complaints in adults, he says, is in the schools. Like Dr. Andry de Bois-Regard over two hundred years ago, he examines the slope of tabletops, the height of chairs, the height of tables, and the slope of chair seats. The critical issue, according to Mandal, is the relationship between the legs and the spine. When that angle is anywhere between 120 and 135 degrees—approximately halfway between sitting and standing—sitting upright is easy, because the work of the muscles in front and in back of the pelvis is completely balanced.[88] His chair also allows the sitter to perch forward or lean back and extend the feet. But to have the legs drop that far away from the body, you need room for the lower leg, a higher seat, and a forward-tilted seat. A higher seat means that table height must also increase. *(Fig. 12)*

Another reason for higher work surfaces stems from our eyes, not legs. Mandal observes that children's visual distance is less than adults'—an average of 12 inches. If the table height is not brought up to within their visual range, children compensate by bending over their papers and books. Of course schoolroom tables are usually not that high. So children are constantly forced to round their backs and distort their bodies in order to see their work. Mandal has found that when children in his lab are allowed to place the tabletop where they want it, they usually put it 6 to 10 inches higher (one-half the child's body height) than the international standard adhered to by school furniture manufacturers. The ideal chair height chosen by children was also higher (at least one-third the child's body height). And how many of the children Mandal studied chose the international standard for chair height? None.[89]

Mandal points out that the average height of children has been steadily increasing over the years, but the height of school tables and chairs (in Denmark, at least) has been steadily decreasing. "The tragic consequence of this misjudgment," he says, "is that more and more flexion and strain are imposed on the backs of our children at a critical period in their lives."[90] He finds the strain of sitting so deleterious, in fact, that he wants to give it up as a routine posture and substitute perching. He lamented that janitorial concerns get more attention than pupils' well-being: "Abuse of children's backs during adolescence could well be the rea-

Figure 12. Dr. A. C. Mandal of Denmark has convinced the school systems in Scandinavia to provide schoolchildren with chairs that protect the lumbar curve naturally through intelligent use of body mechanics. He instructs students to sit on the sloped portion of the seat for reading and writing. The backrest is for use only when listening or resting.

son for the rapidly increasing number of back ailments. Designers of furniture have learned nothing about the anatomy of the seated person, and local school authorities seem to place high priority on low-cost furniture that is easily stacked and compactly stored."[91] Dr. Mandal's campaign has been successful. His research persuaded the rest of the Scandinavian countries, and the European furniture standards committee, that schoolchildren's health will be improved by increasing the standard height of both chairs and desks, and tilting the seats and desktops toward one another. In 1997, the International Standards Organization included this option in their new standards for school furniture.

However, children in Australia, unlike those Dr. Mandal studied, tended to choose chairs without regard to anatomy. Educational authorities there studied twenty kindergartners who were allowed to choose among various chair heights. The kids said they preferred the largest chairs, regardless of their own stature, although 95 percent dangled their feet when sitting.[92] These children have learned that the bigger the chair, the more power and status accrues to the sitter. Studies conducted with American children in the late 1950s found that most of them visualized God sitting on a throne or seat.[93] Most likely Australian children also see God in a chair—presumably a large one.

In the home, in the office, and in schools, social purposes override physiological comfort when it comes to chair design. Even in zero gravity, where there is no up or down, no floor or ceiling, and the body swims in space, the Earth-based designers decided to put a chair into the first space capsule of astronauts in order to make the occupants feel at home. Once it proved absolutely useless in outer space, the chair was dropped from future missions. Maybe after a few more centuries of experimentation, mankind will come to the same conclusion.

When I do sit, I do not sit
to hearten my behind.
I rather do enjoy the fit
of chairs as sculptured by my mind.
The mind, led by its frugal hoax,
when judging chairs, sees style,
leaves "sitting" just to common folks: a use of chairs, so vile!

—"The Aesthete," by Christian Morganstern (1871–1914)[1]

Chapter 2

The Elements of Style

You may easily forgive chairs for relegating comfort to second place, particularly if you have a special fondness for art and beauty. After all, a chair can be viewed as a work of art. Forget class, social superiority, authority, and distinction. Enter line, proportion, shape, materials, decoration, and craftsmanship—all criteria for appreciating chairs as craft, as sculpture, as pure form.

Potentially, an artistic approach to chair design could be more attentive to the body than an approach preoccupied with social position. Custom-made items, especially those made by hand, can be fitted to the individual. Further, when Modernist designers embraced industrial manufacturing processes in the early twentieth century, they sought a new aesthetic, and came up with the slogan that "Form follows function." So it should stand to reason that the form of chairs will accommodate the physical activities of sitting, moving, and resting. And later, in the 1970s, when artists started appropriating furniture for their work, they paid most attention to chairs—much more than to tables, beds, or chests of drawers—because chairs are anthropomorphic. They look like us: with feet, legs, seats, backs, and arms. Surely at least some statements about chair design might take inspiration from the human body, in which case we could expect a spate of idiosyncratic chairs scaled to the artist's or patron's body.

In actuality, artistic approaches to chair design have taken our culture away from the concerns of the body. Surprisingly, as chairs have moved from the workshops of craftsmen to the ateliers of designers to the studios of artists, their form has reflected less and less concern for the biomechanics of sitting. When *Connoisseur* magazine runs an article on the "Twenty-Three Best Chairs," they don't mean anatomically best or even best in the *Consumer Reports* sense of a combination of most functional, durable, and economical. Rather, they mean the personal favorites of important curators, collectors, or art historians who have made their own stylistic judgments.[2] Ironically, the comparatively anonymous manufacturers who have supplied chairs to both elites and the masses may have addressed the concerns of the body more successfully than individual craftsmen, designers, and artists.

Why has an artistic approach taken us away from concern with our bodies? One reason is that we assume that the needs of the body have already been met. Since the chair has been with us for at least ten thousand years, and its basic form has stayed more or less the same ever since, it may be thought to be perfect. This basic perfection would make it an appropriate arena for strictly stylistic play and refinement. In actual fact, the chair is far from perfect, functionally speaking, as we shall see in Part II.

Another reason that an artistic perspective diminishes concern for the body is that style is actually just another form of social differentiation and ranking. Once we start discriminating one form from another, it is very tempting to attach values. One chair is different from another—so isn't it also *better* than the other? Indeed, the most stylish chairs usually belong to those of highest social standing. Benjamin Franklin lamented that sight was inextricably bound to rank when he said, "The eyes of other people are the eyes that ruin us. If all but myself were blind, I should want neither fine clothes, fine houses, nor fine furniture." Accordingly, style readily becomes another way through which we differentiate ourselves from others; we don't just seek to be different but also better. In the end, thinking about chairs as objects of art leads back to appreciating that chairs serve the purpose of social ranking.

Communication is an important part of artistic expression, and communicating the right message can often be more important than what we feel physically. A photograph of President Jimmy Carter at Camp David during a moment of reflection in the Middle East peace talks shows him sitting outdoors on a seat carved out of a log; here a rustic look was more important than real (read physical) comfort.[3] Conversely, when JFK needed a rocker because of his severe back problems, rockers became a stylish fad because people identified them with his charisma, not because rockers are functional. If the shape of a chair communicates the right message, we don't care how it feels physically. How it feels *emotionally* is what counts. Accordingly, we often observe that artists create, sitters select, and collectors buy chairs for aesthetic reasons—it looks better as an object—without regard to how they feel physically.[4] In our age of consumerism, a British observer of pop culture confirmed that a chair was "not just a utilitarian item which performed a service, but a culturally-loaded symbol which helped to express our attitudes, aspirations and identity: it communicates to others our chosen 'lifestyle.' "[5] Sociologists have included chairs as a non-verbal indicator of either social rank or of traditional versus modern identity.[6]

Style eclipses physiology—as paper covers rock—through several mechanisms, including connoisseurship and decorating. Interest in the look of a chair means that some people become enthralled with connoisseurship—knowing which ones are the more authentic expressions of a type and why. A recent *Smithsonian* article described a connoisseur in action:

> Wolfson is transfixed. It is, he realizes at once, a rare exemplar of a line of mass-producible wooden furniture that echoed the gracefulness of Art Nouveau while prefiguring the later austerity of the Bauhaus. Wolfson doesn't have one of [Richard] Riemerschmid's distinctive chairs, but he knows he needs one—it will fill an important historical gap in the inaugural show. . . . "It's the first time I've seen a Riemerschmid that I like," Wolfson tells me excitedly as he circles the piece. "I mean, this chair explains everything."[7]

A poignant account of collecting modern furniture on a much tighter budget comes from *The Washington Post* for June 4, 1992. With a touch of self-mockery, the staff writer in the Style section describes how her family kept faith in the Modernist vision of the "perfect life by design" for over forty years—even though Modernism "costs too much, doesn't wear well and the chairs are uncomfortable." In retrospect, she reports having "recently sat in turn in our hard-sought collection of Modern chairs—each chased down like a Holy Grail in secondhand office furniture stores, want ads, hard-to-find warehouses. And I realized there was not a comfortable place to sit in the house. But Modern is beautiful, and that may be enough."[8]

If not connoisseurs, many of us at least want to know which chair best fits our decor. Chairs are an important component of recognized decorating styles: traditional, Colonial, contemporary, Modern, high-tech, French Provincial, Spanish, Mediterranean, Gothic, and Arts and Crafts, among others. Decorators and image consultants are paid to help individuals hone the unspoken language of their interior furnishings. For those of us who cannot or do not want to pay for such professional help, home-decorating magazines (which designers sometimes disparage as "shelter" magazines) offer advice more readily.

Picking the right chair to communicate the right message is so important that some people experience panic attacks. "We call it sofa/easy chair anxiety," said an interior designer for the department store Marshall Field in Chicago. "It's a very common malady. People will design and build an entire house, but it will take years of indecision before they'll pick that sofa or easy chair."[9] Such status-conscious people are not thinking about issues of physical comfort like whether the chair cuts into the underside of the leg or provides adequate back support. Clearly, this is an extreme example; yet the rest of us do care about style to some degree or another, and to that degree we too may turn from our own bodily awareness to accept various discomforts. The communications design consultant Ralph Caplan has made a similar point, a little more ironically, about chairs being " 'statements' about the social position, wealth, and modernity of the owner. Many of our most elegant living rooms and lobbies are furnished with such statements . . . they can also be sat in, although that sometimes hurts."[10]

THE ABC'S OF STYLE

What can we learn about chairs by paying attention to their looks? Since style is so compelling—enough to override and even shape physical experience—studying it can tell us a lot about which values and concerns have the most powerful emotional significance.[11] Style tells more about people's attitudes toward things than about the things themselves. For example, during the so-called Machine Age between the two world wars, the industrialized societies of Europe and America were valiantly trying to integrate the look and the rhythms of the machine into daily life. As a result, all kinds of household objects, and even buildings, such as New York's Chrysler Building, and large public works like bridges and tunnels, were shaped to look like either heroic or streamlined machines.

Style is the way all the parts of a composition are assembled around its main idea or attitude. Well-designed objects, including chairs, accomplish more than one thing at a time, but if the designer has succeeded, all the different functions look unified. An object looks integrated only because of very deliberate efforts to harmonize its many components. Accordingly, one can evaluate style by paying attention to the relation between the parts. Does it all add up, with a clear hierarchy, to a dominant visual idea? For example, if the dominant idea is an S-shape, a chair designer will compose the back, feet, and seat to contribute to the overall impression of an S. In sociologese, style would be said to perform an integrative function, not only because it integrates all parts into an overall pattern but also because it resolves competing and complementary values into a hierarchical pattern. The implied priority of one value over another is what allows cultural historians to characterize eras by the style of their art and artifacts. Think, for example, of the Time-Life series on American history in which one volume is devoted to each decade—say, the Jazz Age—and its art, politics, and economics. The implicit theory is that the design lines, proportions, shapes, and decorative motifs of the time crystallize the concerns and aspirations of the day. Another example comes from a study of American bathroom and kitchen aesthetics during the forties and fifties: "the fluid modeling of streamlined forms reflected the period's twin obsessions with *bodily* consumption and *economic* consumption. . . . The molded forms of streamlining yielded an excretory aesthetic . . ."[12]

Obviously from this perspective, style is shared, not idiosyncratically personal. Yet in trying to soothe those anxious about selecting the right chair, retailers encourage insecure shoppers to view chair selection as "a personal thing" and reassure them that style is in the eye of the beholder, since "furnishings are a personal matter and shoppers have to trust their instincts." But the reality behind that idea is social, since the same retailers continue, "It's like your clothing, your easy chair says what you are all about."[13] Style has to be shared, even if within a very small group, in order to communicate and be recognized.

What are the codes that make all this communication possible? Broken down to its basic elements, style is the visual synthesis of three aspects: shape, line, and decoration. Shapes are perceptual fields defined by line. The relation between shape and line introduces proportion, which is another element of visual or stylistic analysis. Chair scholars constantly use all these terms in their descriptions. For example, in describing the "sensuous curves" of Art Nouveau, the focus might be on line *(Fig. 13)*; discussing the proportion of Gothic Revival arches requires attention to both shape and line *(Fig. 14)*; and referring to the horizontal panel of Renaissance Revival *(Fig. 15)*, or to the oval and circular backs of the Rococo Revival, involves the concept of shape *(Fig. 16)*.

Decoration is a particularly important component of style because it communicates content or meaning more overtly than shapes and lines. (The word "decoration" comes from the Latin for ornament, in turn based on the Indo-European words meaning "to receive, be suitable, make decent"; from which it has come to mean "adding to make more attractive." The

closely related word "ornament" comes from ordain, meaning "to put in order," and has come to mean "mere external display." Both words share the common synonym "adorn.") Moreover, the materials used for decoration provide yet another medium for expression. Precious materials worked elaborately with inlays or carvings probably signify an elite, while common materials signify or even glorify the modern masses.

Figure 13. Sidechair by the French furniture designer Eugène Gaillard. The fluid lines of the frame and the curving tracery on the leather back are typical of Art Nouveau.

Figure 14. Periods and styles often overlap. These George III chairs are in the Gothic style.

Notice how quickly rank works its way back into the most fundamental discussion of style.

Nevertheless, the communication function of style gives it a measure of autonomy from status. For example, two equally high-status groups might choose different styles: French Provincial or Art Nouveau. One cannot predict the sort of furniture people own solely on the basis of their power or economic status. The term "lifestyle" was invented to acknowledge this kind of free play between economic status and consumer choice. It acknowledges that people's social identity is based on more than their economic standing alone. Because style cannot be reduced to economic status, it usually merits its own category when analyzing designed objects. The Roman architect Vitruvius distinguished between what he called "firmness, commodity, and delight,"

Figure 15. The lines of this walnut Renaissance Revival hall chair emphasize its width rather than its height.

Figure 16. This Rococo-styled chair has an oval-shaped back.

that is, construction, social purpose, and aesthetics. By recognizing that aesthetic style is an indicator not only of social rank but also of other values, we can revisit the social history of chairs in order to see what can be learned from their looks. In this chapter, we will be thinking more about the symbols encoded into chairs by their creators than about the meanings implied by their uses.

FIVE MAJOR CATEGORIES

I see five extremely broad categories of chair styles: handmade, mass-produced, craftsman, designer, and artist.[14] The number of handmade chairs declined when factories began producing chairs in the nineteenth century. During the twentieth century they have come back into fashion, since they are a way of distinguishing the privileged from the ordinary.

Over the centuries, as the number of chairs in the world and the number of people who have access to them increased, chair styles became more finely determined. Chairs first represented their culture and could be described as cultural types: Asian, Medieval, Egyptian, Hellenistic. Then they became identified with specific countries: Italy, France, Great Britain. Since the eighteenth century, chairs have been identified with furniture makers such as Chippendale, Sheraton, Hepplewhite, and the Adam brothers in the same way that paintings are known by their artists' names, whether or not the master artist did the physical work himself. If done in his workshop under his general direction, it bore his signature. In the twentieth century, significant chairs were even more closely identified with individual designers, who were trained as architects but wanted to try their hand at chair design: Corbusier, Aalto, Breuer, Eames. We know their names not just because we have accurate information about who the designers were but also because chairs have become a medium and a subject for artistic expression. Recently, even fine artists have explored chairs as a subject for individual expression, though not necessarily for sitting. In the future, with our emphasis on the individual, chairs may become associated even more closely with the person who designed them. Just as *Megatrends* author John Naisbitt posited that "high touch" may be a compensation for "high tech," perhaps the individual will be revered as compensation for massive numbers and impersonal production processes.

Handmade Chairs

In the West, preciousness in materials and elaborateness of decoration characterized the ancient period in furniture because of the strong association between visual richness and high status. However, the messages communicated on ancient chairs tell us about more than just the rulers' high standing. Egyptian tomb furniture was encased in gold, but this speaks to more than a high standard of luxury. Explicit messages were also worked into the decoration. For instance, one footstool from Tutankhamen is inlaid with nine bound figures, representing the traditional enemies of Egypt.[15] Not only are the enemies bound, but also the sitting pharaoh puts his feet on them. In both Egypt and Greece, intricate pictures and patterns provided narratives about war, domestic life, and myths. Even the apparently purely formal repetitive patterns used for borders and friezes communicate content about the local botany, land forms, and cultural concepts. Admittedly, only elites get such decoration, but the decoration carries information in some measure free of social rank.

As we have seen, the ancient tradition of chair sitting barely stayed alive through medieval times. Even kings and popes received ambassadors while sitting on their beds. The chair was not "reinvented" until the sixteenth century. Historians argue that the printing press was partly responsible for chairs coming back into favor, because the press made possible the widespread dissemination of theoretical texts from classicism. These texts included illustrations of engravings that were used for ornamenting chairs. Even more important, they proposed theories on proportion that were perfectly applicable to chairs, and could be used in more stable cultures. From this point on, the chair moved from a simple utilitarian tool to an object worthy of visual attention and stylistic expression.[16]

The next two centuries of chair design were remarkably coherent. For the two hundred years between 1610 and 1810, English cabinetmakers

Figure 17. An example of Louis XIV masculine Rococo.

generated only ten discernible styles and the French only eight as a result of the constancy of society and design ideology. For this period, in France, and to a lesser extent in England, anyone who could afford expensive furniture copied royal and aristocratic taste, so that particular styles changed infrequently—usually corresponding with the reign of a French monarch. The furniture named after Louis XIV, the Sun King (1643–1715), was classical, but incorporated Oriental themes, was novel rather than historicist, and showed off the artisan's skill *(Fig. 17);* that named for Louis XV (1715–74) was Rococo, meaning profusely and delicately ornamented, small-scale, light, and extravagantly curved in reaction to the Baroque (*see Fig. 16*); Louis XVI (1774–92) has come to be recognized as Neoclassical, full of "right angles, straight lines, architectural proportions, fluting, and decorative elements borrowed from Greece and Rome."[17]

In England, without an absolute monarch, royal taste was not emulated in the same way, so that by the eighteenth century chairs were approached as sculpture, and the signature of the cabinetmaker was for the first time important enough for his works to be known by name: Thomas Sheraton *(Fig. 18),* Thomas Chippendale *(Fig. 19),* George Hepplewhite *(Fig. 20),* and Robert and James Adam. (However, in the next century the English named furniture after Queen Victoria.) During this same period, because it had no royal court, Holland developed a distinctive look in interior decoration, which its painters have made famous.[18] The Dutch relied on their comparatively simple vernacular style for about two centuries. Ultimately, technological, social, and economic changes in the nineteenth

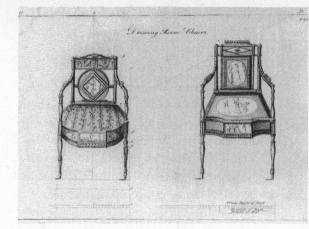

Figure 18. Thomas Sheraton's sketches for two drawing-room chairs.

century disrupted this stylistic stability all over Europe and the Western world.

Mass-Produced Chairs

Once mass production began to dominate chair manufacturing, styles proliferated without regard to nationality or artistic lineage. Thus, the nineteenth century is known as the century of revivalism, without individual furniture makers who distinguished themselves artistically.[19] The earlier styles from England and France, plus vernacular and medieval prototypes, along with Greek and Roman models, were reproduced and combined in endless profusion. Those styles included Gothic Revival *(Fig. 21),* Rococo Revival (Louis XV), Elizabethan (sometimes called Cottage style), Renaissance Revival (Louis XIV), Colo-

Figure 19. A classic English Chippendale-style chair.

Figure 20. An English Hepplewhite shield-back chair.

nial Revival, Japanese, Louis XVI Revival, Neoclassicism, William and Mary, Queen Anne or Early Georgian, Victorian, Craft Revival (often referred to as Arts and Crafts), Frontier style, Windsor, Shaker, and Mission—sometimes with vernacular stenciling. All of these were originally handmade, but all could be copied using machines.

Some contemporaneous and later critics disliked the social significance of revivalism. Specifically, they did not like the fixation on the past, or the sharp distinction between work and home. Remember that in domestic and hotel settings, revivalist models were preferred, while the chief innovation of the nineteenth century, patent furniture, was relegated to the office and other technical arenas such as trains, outdoor camping, barber shops, and laboratories.

However, mechanical improvements did manage to work their way into residential furniture. One such invention was spring upholstery. Earlier, upholstery had meant a thin layer of horsehair, fabric, or tapestry, so the application of coiled springs to upholstery made it deep and changed it qualitatively.[20] This kind of upholstery became a hallmark of the century, criticized in the early twentieth century for

Figure 21. This English Windsor chair has a Gothic back.

obscuring underlying structure. Another mechanical feature that successfully insinuated its way into the present-day American living room was motion furniture, known more commonly by its brand names La-Z-Boy, BarcaLounger, and Lane recliner. These never became a high-status item and were considered stylistically clunky. The number one objective recently has been to restyle them so that they no longer *look* like recliners, but rather like traditional armchairs.

Most of the twentieth-century furniture market continues to rely on industrialized manufacturing, no matter what the look. In addition to revival themes and the various expressions of "efficiency" in office furniture, manufacturers have been churning out "knockdown" and contract furnishings. Knockdown furniture allows the manufacturer to reduce the cost of assembly, and just as importantly, the cost of shipping by having the buyer assemble it at home. The look of this furniture is necessarily full of straight lines, and so lends itself to simple wooden furniture of vaguely modern styles, manufactured almost anywhere in the world. The Scandinavian versions were immortalized in song by John Lennon's "Norwegian Wood," and are marketed today by IKEA. The contract furniture industry produces furniture in multiples, by contract, rather than piece-by-piece selection, for such institutions as schools, offices, libraries, auditoriums, airports, and waiting rooms. The power of mass production has not been harnessed to reproduce historical styles for these institutional settings, but rather to broadcast the "contemporary" look of pleasantly neutral efficiency we know so well from the bureaucracies we inhabit.

Craftsman Chairs

Although industrialization has remained far and away the most important force in terms of number of chairs produced, it has lost its ideological prominence, especially for craftsmen and fine artists, and even for the designers who once looked to it for inspiration. Today, the handmade chair has been revived by craftspeople who value a piece of furniture first and foremost because it is handmade. As early as 1880, the Arts and Crafts movement, led by William Morris in England, was based on the social critique that the easy production of all styles of furniture made possible by industrialization favored the ostentatious and pretentious. *(Fig. 22)* The handmade was a return to authenticity not only for the consumer but also

Figure 22. An American Arts and Crafts–style chair.

for the producer. Critics believed that workers were alienated by mass production because they did not understand how the parts that they were working on fitted into the whole. In contrast, craft advocates then—and now—idealized the American Shakers because they exemplified unalienated labor, and their work, including handmade chairs, was simple, unpretentious, structurally understandable, and carefully constructed.

In the high-minded social ethics of the Crafts movement, beauty is idealized as a goal in itself, not as a means to establishing high status. There are contradictions here, of course; handcrafted chairs are too expensive for most people. The waiting list for one of the chairs by the most famous contemporary American craftsman, Sam Maloof, is long and the people on it can afford to collect paintings. In the words of one critic, "Morally speaking, . . . 'craftsmanship,' far from being synonymous with self-disciplined virtue, [could be] . . . rather a shameless extravagance of human resources."[21]

Another tenet of Arts and Crafts ideology is that art should be part of life, so one should not make a distinction between utilitarian and artistic objects. Creating this kind of unity can produce a meditative state in the craftsperson, which is why former President Jimmy Carter makes his own chairs. Slowing down to make the whole thing, while working with natural materials, certainly can be therapeutic.

Those who believe in the unity of art and life also believe that craft should be viewed as fine art. However, they are probably fighting an uphill battle, because the very categories of craft, design, and art suggest enduring cultural distinctions. Travel guides, newspapers, and city magazines usually have separate listings for craft shows and galleries. Over time this may change because today craftspeople tend to have college backgrounds and emphasize intellectual concepts, in contrast to earlier generations of craftspeople, who emphasized the quality of their raw materials. Further evidence of the possibility of blending categories is that a new category has emerged, that of studio furniture maker, who aims to bridge the two approaches by producing limited editions.

Even though today the Craft movement no longer can hope to replace the organization of the assembly line, it has renewed itself throughout the twentieth century. Since the 1950s, Scandinavian designers have made significant contributions to the movement, both stylistically and conceptually. One well-respected Danish designer, Hans Wegner, views himself as a furniture designer who works with and builds on the strengths of craftspeople. He thinks furniture designers should be familiar with tools, but he does not necessarily build everything himself.[22] In contrast, Sam Maloof twenty years ago turned down a $22 million contract to produce his furniture, saying that he believed that the designer should also be the furniture maker. Here is the essential difference between the craftsman and the designer; when a person provides the ideas that are then executed by someone else, the term "designer" is precisely accurate.[23]

Making chairs by hand usually—but not always—means working with natural raw materials like wood, rush, and occasionally leather, rather than steel or plastic. In the early twentieth century, European and American Arts and Crafts chairs were made of wood, sometimes with leather seats, and in the second half, Scandinavian modern also used wood, usually with seats of natural wool fabric. The way the wood is worked—how it is shaped and joined—is where the craftsman's skill is judged. Craftsmanship is used to assess durability, price, and aesthetic value.

Designer Chairs

In contrast, around the same time, a group of early twentieth-century architects were searching for a new aesthetic appropriate to industrialization, which has been called Modernism.[24] They turned to chairs because they viewed them as a microcosm of the designed environment. Like buildings, chairs are three-dimensional, complex, and need to include pragmatic as well as symbolic functions. Moreover, chairs can stand for people in the photographs and drawings of buildings, which architects often like to depict without the visual interference of real people. Paul Overty notes in *Art in America* the special role of chairs in modern architecture: "Geometric and stylized but at the same time a metaphor for the body, the chair mediates between the human body and the abstract, geometrical forms of modernist architecture."[25] These early architects–turned–product designers desired to show off new industrial materials and the ways they could be joined; but ironically, the details selected—such as the welding required on the famous Mies van der Rohe Barcelona chair—were often labor-intensive, requiring much handwork, (*see Fig. 6*). Unintentionally, custom fabrication became involved, and perhaps for this very reason, these chairs have retained our interest aesthetically and financially as collectors. From a craft point of view, even plastic or metal chairs can be well or poorly made, which is why the architectural historian Vincent Scully noted that early Modernist, pro-industrial chairs actually share a craft orientation with their predecessors. These modern chairs have some of the status of sculpture and antiques, and are collected. In Europe, a Swiss chair manufacturer, Vitra, commissioned the prominent American architect Frank Gehry to design a new museum on the Rhine just to house its collection of Modernist chairs.

The twentieth-century revolt against nineteenth-century furniture design was a twin revolt against revivalism and upholstery. Designers in the twentieth century, starting with proponents of Art Nouveau, were interested in finding ways to express their own age, so they did not want to use historical styles. Whether thinking about architecture or chairs, Modernists hoped to express new ideas and attitudes by turning to the new materials and new construction techniques associated with industrialization.[26] They eliminated surface embellishments like carving, inlays, and moldings, and replaced the traditional wood and fabric with laminated wood, canvas, stainless steel, steel coated with alloys or enamel, plastic, rubber, latex, foam, and other resins. Stylistically speaking, they were still working with shape and line, but they were much less obviously working with decoration. Twentieth-century decoration is subtle indeed. It lies in the nature of the materials that the designer chooses to explore and the construction techniques used for joining those materials. According to the British art historian Edward Lucie-Smith, the disappearance of animal, vegetable, and architectural ornaments indicates that the chair had become a thing in itself, not an allusion to something else, like royalty, national his-

tory, flora, or fauna.[27] These forward-looking materials of the new indus-
trialism were meant to communicate simultaneous references to the new
industrial order as well as nose-thumbing disdain for the backward-looking
nineteenth century.

The Modernist attitude toward materials actually had roots in the
late nineteenth century, when the Austrian furniture maker Michael
Thonet applied steam to wood
and molded it into Bentwood
chairs *(see Fig. 32)*. Consistent
with that tradition, twentieth-
century chairmakers utilized
newly available glues and
steaming and lamination
processes to explore plywood as
a medium. Metal was also
shaped in new ways. The German architect Marcel Breuer
looked at bicycle construction
in the early 1920s and thought
of using bent metal tubes for
chair structure. *(Fig. 23)* New
metals such as steel were strong
enough for this kind of construction, so he and others like
Mies van der Rohe, Mart Stam,
Le Corbusier, Charlotte Perriand, and George Nelson explored metal
in combination with leather, canvas,
wood, and rattan. Ray and Charles Eames
along with architect Eero Saarinen
molded plywood to create new kinds of
laminated wooden chairs. Fiberglass and

Figure 23. Marcel Breuer designed arm and armless
versions of this cantilevered chair (1924–25), which
has come to be known as "Cesca"—the nickname of
his daughter, Francesca.

plastic stimulated Saarinen and Eames to explore integrating seat, back, and arms into one eggshell-shaped unit—much to our anatomical detriment. *(Fig. 24a and b)* Frank Gehry explored cardboard in the 1970s, and these chairs are now collectors' items, still in production by Vitra today. In the early 1990s, the design magazine *Metropolis* still found the challenge of building a chair from an unusual material like shredded paper provocative enough for a front cover. Note, however, that modern chair

designers have not invented new technology, but rather have adapted technology from other fields. They do not first see the need for a cantilevered chair and then invent the materials and processes that could facilitate their vision. This is yet another way of saying that design has integrated culture, rather than forcing it to change.

As designers began to exploit the qualities of new materials, these materials formed the very categories for this century's aesthetic understanding of chair design. For example, elasticity came from the use of leather, plastic, or cloth in tension. Cantilevering was the outcome of new metals (steel or aluminum) in thin tubes or sheets. Moldability emerged from the properties of plywood and plastic resins. Strength came from new glues, as well as from

Figure 24. (a) The tulip pedestal chair by Eero Saarinen (1956) is one of a series of fiberglass molded chairs he and Charles Eames designed together after World War II. *(b)* Earlier (1948), Eames designed the ubiquitous one-piece shell chair with metal rod legs.

steel. The architect Allen Greenberg notes that these aesthetic categories were "simple and expository" because they emerged from the "expressive characteristics of materials or related techniques of jointing."[28]

Since the technical construction of the chair and the sociological expression of modern values influenced the form of early twentieth-century chairs, does that mean that the Modernists followed the dictum that form follows function? Surprisingly, these designers were not particularly interested in responding to the functions of their own bodies. The British curator of the museum show on chairs, Deyan Sudjic, has made a similar observation that early modern chairs "obviously owed a lot more to architectural slogans than to the principles of ergonomics."[29] As Greenberg also explains, in Modernist chair design, the expression of aesthetic ideas "requires clarity and conciseness, and compromises in design, for the sake of comfort, especially in details, are often difficult for the designer to accept." Greenberg cites Bruno Taut, the early twentieth-century German architect, who wrote, "Beauty originates from the natural qualities of the material and from elegance of construction."[30] All of the Finnish designer Alvar Aalto's work exemplifies the exploration of wood as decorative material. Aalto in turn influenced Gerald Summers, a British designer who "pushed the idea of the plywood chair to a logical extreme," cutting and folding a chair from a single sheet of plywood, "almost like an origami conjuring trick."[31] *(Fig. 25)* I would add that sitting on it also requires a trick of some sort.

Early twentieth-century modern chairs are now classics. The contemporary postmodern scene has not generated the passionate ideas about proper form that early Modernism did. Those who have the most fervor about getting things right these days are the designers who are investigating the implications of ergonomic science for chairs. The categorical split between furniture for the office versus the home

Figure 25. Birch "Summers" plywood chair by Gerald Summers (1933–1934).

Figure 26. Emilio Ambasz and Giancarlo Piretti's "Vertebra" chair.

means that virtually all of this experimentation is focused on office furniture. Ergonomic styling aims to communicate sleek efficiency, look-alike shapes, utilitarian textures, subdued colors, black or gray with varying amounts of chrome. Emilio Ambasz, an Argentine-American designer and former curator of design at the Museum of Modern Art, with the Italian designer Giancarlo Piretti designed one of the first office chairs that automatically adjusts to a conventional range of seated postures while continuing to support the spine. *(Fig. 26)* The designers wanted to express the movement and flexibility of the chair as a visual idea, so they equipped their chair with a distinctive black corrugated plastic tube. Of course, the look could be and has been copied without its ergonomic substance.[32]

Today, we are left vacillating between the non-aesthetic aesthetic of the ergonomic chairs and the bold experiments of earlier designers. Designers today such as the French Philippe Starck and the Americans Dakota Jackson and Robert Venturi either exaggerate one of the lines of the classics, or parody it, even to the point of mocking themselves. Consumers and designers alike share a retro-interest in the twenties, thirties, forties, and fifties, with no commitment to any one decade. The nineties seem to have no particular style—except minimalism and simplicity to the point of austerity—but a decade or two from now a characteristic profile will undoubtedly emerge. For the present, we experience a disparate mix, including a nostalgic Ralph Lauren Frontier style, African stools, art from preindustrial societies, fancy Louis XIV chairs, and industrial knockoffs. As the art critic Sidney Tillim puts it, "Flea-market '50s taste is everywhere today; at its best it comes off as a kind of high kitsch that criticizes our lack of true style while masking its own emotional investment in style by mocking it."[33]

A more tolerant view of this eclecticism is provided by the American sociologist Fred Davis, who explains that our social identities are amalgams to start with and ever-changing thereafter, so that fashion in clothing expresses our multiple and conflicting identities; insofar as chairs are like clothing and other art codes, we use them to assemble and then reassemble our definitions of ourselves.[34] Edward Lucie-Smith makes a similar point when he says that interior decor today has to do with assembling still lifes in the artistic tradition. He thinks that we are more interested in what some historians have called assemblage, or collage. When it comes to the chair, it is part of that ensemble or collection of objects in our rooms, part of an artistic tableau.

But does this eclecticism offer the possibility of expanding our visual repertoire to include a body-inspired sensuousness? Even though the industrial design approach to chairs has taken a turn down the path of ergonomics with little expressive symbolism, the artistic approach, in contrast, might have articulated or celebrated the mechanics of the human body more delightfully.

Artists' Chairs

Artists have played with the communication function of chairs more overtly than either craftsmen or designers. They have used chairs as an opportunity to engage in social criticism and comment on social arrangements, including status, even to make visual puns. Many artists have used chairs as the "apparent subject matter" of their paintings and sculpture. In the early 1970s, some artists unsuccessfully attempted to do away with making objects. Consequently, as Naomi Gilman, the curator of an American show on chairs called "Form, Function and Fantasy," which took place in 1978 in Sheboygan, Wisconsin, explains, "without the possibility of creating meaningful new objects or non-objects, painters and sculptors began turning to the banal: common things that already exist in such abundance they cannot be seen as precious or profound. The chair suits this purpose perfectly."[35] One artist in this show split a chair in two, while another created a wearable chair.

In the nineties, artists continue to use chairs to make statements about society. One local installation of five chairs in Oakland, California, is intended to increase awareness of the stages of a person's life or social roles: high chair, desk chair, wheelchair, office chair, and rocking chair.[36]

Group shows have been organized on chair themes. In "The Chair: Deconstructed/Reconstructed," a show held at the Sybaris Gallery in Royal Oak, Michigan, each artist was asked to take inspiration from a "found" chair to create "their own incarnation either functional, sculptural, or frenetic."[37] One made rubbings of an old-fashioned wooden dining chair onto a white damask tablecloth and disassembled the entire chair into its components, which were displayed below the fabric images. Another artist covered a chair in furlike shag that was partially clipped, presumably by the clippers lying on its seat. A 1996 benefit for an AIDS-related project involved giving one hundred chairs to artists, who had three months to "decorate" or redesign the chairs, which would be photographed along with their creators for a catalogue and auctioned as a fund-raiser. Promosedia, an Italian organization that represents about one hundred chair-manufacturing companies in Italy, invited twenty artists to "interpret" chairs, which were auctioned in 1997, also to fight AIDS.[38]

Lucie-Smith observes that furniture has become visually so significant that it can challenge sculpture. The modern movement in art, he explains, taught us to look at forms attentively. "This means that we look at an artefact such as a chair with entirely new eyes. If it is old, we are conscious not only of the talismanic properties . . . but of its qualities as pure form. If it is new, we automatically compare it to the contemporary sculpture it so closely resembles."[39] If they are unique pieces, chairs by sculptors may not really have "style" in the sense of a shared code. *(Fig. 27a and b)*

For the body, do the chairs by sculptors and artists work better than those by designers? Imagine a continuum from designed chairs to highly expressive or critical art works. Two different exhibits mark the ends of this continuum: the Cooper-Hewitt National Design Museum in New York City, a branch of the Smithsonian Institution, held an exhibition entitled "The Outdoor Chair" in 1988. In that exhibition, even though most of the chairs featured are not in production, and in that sense are unique prototypes, they would still have to be described as "responsible design," oriented toward the seated body. Providing high-status elites with freshly interpreted or highly refined versions of Modernist principles, these chairs are architectonic in attitude. They emphasize orthagonal, right-angle lines within another set of rectangles or squares, and the small refinements come in the materials or the proportions. By contrast in the earlier exhibition, the chairs were idiosyncratic. They were used as criticism, cultural commentary, and envisioning—one flexible vinyl simulating wood, another motorized to go through a cycle of automatically breaking down and building back up. They usually mock the body or ignore it altogether.[40]

Somewhere along this continuum are the "one-off" chairs by architect-designers

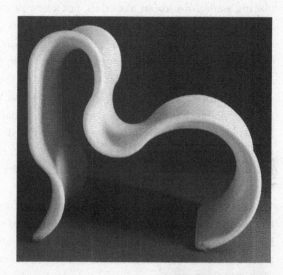

sold in galleries, which blur the distinction between artist and designer. Rather than merge the two identities, collaboration between designers and artists has been a recent practice in several arenas, including that of chair design. Such collaboration started in the 1980s with federal and then state legislation that required 1 percent of

a public building's budget to be spent on art. Artists usually feel that if they were given a greater role in such collaborations, the resulting work would be more specifically fitted to the site. For chairs, rather than getting a standard designed look for a home or office or park, the public would get a more individual, fresh and distinctive treatment. Thus, their motives include commitment to improving

Figure 27. (a) The chair as sculpture is often still usable, but just as often (b) it is unusable because the artist is making a social commentary.

the built environment. But from the point of view of the body, putting two heads together still has not generated any particular interest in the experience of the body—outside the traditional interest of artists in visual scale and proportion.

If someone is making a one-of-a-kind chair, what is it that they are exploring? Worldwide, when artists create a chair, they are usually exploring something about materials, not a new posture. In New York City, design galleries represent international designers who offer "limited editions" of chairs in order to capture part of the fine art market. In Europe today, Ron Arad, avant-garde furniture designer, explores sheet metal as a medium for armchairs meant to be viewed as sculpture. Occasionally a sensuous rationale is offered, as in the case of Zadik Zadikian, an Armenian émigré living in New York, who is making chairs out of plaster of Paris because it feels "organic, sensuous" against the skin.[41] But, as this example shows, the emphasis is on materials—plastic, metal, and wood in varied applications—rather than on the effect of the chair and its structure upon the body and *its* structure.

These various sculptural manipulations for one-of-a-kind, handmade chairs have not been customized to an individual's body or used to establish new prototypes for mass production. Chairs are indeed anthropomorphic, but a chair in a gallery is more likely to have a CAUTION, DO NOT SIT sign than to invite one of us to sit on its lap. Ironically, artists have used chairs, by and large, to address more abstract sets of concerns—as a social, psychological, or cultural commentary.

Given this tendency toward conceptualism, and the recent scholarly attention to the body, I suspect that some artists may eventually try using chairs to express ideas from social theory. One such idea is that the body is a salvation from the repressions required by our modern bureaucratic society. Nineteenth-century industrial capitalism imposed its own specific controls on the human body regarding, for example, sexuality, rest, eating, and leisure. Correspondingly, social thinkers of the day conceptualized people as significant for their thoughts and feelings, while relegating the body to the role of mechanical support for the mind and soul. A second notion popular by the mid-twentieth century is that the body is interesting as the battleground where tensions between social codes and the self are experienced and eventually resolved. A third concept is that the body is a text—

a complex social reality used for social communication through gesture, marking, and costume.[42]

Intriguing as all these ideas are, the challenge when communicating any such ideas about the body is how to stay with the experience of the body itself. Since chairs are so physical, they could be a vehicle for embodying these ideas—particularly the resolution of tensions between social codes and the self—in a way that could be directly appreciated. One idea that *has* been clearly expressed, by paying so much attention to the chair rather than the sofa or table, is the cultural importance of the individual.[43] Because the chair seats only one human being at a time, it responds to the body. Otherwise, none of the approaches to style—historicist, craft revivalist, Modernist, abstract sculptural—that have flourished since the nineteenth century have taken inspiration from the finer points of human morphology or individual differences. This neglect has consequences we feel every day.

Yale professor Vincent Scully in his *New World Visions of Household Gods* offers three important ways to evaluate a chair: its craft, its relation to the body, and its emblematic or communicative function.[44] In his view, twentieth-century chairs share a craft orientation even though they use industrial processes, because of the emphasis on the nature of the materials and how they interact—the tensions between steel and leather, for example. He also judges these chairs as strong on the emblematic/communicative function. However, he thinks they are quite weak as, in his term, "an active physical object," because of an "underdeveloped relationship" between the chair and the body. As we go on to examine what's wrong with the chair, I hope to clarify just what an understatement he has made.

PART II

What's Wrong with
the Chair?

Most people don't think about chairs much one way or the other, because they are part of our surroundings, meant to support us silently and constantly, without attracting much attention. But when stimulated to do so, people often ask me if I recommend a specific brand or if I have designed a chair available on the market. Disappointed that I don't and haven't, they usually follow up with an even better question: What makes a good chair? Often they have a favorite chair, but just as often they wonder why they can't find a chair they really like.

I too wanted to know what might be the best of all possible chairs, so I turned to the scientific literature on chair design, now dominated by the work of ergonomic researchers (Chapter 3). These specialists describe and measure the relationship between human activity, usually work-related, and the immediate environment, which includes chairs. Yet I learned that this field does not have all the answers. Ergonomic criteria need to be applied selectively, because many of them are contradictory. However, joined with a holistic perspective (developed in Chapter 4), the two disciplines provide a powerful standard by which to evaluate almost any kind of chair, including some of the most famous pieces of the twentieth century.

To know a Chair is really it,
You sometimes have to sit.

—from "The Chair," by Theodore Roethke[1]

Chapter 3

An Ergonomic Perspective

THE CHAIR AS A HEALTH HAZARD

In the early 1970s, I ran across what I thought was a brilliant article. It purported to explain why people always fidget so much when they sit in a chair for more than a few minutes. The argument went like this: When a person leans backward into the chairback, that initiates both a backward and a downward force. The downward force pushes the bottom of the pelvis forward. Eventually, the sitter finds himself sitting on his tailbone out at the edge of the chair with the spine as a whole transformed to a C-shape slouch. Sound familiar? We've all been there.

This particular slump proves to be uncomfortable in several ways: congestion is created in the lungs and in the guts; the ribs fold down over the diaphragm toward the belly; strain is created in the lower back. In order to try to relieve themselves of this discomfort, people sit up straight and perch on the front edge of the chair without back support. In short order, they also find this position tiring, so they scoot all the way back into the seat to take advantage of the chairback. Once they lean back, they recreate the twin forces that eventually push the pelvis forward once more, initiating the cycle all over again. *(Fig. 28)*

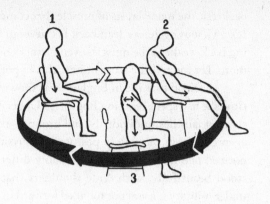

Figure 28. The inherent instability of the seating posture is diagrammed here. Note that Westerners assume the third position is too tiring to maintain.

What a revelation! If the seated posture is inherently unstable, no wonder designers have not been able to design the perfect chair. If there is no stable posture, it cannot be supported. Doug Stewart, in *Smithsonian* magazine in 1986, apparently without the benefit of reading this analysis, observed in his title that "Modern Designers Still Can't Make the Perfect Chair."[2] After all this time, despite scientific rationality, modern designers have not been able to keep pace with their counterparts in other professions and occupations. But designers are excused once we understand that the body itself is to blame. Its inherent instability makes the perfect chair forever elusive. Blaming the body frees the designer from anatomical constraints and leaves the door open to self-expression and artistic experimentation with form, materials, and symbolism. Early on, therefore, I dismissed chair design as an area for rational inquiry.

I have since developed an opposing view: the chair, not the body, is the problem. Bodies were here first, so chairs should respond to bodies, not vice versa. Thus, if people are "unstable" because they move frequently, chairs should accommodate that movement. Chairs that fail to offer that flexibility can harm our bodies.[3] I have come to believe that chairs are hazardous to our health, and I do not believe that our bodies compromise the success of our otherwise skillful design solutions.

After many years of training in various body-mind disciplines, I finally recognized that a cultural assumption lay hidden in the first explanation. The assumption is that sitting at the edge of a seat upright, without support, is too tiring to sustain. But in other cultures, people sit upright by the hour. I wondered why we couldn't do that. A radical thought kept surfacing: we can't sit upright simply because we have grown accustomed to being supported by chairbacks. Because we lean against the backrest, the many layers of muscle that comprise the torso get weakened. It's a vicious cycle: we lean back because our muscles are weak, and leaning back weakens the muscles even further, so that we "need" support even more. Let me tell the story of how this hypothesis was born.

A friend of mine in England was showing me photographs from the time she had spent teaching English in Upper Volta, Africa. I scanned snapshots of families, individuals, and groups—men, women, and children of average stature, varying in posture and physical development. Suddenly I noticed one man who was remarkably different from all the others. He stood beautifully, with wide shoulders that were neither pressed back under military tension nor rounded forward in a clerical stoop, and his chest was deep. His spine was erect and his head balanced, with no strain apparent in his neck muscles. I exclaimed at the perfection of his physical development. Then I found a second such person. *(Fig. 29)*

Without knowing anything about my interest in chairs, my friend commented that the two men I had singled out were the only two who had grown up in a village without a missionary school and its tables and chairs. Of course, there may have been other differences between these two

and the rest that I will never know, but my friend's comment served to precipitate my suspicions into a hypothesis. Here was a dramatic sign that the entire scientific paradigm for chair design was misguided. Chairs *in and of themselves* are the problem; not poorly designed chairs.

I began to look for research evidence that sitting in a chair itself generates physical problems and deforms the body. I found diverse evidence from

Figure 29. This snapshot of an African of Guinée, shown to me by my English friend, confirmed my suspicions that chair sitting cumulatively deforms our bodies.

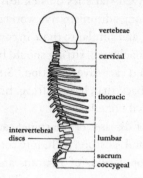

Figure 30. A diagram showing commonly used anatomical terms. Note the natural elongated S-shape of the human spine in side view.

vertebrae
cervical
thoracic
intervertebral discs
lumbar
sacrum
coccygeal

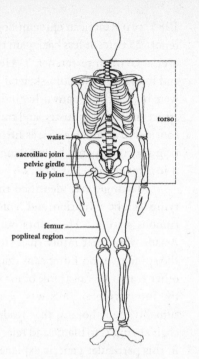

torso
waist
sacroiliac joint
pelvic girdle
hip joint
femur
popliteal region

many countries that such sitting has been associated with numerous problems: back pain of all sorts, fatigue, varicose veins, stress, and problems with the diaphragm, circulation, digestion, elimination, and general body development. (*Fig. 30* offers a glossary of anatomical terms used to describe the musculo-skeletal system.) Most of this research is published in journals devoted to rehabilitative medicine and ergonomics. The term "ergonomics" comes from the Greek *ergon,* meaning "work," and *-omics,* meaning "to manage." Thus, ergonomics is the study of the relationship between the person and the immediate work environment. It is primarily a twentieth-century discipline developed during World War II, first in cockpit design and thereafter in factory production facilities, and is now applied in office workstations. Because the chair is part of the immediate work environment, it has received plenty of attention from ergonomics researchers.[4]

First of all, I learned from ergonomic and occupational health perspectives that sitting is hard work. This is true whether we sit well or badly, because the pressure on the spinal discs is 30 percent greater when sitting than when standing.[5] In consequence, sitting strains the spinal column, back muscles, lower back nerves, and diaphragm. If sitting is so stressful, why do so many people prefer sedentary office work to physical labor? In

1985, two American epidemiologists found that sedentary office workers report 25 percent less back pain than people who do physical labor.[6] However, a German researcher, T. Hettinger, analyzed statistics on sick leave and found that musculo-skeletal problems among administrative workers were higher than in any other industrial sector, and similar to those in construction, metal industry, and transport. His conclusion: sitting should be considered as much a risk as lifting weights and excessive vibration.[7] Sitting may or may not be less dangerous to the back than heavy lifting, but if it is merely the lesser of two evils, it is an evil nonetheless.

Hettinger has identified three sources of diseases of the spine: carrying weight, vibration, and "enforced (unnatural) posture, including continuous sitting." He points out that two populations of Africans and Asians who squat rather than sit on chairs report far less compression of the spine than do Europeans doing either light or heavy work. The only other reason he can think of for this finding is that perhaps the tissue of the intervertebral discs was "genetically" stronger to begin with.[8] Presumably, he is hoping that readers will accept his first explanation that chair sitting is to blame and reject the subtle racism that would be at work in this particular genetic explanation.

Unconscious racism is all too often involved whenever people seek genetic explanations for social differences. Certainly, it lies behind statements to the effect that "Westerners can't squat." That is anatomical nonsense. Westerners have simply lost the flexibility required for squatting through lifetimes of not squatting. Remember, as children we all squatted beautifully. And if we work at it as adults, we can regain the ability. In societies where squatting continues as an adult practice, medical researchers have observed lower rates of disc degeneration than in sitting cultures.[9]

A team of Swiss researchers were among the first to confirm that the constrained sitting postures used at video display terminal (VDT) workplaces and in full-time typing were associated with physical impairment of the hands, arms, shoulders, and neck.[10] Despite all this diverse evidence that prolonged sitting is the problem, when trying to account for low back pain, medically oriented epidemiologists still seek structural rather than behavioral explanations. That is, they look for explanations such as leg-length difference and whether or not a person has been in an automobile crash. Tautologically, they find that the best single predictor of back pain is previous back pain. One such researcher concludes that lower back pain is a mystery, even though others have very clearly shown that sitting is implicated as a major cause.[11]

Complicating the issue further, psychological causes also have to be considered. In the mid-1980s, John Sarno, an American physician, published a popular book, *Mind Over Back Pain,* in which he argued that back pain has a psychosomatic basis.[12] He developed a comparison with ulcers, which he reasoned used to be the way people expressed tension, until its psychological base was discovered, at which point people began to express their tension through their backs.[13] He did not consider posture, and certainly not chair sitting, as a source of tension.

Wilfred Barlow, a British medical doctor and Alexander Technique teacher, has clarified what lies behind the confusion over sources of back pain. "Conflict of opinion on the subject of low back pain will be with us forever," he wrote as early as 1955, "unless we realize that it is behaviour which disturbs the mechanics of the back, all day and every day, and that it is only through a re-education of behavioural attitudes that we will alter these mechanical faults." If the body is analogous to an automobile, the standard medical approach often would be to provide new brake linings. "But," Barlow goes on, "if the driver insists on putting on the brakes on the front wheels whilst he accelerates with the rear wheels, it is no solution to provide new brake linings; the driver needs to learn how to integrate his performance so that he brakes or accelerates at the right time."[14]

More recently, a massage therapist wrote a letter to *The New York Times* responding to medical columnist Jane E. Brody, who suggested that strenuous activity and overuse were the main culprits in muscular pain and spasm. The therapist objected, to the contrary, that poorly coordinated action or sitting still—in chairs—is the actual cause of such pain:

> As a massage therapist—with a clientele ranging from world-class athletes to the chronically disabled—I have learned that under-use contributes to significant muscle pain, spasm, and, if they are untreated, disability.
>
> Anyone who sits before a word processor for six or seven hours a day might have significant pain and spasm in the muscles of the posterior neck, shoulders, lateral hip, hamstring, and sacroiliac regions. Not infrequently, such people are unaware of their pain condition and will be perplexed about the cause

of sore muscles. They'll say, "I didn't do anything out of the ordinary to have caused this pain." Precisely. Holding any posture for prolonged periods without redress or remedy is, I'm convinced, a major cause of chronic muscle pain and spasm.

As a taxpayer and the mother of a child in primary school, I am disturbed that sitting still is still considered an essential component of public education. We should be teaching our children the habit of shaking loose five minutes in every hour, from the insidious vice grip of the common chair.[15]

As a single practitioner, her views are not conclusive, of course, but in general they corroborate the experiences of Alexander teachers and other somatic practitioners, that malcoordinated action or sitting still, rather than too much exercise, gives us muscular pain. Sitting certainly does not relieve it. To the contrary, the 1985 medical research reported earlier states, "Lying down or walking provides relief for most sufferers." The same report specified that stooping is the most aggravating factor in back pain, followed by sitting.[16] And many people manage to stoop while they are sitting.

The head of a Norwegian furniture company has confessed that he felt guilty about making his living from producing chairs after he learned about the health problems they create: "Being a chair manufacturer, it was a very unpleasant experience when I realized that humans were not created to sit: humans were created to walk, stand, jog, run, hunt, fish, and to be in motion; when they wanted to rest, they lay down on the ground." He bravely soldiers on, summarizing the health problems (in addition to low back pain) that are associated with traditional sitting posture: "The ninety-degree sitting angle at the hip joint exerts pressure on the diaphragm and all the natural functions of the internal organs in and around the stomach area are restricted. The lower the chair, the worse it is. This again means that by restricting the natural functions of the internal organs the blood circulation is reduced, which in turn causes a decreased oxygen supply to the head. This results in a person becoming tired more quickly."[17]

As we saw in Chapter 1, Dr. Mandal of Denmark is especially worried about children's health—in particular, their eyesight and spines—being undermined by years of sitting in chairs. He knows that adults suffer back and neck pains of all sorts, but he has judged that the long-term solution to back problems is to protect people earlier. He hopes that if children's health can be protected in schools, they will not only be better off physically but also psychologically prepared to expect and demand improved work environments.

Other indications of the deleterious effect that sitting has on our internal organs comes from research on a common affliction of infants, gastro-esophageal reflux. The involuntary bringing up of food or liquids is sometimes associated with pulmonary aspiration, pneumonia, bronchial spasm, apnea, asthma, and even death. Since gravity helps prevent reflux in adults, infants younger than six months have routinely been placed in an infant seat since the 1950s. But medical research concludes that the seat, rather than being therapeutic, is actually detrimental. What's a better approach? Simply placing the infant prone. Babies younger than six months do not yet have strong torsos, so sitting them upright prematurely allows the junction between esophagus and stomach to become constricted; when prone, their digestive apparatus lengthens properly.[18]

An Australian doctor, Colin J. Alexander, reports that varicose veins are common only in chair-sitting cultures; conversely, they are uncommon in cultures where people sit on the ground. The chair-sitting posture holds the sitter in a static right angle between the foot and the leg. That angle opens the saphenous vein in the ankle to its maximum, subjecting its walls to constant pressure, so that they lose their elasticity. After years of sitting in school in that posture, the vein is permanently dilated. Later, an adult who works for hours on his or her feet or experiences pregnancy may need that elasticity. But when the elasticity is not available, the walls of the veins rupture.[19]

After reviewing all the havoc sitting in chairs wreaks upon the body, it becomes less surprising that this cultural practice could impede overall morphological development.[20] No wonder the two African men who did not grow up in a table-and-chair culture developed so differently from those who did.

ERGONOMIC CONSENSUS

How does the science of ergonomics help us overcome the deleterious effects of chair sitting? Some ergonomic recommendations are straightforward and self-evident, and following them would actually minimize, but never completely eliminate, the damage caused by chair sitting. Many chairs fail to meet at least some of these basic standards. These guidelines are termed "performance guidelines," meaning that the criteria are meant to enhance behavior, and that the measures in inches are not ends in themselves. How many criteria from this simple checklist does your workaday chair violate?

• Chair seats should not be too high

For conventional right-angle seating, the Swedish chair researcher Bengt Akerblom argued as early as 1948 for a lower seat height in order to accommodate the shorter half of the population. Today, the standard seat height for an ordinary task chair with a flat seat is 18 inches from the floor, but that is a distortion for at least half of the population. In other words, it suits some sort of mythical "average", body, which turns out to be a tall male body. So, for all children, most women, and a healthy percentage of men, chairs are too high.

If a chair is too high, it cuts under the knee, pressing the thigh muscles up from below on the edge of the seat. This forces the muscle tissue to take on a load-bearing function for which it was not designed.[21] *(Fig. 31)* If you are sitting now, do you feel pressure under your thighs? If so, your veins and arteries cannot circulate blood properly. An easy way to tell if your seat is at the right height is that your heels should reach the ground. Your entire foot, including the heels, should rest securely on the floor or other underpinning. If the heels are pulled up, your thighs are probably being compressed against the front edge of the seat.

Chairs can also be too low; if your knees are higher than your hip sockets, that jams your hip joint, and worse, reverses the natural for-

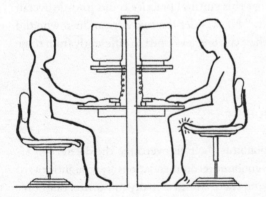

Figure 31. An example of ergonomic consensus: the seat should not be too high; both feet should be able to rest fully on the floor or support bar.

ward curve of your lower back, stressing the discs. The height issue is further complicated by one of the ideas for seating reform, namely, that one's knees should be lower than one's hips in order to preserve the natural curve in the lower back. In this case, one can "walk" the sit bones out to the very edge of the chair and perch there. Higher is better until the sitter approaches a half-sitting/half-standing position (discussed below).

For now, our focus is on traditional chairs. Seventeen inches might be a safe compromise, but multiple sizes or adjustable heights are preferable. Like Goldilocks, you want a chair that is not too high, not too low, but just right.

• The front rail of the seat should be curved downward

The reason for curving the front rail of the chair is to eliminate the sharp edge that might cut into flesh under the knee, called the popliteal region. All ergonomicists agree on this simple rule, but it is violated in chairmaking fairly often. *(Fig. 32)*

• The depth and width of the seat should be 17 inches

Most ergonomics researchers recommend that seats be about 17 inches deep and 17 inches wide. This would fit a surprisingly wide range of body sizes, probably because the thigh bone has the lowest standard deviation of any bone in the body. However, one ergonomic specialist, Anne Shihadeh, reports that in actuality, "most chairs don't have 17 inches of *usable* seat depth." She explains that "many chairs have lumbar supports that extend so far forward that people cannot get to

Figure 32. The ubiquitous Austrian Thonet chair has a rounded front rail, but the raised rim around the seat edge cuts into the sitter's thighs.

the back 2 inches of the seat . . . [or] . . . the waterfall contour is so gradual that the usable depth is diminished another 1–2 inches."[22] Also, many club chairs are deeper than that, which is fine for a long-thighed man, but most of us would need to adjust it by using a pillow at our backs.

• Weight should be distributed through bones, not flesh

When seated, you should be able to feel your sit bones on the seat. That's another way of saying that flesh is not supposed to be load-bearing; bones are. This means that both sitter and designer should avoid deep padding for sitting. An overpadded chair forces the sit bones to rock in the padding rather than make contact with a stable surface, thereby forcing the flesh in the butt and thighs to bear weight. Ergonomics researchers say the padding should be "just right," but they don't explain exactly what number of inches they would recommend at what density and for what weight. I prefer one-quarter-inch padding and find one-half-inch padding okay, but any more than that seems to create instability for the sit bones.

You should be able to feel the sit bones doing their job—carrying about 60 percent of your weight. (When properly seated, the other 40% is transferred down to the heels, which is why they need to be set comfortably on the floor.) To find your balance of weight internally, sit on bare wood. Rock on your sit bones from front to back about 1/4–1/2 inch. Remember that feeling when buying a chair.

• Space between seat and back is preferable to continuous support

Many ergonomicists agree that there should be some space between the seat and the lower edge of the back of the chair. Without that space, the sacrum and the pelvis are pushed forward. That eliminates the natural curve in the lower spine and makes the spine unstable. If there is no space for our butts, we lapse into a C-shaped posture. This is true even in lounge chairs if they don't offer an adequately articulated joint between seat and back for our hips and pelvis.

Unfortunately, these sensible recommendations, backed up by scientific studies, are ignored by many, many designers. If consumers were to refuse to buy or use chairs that ignored even these criteria, chair design would be reformed remarkably, and there would likely be an enormous benefit for public health.

CONFUSED ERGONOMICS

The problems associated with chair sitting will never be completely resolved by following ergonomic guidelines, however, since it turns out that several ergonomic guidelines create their own problems. For example, most researchers recommend a very wide angle between the seat and the back of the chair—usually approaching 110 degrees—especially in chairs used for socializing. The wide angle is recommended to reduce intradiscal pressure and decrease lumbar muscle activity. Yet it is not entirely clear that reducing disc pressure or muscle activity is beneficial in itself, as we shall see in discussing design for movement in Chapter 5. But even if we provisionally accept this rationale, it also has negative consequences. If the head followed the trajectory set by the spine leaning at that angle, the neck would be under tremendous stress because it would be thrust back in space without any support. *(Fig. 33)* Naturally, people bring their head forward, instead, over their center of gravity. Meanwhile, since the spine is still traveling backwards while the head is being brought forward, the thoracic bend of the spine is exaggerated. After years of holding this position, people develop a hump in the thoracic spine.[23] Even task chairs are recommended to have a wide angle between seat and back, with the same outcome of exaggerating the thoracic curve. Most people attribute this deformation to old age, whereas the community of somatic practitioners believe the problem comes from misuse, which this ergonomic guideline inflicts.

Another worrisome example comes from the research by A. Grieco, director of the Institute of Occupational Health in Milan, who gave the annual lecture to the Ergonomics Society in 1986. He reported that his research group studied telephone operators in their old workstations and in their new workplaces with video display terminals, and learned that their movements were cut in half. He had the courage to conclude not only that ergonomically designed furniture could not resolve all the problems of sitting, but also that the ergonomic furniture itself contributes to "a new problem, postural fixity. . . ."[24] Ergonomic furniture has created back problems because it succeeds too well in supporting the body in one position.

Figure 33. Chair sitting actively creates a hump in the upper spine. The diagram traces spinal deformation in the photo. (The dotted line shows the trajectory of the head established by the angle of the backrest.)

Perhaps an even more profound reason that ergonomically designed chairs have not been able to solve most of the problems of sitting is that they are *intrinsic* to the right-angle seated posture. Grieco came close to saying as much, but not quite.

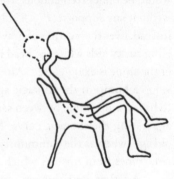

He was absolutely right in stating that holding any posture for long periods of time is the ultimate problem; but holding the classic right-angle seated posture in particular has its special stresses, which no amount of ergonomic tinkering can eliminate.

The entire scientific specialty of ergonomics has remained naive in assuming that a problem-free chair is just a matter of time and effort. The cultural assumption that chair sitting is natural, civilized, or somehow beyond question has kept ergonomicists' efforts confined to a narrow circle. It reminds me of a "conceptual blockbusting" exercise in which one is asked to connect five dots without lifting one's pencil in one continuous line. The trick is to allow oneself the possibility of extending the line beyond the box in which the dots are arrayed. In Western culture, we cannot imagine life being conducted without tables and chairs, so we stay within the box, trying to become comfortable within the constraints of the classical right-angled seat, struggling to resolve what I have come to see as irresolvable tensions.

Ergonomics researchers assume, like most of us, that right-angle sitting is rational, that we need back support, and that we all value comfort. These assumptions get them into trouble—spawning contradictory concepts, invalid research methods, and conflicting recommendations.

SUPPORT

The whole issue of back support is controversial, and I want to make it more so. Bernard Rudofsky, in *The Unfashionable Human Body,* drove a wedge into this issue by slyly pointing out that in the nineteenth and early twentieth century it was common knowledge that ankles "had" to have support. Therefore, everyone wore high-top shoes. Since we now know that you don't have to have ankle support to walk around, Rudofsky subversively undermines two of our current assumptions about support. First, if we don't need ankle support, then perhaps we don't need arch support in shoes; but, more importantly, if support is overrated in general, then back support might not be necessary in chairs. Having introduced this provocative thought, he proceeds to extol the virtues of the Eastern practice of autonomous seating—that is, sitting upright without back support.[25] But Rudofsky is unusual. Almost everyone else, from Sweden to California, believes that back support is necessary. And they usually add: "Especially if you are going to sit for any length of time." After all, what distinguishes a chair from a stool is its back, and that assumes that you are going to lean on the back of the chair at some point. So, it is logical to care about the shape of the chair back.

Etienne Grandjean, an influential Swiss ergonomic researcher, spelled out the logic of lumbar (lower) back support.[26] Faced with one of the major problems in the research literature—how to define comfort—he settles for an objective rather than a subjective definition. That is, rather than rely on unreliable accounts of whether or not people feel comfortable, he starts out from the more objective criteria of whether or not muscles are working. He asks: What position in the seated posture requires the least muscular work? His answer: A C-shaped slump. Amazingly, Grandjean starts with the slump as a goal. However, he acknowledges a conflict of interest between the muscles' comfort in doing nothing and the health of the discs. That is, he knows that when the forward curve in the lower back is flattened, as in his "desirable" stoop, problems ensue for the discs. The front edges of the large vertebrae at the bottom of the spine get too close together, which makes their back edges flare apart too much; this puts uneven pressure on the discs between the vertebrae. They are poorly nourished and likely to thin or rupture. Most discs rupture dorsally—toward the back. I suspect that slumping in a C-shaped configuration could be responsible for rupturing the discs in the first place, and certainly for the direction of their bulge.[27] *(Fig. 34)* Ruptured discs cause pain and nerve damage, sometimes requiring surgery to replace the discs between the vertebrae or other procedures to get them back to their proper function.

What should people do if the most "objectively" comfortable position—the no-work slump—is also bad for them? Here enters the concept of lumbar support. By configuring the seatback so that it sticks out at the sitter's lower back, the sitter (as long as he/she is right up against the seatback) will not be able to lose the natural forward curve in the lower back. Yet since Grandjean's goal is still the no-work slump, the lumbar support pushes the lower spine forward, while the upper body is still supposed to maintain the top half of the C-shaped curve, that is, a caved-in chest. This is why you encounter professionally designed seats in some airplanes and cars that have a C-shaped curve, pushing your upper body, head, and shoulders forward and down, while at the same time pushing the lower back region forward with a specialized contour. *(Fig. 35)*

I was surprised to find that someone was willing to put this poor reasoning in writing, but I was also relieved to find a logic of sorts behind such contorted furniture. This means there's hope, because if such designs are a response to bad reasoning and faulty conceptual models, they can respond to better reasoning and better models.[28]

Figure 34. When we sit in a C-shaped stoop, the lumbar vertebrae force uneven pressure on the pulpy discs, which tend to slip out toward the back.

Healthy Discs

Slump Position

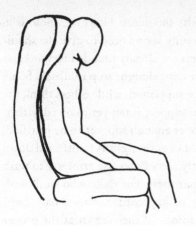

Figure 35. Does this diagram of an airplane seat look familiar? The spine is unhealthily curved at both the bottom and top.

Dr. Mandal, not an ergonomist by education but a surgeon, was the pioneer in challenging the logic of back support. For nearly thirty years he has observed that most people ignore the backrest, no matter what its angle, 90 degrees or 110 degrees, because they lean forward over their tasks. While most ergonomicists worry about how to get people to use the back support, the maverick Mandal insists that empirically speaking their concerns are at best irrelevant to actual behavior, probably wishful thinking, and perhaps even a moralistic throwback to Victorian times. A recent (1996) Danish study by a team of ergonomic researchers tackled some of these same issues. They dated this long-standing belief that a backrest facilitates lordosis, the natural curve of the lower back, to 1913, and decided to test it by studying people using three different kinds of workstations: one without any backrest; the second with a flat vertical lumbar backrest; and the third with curved lumbar support.

Their various findings challenge the logic of back support. The flat backrest was worse than no backrest at all, a victory for autonomous seating. However, at first the lumbar support looked better than the flat support; but when the task of reading was introduced, people rounded their backs regardless of the type of backrest—another score for Mandal's contention that the classical right-angle posture is an abstraction, irrelevant once forward-oriented tasks are involved. Ultimately, the third workstation with lumbar support induced the greatest load on the spine. Mechanically forcing the spine to go forward while the musculature of the body is pulling it backward is probably the reason for the stress. These researchers concluded that "the traditional conception that a backrest facilitates lordosis is apparently not true," thereby confirming Mandal's contention.[29]

Other conflicts surround the issue of support. Some ergonomic researchers think you need to support the shoulders. However, those who follow the no-work slump line of reasoning see no need to give the shoulders extra support because the shoulders are already rounded forward and droop over the torso. In any case, most chair designs stop midback. Some researchers think that thighs need to be supported, while others think the thighs should be free. The issue of arm support is not yet resolved, either. Some think that an armrest does not offer enough support to be justified, because on average only about 4 percent of our weight is transferred down through armrests. Although the elderly sometimes use armrests to push up on, this is not the case for most chair users. For those who work with their arms extended in order to type or keyboard, armrests have been demonstrated to relieve stress on the spine—if they are set at the proper height for each person. In these cases, office seating experts recommend that they fold out of the way so that employees don't feel constrained.[30] But the reason we have arms on selected chairs at dining-room or boardroom tables has more to do with status than physical support. The head of the table, traditionally the man of the house, has arms on his diningroom chair to communicate his importance, not to carry the weight of his arms while eating or to help him push up after a meal.

Other contradictions also permeate ergonomic research. At the opening of this chapter, I described how using a chairback takes a person's body back and then down into a forward slide. There are other responses to this problem. For example, people themselves often cross their legs to stop sliding forward. What designers do is cant the front of the seat up, which cuts under the knees and jams the thigh into the hip socket—two fundamental violations of good ergonomics in one move. To correct these problems, that is, to take pressure off the underside of the thigh and open up the hip socket, they increase the backward slope of the chairback. However, this adjustment sends the spine and head diagonally backward. If you follow that trajectory, your head will be behind your chest. Holding it that far back puts tremendous stress on the neck, so naturally you bring your head forward. This only *recreates* the infamous C-shaped spine, collapsing the rib cage over the guts and creating a series of internal problems and a nasty hump in the back.

Instead of challenging the logic of back support, ergonomic researchers argue among themselves about the direction of the angle of the seat to the floor. Some want the seat canted backwards almost five degrees;

others want it tilted *forward* about five degrees or even more. The dis-agreements are the result of responding differently to the problems intro-duced by chairbacks. The people who recommend tipping seats back-wards are trying to counteract the tendency of the body to slide forward in a chair. The people who want to tip the seat forward are trying to open up the hip socket in order to preserve the lumbar curve and allow the head and spine to remain erect. While they seem to have persuaded the manu-facturers of office chairs to produce some forward-tilt seats, the flat-seaters are still in the majority, following convention without much justification.

When the upper body is extended far back behind the sit bones, an alternative response could be to run the chairback all the way up past the shoulders and to support the head behind the shoulders, rather than re-quire it to be drawn forward. This would eliminate the exaggerated for-ward curve of the spine. But then we have a different entity, a lounge chair. Probably we should use lounge chairs more often than we do. But if the designer wants to retain the classic chair, he or she only chases the prob-lem throughout the body from lower back to hip joint to neck to rib cage. As a culture, that's where we stand right now: we have chased the contra-dictions intrinsic in the right-angle seated posture to the front of our rib cages, by and large. Cultural critics could probably characterize an era by where its quintessential chair design chases and leaves the physical prob-lems it creates. Currently, we accept sitting collapsed into our chests like the man in *Fig. 33* as normal and even pleasant. Of course, we can find ex-amples of chairs that let the problem stop at all those other anatomical points, too. Some famous twentieth-century chairs cut under our knees, jam our hip joints, or stress our necks, as you will soon see.

Ideas about support continue to confuse the research specialists and our culture at large, making design for healthy sitting unlikely. Snarled up with these competing ideas about support is an even bigger confusion about comfort.

COMFORT

What is comfort? How should it be defined? In his popular book, *Home,* the architectural historian Witold Rybczynski noted that architectural education glosses over the topic without ever defining it.[31] One might think that furniture designers would have been forced to tackle and resolve the issue. Yet resolution eludes not only designers but ergonomics researchers, too. In a review article in the ergonomics journal *Human Factors,* the office consultant Rani Karen Lueder concludes that the field has "no universally accepted operational definition of comfort."[32] Moreover, Lueder finds that the "experts" have not agreed on whether comfort and discomfort are two ends of a continuum or two distinct dimensions. She cites an early (1958) operational definition of comfort as "the absence of discomfort." But comfort surely involves more than an absence, so in order to find a more satisfying definition, Lueder turned to Webster's 1964 definition of the word—"support and assistance"—paying no attention to the original Latin roots, "to strengthen." Comfort and its synonyms, like ease, are problematic because its two components, support and freedom, could be in conflict; for instance, a concave seatpan could support the buttocks while restricting movement. An ergonomics advocate herself, Lueder reiterates that ergonomics researchers have tried, and failed, to define comfort in a way that can be measured either subjectively or objectively.

Researchers have tried to measure "what people *think* is comfortable," but, not surprisingly, this varies from trial to trial. A chair that is described as being comfortable one day is described as not being comfortable the next. In one test, in which subjects were asked to rank the comfort of nine chairs, they produced an order that was radically different a week later.[33] One's memory is not trustworthy enough to compare one sensation of comfort with the sensations of comfort from previous experiences in other seats. You could object that kinesthetic memory is not the issue, but rather what the person needs, which might change depending on what the person has been doing with their body most recently. However, another researcher found that the rankings began to shift after only five minutes.[34]

Other researchers have found that the number of body parts experiencing discomfort is more important than the intensity of the discomfort.[35] Still others maintain that the comfort of back and buttocks is more important than the comfort of neck and shoulders, which, in turn, is more important than the comfort of thighs and legs.[36]

Most disconcertingly, what ergonomics researchers recommend—support of the sit bones, not cutting under the thigh, support for the lower spine, etc.—never translates into chairs that all human beings describe as comfortable. The researchers defend their conclusions by responding that people employ thoughtless generalities, such as, "I never like a chair that is not padded," or, "That leather chair must be comfortable," or just the notion, "That looks cozy." People seem to respond more to their *ideas* about comfort than to their actual physical experience of it. Advertisers, of course, capitalize on the difference between the reality of comfort and its image in the marketing process. The most likely illusions and allusions are to luxury, power, and prestige. Remember, the executive model of an office chair often costs less to manufacture than the secretarial model, but the company can charge more for the larger, leather model. Retailers can also get people to buy physically awkward if not outright damaging chairs if they look right. Many different genres can look right to the right person; stylish, avant-garde, traditional, comfortable, sensible and rational, technologically sophisticated—all have rhetorical appeal and power.

Behind those subjective variations in the judgments people make about what is comfortable in a chair are still more assumptions. One is that respondents are aware of their feelings of comfort—though they may not be at all. Because individuals vary enormously in how aware they are, one cannot assume that the description "pleasant" or even "comfortable" means the same thing, physically, to different people. Another assumption is that feelings of comfort can be verbalized, when in actuality such feelings are difficult to express. P. Branton, an ergonomic researcher, observed that awareness of posture is "very primitive and deeply ingrained . . . not readily accessible to introspection and verbalization."[37] Yet another dubious assumption is that people are able to single out aspects of the chair or seat that are the sources of their discomfort.

Ideas about what is comfortable also seem to vary from one historical era to another. This raises the unsettling possibility that comfort has become so detached from our human experience that it has become fashion. In fact, Rybczynski claims that each historical period has had consensus about what is comfortable and what is not.[38] Of course, people are much taller now, which might affect the assessment of chair designs from the past, but most judgments about seating do not have an obvious link to height. For example, an upright horsehair settee was judged comfortable in the eighteenth century, but by the nineteenth century people expected luxurious fabric, springed upholstery, and a more open angle between seat and back.

Since individuals vary from trial to trial as to what is comfortable, and societies also vary from era to era, one can understand why ergonomics researchers throw up their hands in dismay in trying to find a universally experienced definition. Electromyogram tests (EMGs) have even been used to determine whether a muscle is doing any work, but researchers admit that interpreting the test results is problematic. Comfort, defined as rest for one muscle, may require extra work, hence less comfort, for other muscles. In their words, "a low level of activity in one muscle group may signal an increased level of activity in all the other groups." Theoretically, one might measure the average of all muscle activity in the body; but this research technique is inadequate for the task because needle electrodes are only able to tap single motor units.[39]

Another approach tries to measure stresses along the spine, using needles in the discs or pressure-sensitive pills which emit radio waves that are measured remotely. But these are fairly indirect measures and are open to error themselves. Seated pressure distribution can be measured, but researchers have learned that the pressures noted never correlate with experiential comfort.

Aside from these ambiguities, the absence of muscle work may not be a valid way to define comfort. Instead, an equal distribution of muscular effort, called "tonus," would capture more of the meaning of the concept. But tonus, again, is hard to measure objectively because it is a measure of how the system as a whole is working. This is why "holistic" practitioners often give up on the scientific method. They figure it's better to have no measures at all than to have inaccurate ones.

Teachers of the Alexander Technique specialize in teaching posture and movement, so they prefer to make postural and behavioral assessments of comfort. Some ergonomic researchers have also learned that "Postural analysis is at least as good an index of comfort as are subjective estimates."[40] More generally, observing behavior has proved to be as good a measure of comfort as verbal judgment.[41] Specifically, if people are restless or fidgeting, an observer could presume that they are uncomfortable. But is this actually so? It turns out that measures of posture and behavior also have problems of interpretation. Is the *furniture* uncomfortable, or is the *person* needing activity in order to release internal emotions? In fact, fidgeting could mean that the person is comfortable and moving in order to remain so. But most observers assume that if a person does not fidget, then he or she is comfortable—an inaccurate assumption if the furniture is constraining movement. A further problem with relying on restlessness as a measure of discomfort is that restlessness is also influenced by other variables—age, time of day, as well as genetic factors.[42]

Another logical possibility for a researcher would be to compare postures to some normative standards. But such norms are not established or agreed upon; they vary by gender and by individual. The Alexander Technique offers idealized standards, but until recently the technique has been known primarily among performers and therapists, not scientists. Objective postural analysis could be used to assess degrees of comfort for scientific studies, but this would require training in one of the systems of comprehensive postural analysis from F. M. Alexander, Ida Rolf, Rudolf Laban, Bonnie Bainbridge Cohen, and other somatic practitioners. One notable scientist has confirmed that these techniques are appropriate to the scientific method, especially observation. The animal ethnologist Nicolas Tinbergen devoted his Nobel laureate acceptance speech to the Alexander Technique, citing it as a first-class example of the scientific observation of behavior, which he thought should be emulated.

Office workers often claim that comfort would increase their productivity, but the relationship between comfort and productivity is elusive. The further up the organizational hierarchy the person rises, the harder it becomes to measure performance, even though he/she is becoming more costly to the organization. The literature on productivity sometimes focuses on the physical office—open-plan versus traditional—but the productivity difference between these settings is related to their flexibility, communication, and distractibility rather than to their physical comfort. The famous "halo effect" may also be at work: if workers think that management cares about their comfort, their productivity may go up, but the perception of caring may be more effective than whether or not the workers are actually comfortable. The upshot of these ambiguities is that researchers have concluded that performance is a relatively insensitive index of comfort.

A BRIEF LOOK AT THE NEW ERGONOMICS

In the last decades a few people studying ergonomics have tried to rethink the tenets of chair design because they recognize that ergonomic science is at best partial and at worst confused and even silly. Rather than throw the baby out with the bathwater, they are trying to create a "new ergonomics." This small but important group is disparate, but shares intellectual premises about the value of movement both socially and physiologically.[43]

A radical view held by a very few furniture designers is that back support is not necessary at all if your thighs are not at a 90-degree angle to the spine but at an oblique angle. When the legs are at an angle of 135 degrees to the spine, the work of sitting upright is distributed between the front and back of the spine and along its length most evenly, so that sitting upright is easy, one doesn't tire, and therefore one doesn't need or want back support. The chief application of this idea is the Norwegian Balans chair, designed by Peter Opsvik, often called the kneeling chair, and more recently used as a computer chair. This chair requires the sitter to fold his/her legs and rest partially on the knees. *(Fig. 36)* The practical reason for this unusual posture is to take advantage of the biomechanical benefits of dropping the thighs significantly in relation to the spine, while still allowing people to work at tables and desks of conventional height.

In contrast, Dr. Mandal is willing to advocate change not only in the basic chair design but also in the height of work surfaces. *(Fig. 37)* He recommends perching—a stance halfway between sitting and standing.[44] *(Fig. 38)* Perching does not require resting on one's knees, but creating a kind of tripod between the left and right feet and the sit bones. All the standards for conventional right-angle seating become irrelevant because one does not sit on one's thighs. Almost none of the ergonomic seating criteria apply: chairs using forward-tilt seats should be significantly higher

Figure 36. The Norwegian Balans chair by Peter Opsvik has been called the most radical chair design of the twentieth century, but it accepts conventional height for work surfaces, thereby stressing the head-neck joint.

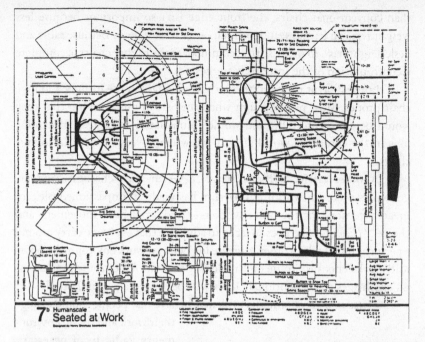

Figure 37. Mandal calls this drawing "the Bible" for furniture designers worldwide, but insists that the right-angle seated posture is unrealistic, possibly unhealthy.

Figure 38. Dr. Mandal's chairs are higher than standard to ensure that the legs are at an oblique, not a right angle, to the spine. Note the complementary forward slope of the desktops, essential to reduce neck strain.

than conventional chairs; the front edge isn't so important because less weight rests on it; and seat depth can be narrow or deep. Because table and desk height have to increase to accommodate the higher chairs, a complete reconfiguration of the interior is suggested.

I myself favor the open trunk to thigh angle in the form of a lounge chair proper. Most people laugh when they sit in mine, saying that they would be too comfortable and would immediately fall asleep. But some jobs in the computer world already allow employees to work in lounge chairs.

Another critic, Barbara Tietze, a German psychologist and ergonomics professor working in Berlin, has made an impassioned plea for greater freedom for the office worker—freedom of both movement and choice.[45] *(Fig. 39)* She goes so far as to advocate that everyone carry around a personal roll of felt in order to create his/her own work environment physically, even choosing to lie on the floor if desired. All of these fundamental challenges to conventional chairs will be visited again in Part III.

These new ergonomicists evidently believe that people should change their work and living environments, radically if necessary, to put their physical comfort first instead of meeting traditional cultural expectations. They want to change traditional workplace design. For them, the beginning and the end of design should be the body.

Figure 39. This floor-based office in Berlin was a project by students of Professor Nick Roericht at the Hochschule der Künste.

" . . . the chair, the most atrocious institution
hygienically of civilized life."

—C. F. Coghill, Introduction to F. M. Alexander,
Universal Constant in Living (1941)

Chapter 4

A Body-Mind Perspective

Supposedly, ergonomics is the study of the relation between people and the machines in their immediate environment, but somehow the people in this equation get left out. Most ergonomic research implicitly treats people as if they too were machines with interchangeable parts. In reality, we all know that our bodies are interdependent systems; we even have a popular song to remind us that "the knee bone is connected to the thigh bone . . ." Nevertheless, ergonomicists are willing to study disconnected parts of the body. In order to study pressure on the discs between vertebrae, for example, one researcher cut out a section of several vertebrae, clamped them between two surfaces to measure pressure, and proceeded to record when the soft, pulpy discs began to bulge and deteriorate. The problem with this approach is that dead tissue no longer functions like living tissue, so that the supportive functions of fascia, tendons, and ligaments are ignored, and the support from the rest of the spinal column, torso, and the body as a whole cannot be measured. This desire to isolate variables is understandable but misleading. The body is a complex, interactive system; when supporting its movements and postures in furniture design, we cannot concentrate on one part at the expense of the whole.

Even more complicating, our minds also affect our bodies, and vice versa. Obviously, a good experience might make us smile, but less obviously, the physical act of smiling can change our biochemistry and hence our mood. Ideally, then, a new theoretical model would be helpful if it could acknowledge the reality that the different parts of our bodies and minds work together in very complex ways. The integrated body-mind perspective arising out of the somatic disciplines points toward such a new model, which could expand and improve the current ergonomic approach to chair design.[1]

SOMATICS AND THE ALEXANDER TECHNIQUE

Over the last twenty years an integrated body-mind perspective has emerged from a field of inquiry and practice, termed "somatics," that differs from medicine, osteopathy, chiropractic, and physical therapy in its focus on the relationships between body and intellectual thought, cultural belief, individual feeling and will.[2] Essentially educational, one definition is that it "involves the whole human being, focusing in a practical way on the interactions of posture, movement, emotion, self-concept, and cultural values."[3]

An example illustrates how somatics bridges several fields. Paul Linden, a somatic practitioner, described his experience with a jazz pianist who had "disabling pain in his upper right arm when he played." First, Linden observed that "rather than using his body as an evenly balanced, unified whole, his posture was lopsided and tensed. His left shoulder was higher than his right. His left leg was stronger than the right, and he used it more for weight support. When he played the piano, he sat hunched over the keyboard." Linden helped the pianist become aware of his posture, taught him how to relax and how to sit straight.

Once the pianist could sit well, Linden asked him to add movement involving effort, at which point his movements hardened and constricted. When Linden asked him why, the pianist realized two things: "that trying *hard* was part of what he envisioned strength to be and that it created excess tension in many of his movements." Linden comments: "The idea that strength is tough and hard is, of course, very common in our culture."

Linden continues, "We talked about how this habit of constriction affected his playing . . . [that] he was forcing his muscles to move against internal resistance, creating strain just when he needed to move in the freest possible manner. He realized that was a major factor in the pain he experienced while playing, and he found that he could keep his body free and open and still generate the power needed to play the piano . . . [but] when I asked him to play something . . . he lost his awareness of his pelvis and breathing." Instead, the pianist's attention shifted to head and hands: "when he played, he felt that eyes to see, ears to hear, and hands to play contained all of his musical being, and the rest of his body was inconsequential." He went back to the initial patterns of muscular tension, so Linden reminded him "that music came from *all* of himself and that he needed to feel his whole body and use it well. . . ."

At home, the pianist reported that his arm worked better when he used his body the new way. However, when Linden watched him "really get into the music," he reverted to hunching over the keys. In talking about this, the pianist explained that he often played in bars where people were drunk and unpleasant, so that he wanted to "go into" himself, the piano, and the music in order to create a barrier between himself and his audience. He also explained that part of jazz improvisation required listening closely to the piano to find the next notes to play. Of course, his musical "thoughts" actually "came from deep within himself." Once he recognized this, he was able to create a new symmetrical and expansive shape, perform with new power and sensitivity, and reduce the strain on his arm. With this case study Linden explicates beautifully how somatics bridges several fields, but cannot be reduced to any one of them individually:

> The pianist came with a legitimate physical trauma, but one which was not treatable medically because it was not really a *physical* problem. It involved numerous cultural, emotional, and spiritual elements. However, it could not have been treatable psychologically because it was indeed a physical problem, and the musculoskeletal analysis was a key to solving it. In actuality, it was a somatic learning problem and only somatic re-education could have solved it.[4]

Somatics covers many different specialized practices, including Trager, Hellerwork, Bonnie Bainbridge Cohen's Body-Mind Centering, Rolfing (also known as Structural Integration), Rosenwork, the Feldenkrais

Method, and the Alexander Technique. My own knowledge of somatics as a general field comes chiefly through my experience with the Alexander Technique, first in 1978 as a pupil, then as a trainee, and finally as a teacher. Initially, my motive was to find a way to cope with severe scoliosis (curvature of the spine). I found the help I was looking for, which was compelling enough; but it was the intellectual and philosophical implications of the technique that engaged me completely.[5] I had tried—and benefited from—several other disciplines. The older traditional Asian systems are more comprehensive than the Western somatic disciplines, but they share with somatics the view that body and mind are part of a system. I have practiced the Chinese martial art of tai chi chuan daily since 1976. I have experienced two years of jin shin and twenty-two years of acupuncture as a client, and have practiced Iyengar-style yoga intermittently as a student for fifteen years. My reading and experience, combined with discussions about the broader field, have enabled me to make connections between most somatic practices. Because my own professional certification in this arena is as an Alexander teacher, it forms the basis for the somatic point of view presented in this chapter.[6]

Michael Murphy calls the Alexander Technique the grandfather of the somatic disciplines.[7] The technique was developed by an Australian, Frederick Matthias Alexander, at the end of the nineteenth century. Alexander was a young Shakespearean reciter who found that he lost his voice after performing. When no doctor could remedy the condition, he undertook his own investigation. Alexander reasoned that his vocal cords must be stressed by something he was doing when he performed, so he set up a series of mirrors to monitor his own behavior. What Alexander discovered was that his laryngitis was in fact related to certain physical movements he made in trying to project his voice in the standard manner. Specifically, Alexander found that when he addressed an audience during a performance, he moved his head backward and downward in an effort to achieve dramatic power. This resulted in undue physical pressure on his neck and larynx. However, Alexander found that he could relieve this pressure by freeing the connection between his head and neck—what anatomists refer to as the Atlanto-occipital joint (the occiput is the bone that forms the bottom and back of the skull, and the atlas is the top vertebra of the spine). By inhibiting his old pattern of behavior, he could perform without stress to his voice. As a result of this new relationship between head and neck,

Alexander cured his laryngitis; in fact, his voice became so powerful and attractive that people started coming to Alexander for voice lessons, and he even became known as "The Breath Man."

As the story goes, at a dinner party during this period, a doctor told Alexander about a patient with a back problem without an obvious physical cause and asked him to see if his behavioral approach could help. Alexander helped her, and the technique started to be used to aid people suffering from various biomechanical problems throughout the body— ankle, knee, hip, back, neck, shoulder, elbow, and wrist pains. In 1904, Alexander moved to London, where he continued to teach the technique privately, eventually establishing a school in the 1930s to teach others. Today the Alexander Technique has two chief applications: performing arts and healing. Musicians, actors, singers, dancers, and performers of all kinds who use their voices and bodies expressively learn the Alexander Technique in order to perform more powerfully. And as a form of healing, people who have pain in any part of the body benefit because the technique works with the mind to reorganize and realign the entire body. However, teachers of the Alexander Technique do not call it either therapy or performance, because Alexander was adamant that his technique was a form of kinesthetic education; more precisely, reeducation.[8]

The term "somatic" is useful in part because it includes both the educational and the therapeutic components of body-mind practices like the Alexander Technique. A somatic perspective expands the problem of chair design beyond discrete ergonomic measurements. At the very minimum, a somatic approach would require working with the entire body.

SOMATIC PRINCIPLES AND CHAIR DESIGN

Ergonomic and somatic perspectives converge on some points, but they diverge in regard to many more. I have organized the somatic principles into three clusters: (1) philosophical ideas about the human body; (2) ideas about anatomy; and (3) ideas about psycho-physical processes. The most general idea of somatics is that the body and mind are one system. Working on one aspect affects the other. This is an ancient as well as a contemporary observation. Eastern religious and philosophical traditions are still absolutely explicit about posture being an essential part of one's worldview. For example, zazen, the Zen Buddhist practice of floor sitting for meditation, encompasses both the posture and the attitude associated with that posture.[9] A consequence of this perspective is a greater interest in the entire system than in any discrete symptom. A somatic practitioner seeks to get the whole system—the fascia, the bones, the muscles—organized so that the body can heal itself. The practitioner does not concentrate on scoliosis or sciatica or any other ailment. Instead, he/she concentrates on establishing a balance and on maintaining an unobstructed flow from one system to the next, whether by a biomechanical approach or by an energy system such as polarity therapy, jin shin, shiatsu, or acupuncture. Because the body functions as a *system,* problems in one part of the body can be expressed in another part. Problems in the knee may in fact express problems stemming from the pelvis. The pelvis problems may, in turn, come from imbalance in the connection between the head and neck. *(Box 1 and Fig. 40)*

The implication of this systematic viewpoint for chair design is that you should not focus exclusively on one part—is the seat hard or soft for the sit bones, or tall or short enough for the heels to reach the ground? Instead, you have to go through the whole system.

Let's start at the top: As you sit in a chair, does it make your head droop? Does it push your head so far forward that your chest caves in? Does the head pull the neck forward? The position of your head should allow the neck to continue as a vertical extension of the spine. Are your eyes forced to look too far up or down? Is the weight of the head rotating back and down, compressing the spine? How about your chest, is it rounded forward? In addition, you need to think about what sitting in that chair does for the heels, ankles, knees, hip sockets, and spine. If you create more length from head to foot, you make more space in the joints, rendering movement easier. What sort of movement is allowed in the arms when you are working on a surface? Basically, you want the possibility of choosing either movement or stability in any part

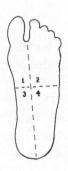

Figure 40. By starting with the foot, a person can eventually experience how the entire body works as an interrelated whole.

of the system at any time. A chair that creates bad posture even in one part of the body inevitably creates problems for the whole body. As we have seen, measuring such a complex interactive model has been a challenge to the field of ergonomics.

Mini-Exercise in Experiential Anatomy

Students have told me that anatomical terms strike them as technical. To help them get over this distaste for the technical, I introduce them to anatomy through direct experience of their own bodies:

Start with your feet. Stand on both feet and figure out which foot carries the most weight—the right? the left? Now focus on one foot, the right. Draw an imaginary line from the space between the big toe and its neighbor straight through the heel. Then ask if the inside or the outside of the foot carries more weight. Now divide your foot the other way across the middle. Does the front where all the toes are or the heel at the back carry more weight? Now combine the two lines and you get four quadrants. Which one carries the most weight? Every combination is possible, and in my classes someone always represents each possibility.

Still standing, try to balance the weight equally between all four quadrants. Notice what happens to the rest of your body to make those changes. You might have to make adjustments in your pelvis or lower back or even in how you carry your head in order to even out the way weight is transferred to your feet.

This demonstrates how the entire body is interrelated, and it also helps you feel from the inside that anatomy is just a way to talk about (give labels to) experience we have inside our own bodies. We are not undifferentiated, homogeneous lumps. Once you experience that the heel is different from the toes and the bones leading to the toes (metatarsals), thinking about the rest of the body's internal differences becomes easier. For example, we can easily recognize that our spines are different at the top than at the bottom. The top is thinner, made of smaller bones, the bottom thicker and heavier, made of bigger versions of the same kind of bones (vertebrae). The spinal column curves forward at the neck (cervical region), backward at the upper back (thoracic region), forward again at the lower back (lumbar region), and back out again at the arrowhead-shaped plate at the base of the spine (the sacrum). ●

Believing in the integrity of the psycho-physical entity, Alexander teachers tend to avoid the term "posture" in favor of the term "use." "Use" is different because it implies movement over time, a pattern of coordination and volition. "Posture" suggests for many a static, fixed position. Furthermore, "use" is as much mental as physical. (Slouching, for example, may carry the emotional satisfactions of making us feel socially hip or "cool.") Here I employ the term "use" to mean overall, coordinated use of the body, working in concert with thought. According to the principles of the Alexander Technique, when people in contemporary Western society are young, for the most part they use themselves correctly. Children have excellent use until about age two. Thereafter, they lose good use at differential rates, depending on their particular cultural and family influences. Chairs are one of the most direct negative cultural influences on children's use, hence on their morphological development.

Good use means that the neck joint is free so that a person is able to initiate motion with his/her head. Good use refers to an underlying pattern of coordination present no matter what the specific movement. The scientific basis of the Alexander Technique is that all vertebrates initiate action with their heads. You might think you initiate the act of walking, for example, with your feet. But, in fact, the head initiates all actions, a physiological observation first demonstrated a century ago by Sir Charles Scott Sherrington, the British anatomist.[10] The head is where four of our senses are housed, and therefore where we pay attention; we make movement choices from there. People perceive and are curious, then their bodies follow. But many people, instead of leading with their face and front of the cranium, lead with some other part of the body, like the pelvis, while their head rests on the top of the neck rotated backward and downward. The weight of the head so held compresses the entire spine, creating problems along the spinal column and in all of the joints of the body. When someone is sitting down, their head should still lead; but a soft seat makes it all too easy for sit bones, pelvis, spine, and head to sink. In this case, in order to see, people often rotate the head further back and down. Many chairs make good use extremely difficult, if not impossible.

A therapeutic corollary of body-mind integration is that we hold our mental and emotional stress in the body. Conversely, freeing a tight muscle or other tissue may release emotional feelings or memories that seem to come from nowhere. We do not have to confirm the mechanism involved, but rather simply observe that the muscular condition relates to habits that stem from an emotional commitment to a way of doing things: anxiously, fearfully, viciously, gently, certainly, and so forth. The inverse of the therapeutic premise is that by stressing the body, you can lower your feeling of well-being. The implication for sitting is that a chair that forces you to sit badly has both physical and mental consequences. Since some chairs exact more physical damage than others, a somatic inference is that some will be less depressing and mentally stultifying than others. Even though all chairs are problematic, some chairs *are* better than others. Nevertheless, sitting in *any* chair for more than a short (ten-minute) interval is likely to begin to have negative effects on your physical self, hence your mental self, and at a minimum reduce your awareness of physical and emotional sensations.

The somatic perspective challenges some of our conventional ideas about comfort, gravity, the structure of the body, the separation of mind and body, and healing, as well as related ideas about how we can change personally and culturally. Starting at the top of this list, one might wonder if somatic practitioners can do any better than their ergonomic colleagues have managed so far. Certainly, they are not going to define comfort as "no work." Rather, for them, comfort means balanced work throughout the whole system. The subjective counterpart to this "balanced work" would be a feeling of vitality and ease. A somatic perspective on comfort, which seeks balanced work, is closer to the original Latin meaning of the word, "to make strong." Perhaps the scientists who have been frustrated in trying to define comfort for purposes of scientific study should consider adopting this older notion.

Another challenge to contemporary ideas about comfort is inherent in what the architectural critic Bernard Rudofsky calls "autonomous sitting"—when the sitter sits upright without any kind of back support.[11] Autonomous sitting is still comfortable by contemporary Eastern standards, but not by contemporary Western ones.[12] *(Fig. 41)* Sitting without external support is not easy for people unused to it; it requires work, even though that work might be distributed evenly. Regarding comfort, Alexander teachers are not particularly interested in immediate sensation, even a nice one like softness. Instead, they are more interested in ease or vitality over the long run. Similarly, they are less interested in the comfort of any single part of the body—making sure the sit bones, for in-

Figure 41. The ease in Buddha's posture exemplifies the potential comfort in autonomous sitting.

stance, are on thick cushioning—because they are more interested in the well-being of the whole body. When selecting a chair for comfort, then, a somatic practitioner would look for an entire sequence of measurements in relation to one another: appropriate seat height, proper ratio and good angle between the seat and the back (if there is a back), firm support, and other details discussed in the next chapter on body-conscious design. A very few custom chair designers offer a service like this, taking into account some dozen measurements of the individual for whom the chair is being made. In summary, somatic theory defines comfort as a shifting distribution of effort balanced over time.

What about gravity? Are we constantly fighting it? People ordinarily assume that gravity is bad, because it pulls us down. But if we take the systems approach seriously, then we have to assume that human beings are constructed to use gravity in order to be upright. Ida Rolf, the chemist who turned to structural analysis of the human body and in the process invented Rolfing, claimed that gravity was essential to the upright posture. If we look at what happens to the body without gravity in outer space, a number of interesting health and postural problems emerge. After about ninety days in zero gravity, humans begin undergoing osteoporosis; without tension on the bones, they start losing calcium. Their bodies begin to elongate. This kind of evidence indicates that gravity is not our enemy, even though improper and unnatural alignment can cause it to exacerbate collapsed structures. That's why proper alignment is so important; it allows gravity to help us retain our full volume and stature. Chairs obviously can and do have an adverse effect on our dynamic structure when they allow gravity to deform us.

If a designer thinks gravity is the enemy, he/she will design chairs like bags to hold our collapsed structures. But if the designer believes that gravity is useful to us, the sitting surface can function more like a platform so that the structure of forces and counterforces helps us spring into the body's natural volume—as opposed to being stacked from the bottom up like a wall or collapsed into a heap.

What is the nature of the human body's structure? Is it a compression structure, like a wall? Is it a tension structure, like a tent? Or is it some combination? Ida Rolf sees the fascia—the connective tissue made of collagen, a protein, that wraps around every muscle spindle, bone, and organ—as the critical element in the body. Indeed, it is so pervasive that the anatomy teacher Deane Juhan says that if one were to take out all the muscles, tendons, and bones, but leave the fascia, one would have a spongelike structure that could still hold our human shape—before it collapsed, that is.[13] Since fascia is so widespread and wraps around everything, Rolf believes that it, not our skeleton, is responsible for our structure. She reduces the function of bones to spacers. Traditional anatomists would not necessarily disagree with this formulation, since they understand that the relationship between bones depends upon ligaments, muscles, and the membranes enclosing our organs.[14] Each specialist might prioritize the relationships differently. Embryologists and internists would be more likely to see bones as less important than soft tissue, but orthopedists would obviously focus more on the supportive function of bones. Certainly in our culture at large, we see bones as more important than soft tissue.

Because of the critical role of fascia as structure, Rolf, Bonnie Bainbridge Cohen, and others conceive of the body as a tension structure (like a tent) as much as a compression structure (like a wall). One of Rolf's students has argued that the body is a "tensegrity" structure—a term Buckminster Fuller used to describe structural systems that combine elements of compression and tension.[15] *(Fig. 42)* Plausibly, our body's system of cantilevers and counterbalanced forces, like Fuller's geodesic dome, requires gravity to create our upright volume. This metaphor for human structure

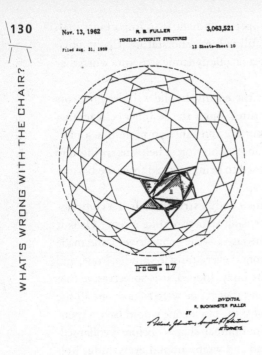

Nov. 13, 1962   R. B. FULLER   3,063,521
TENSILE-INTEGRITY STRUCTURES
Filed Aug. 31, 1959   13 Sheets-Sheet 10

FIG. 17

INVENTOR.
R. BUCKMINSTER FULLER
BY

ATTORNEYS.

Figure 42. Buckminster Fuller's tensegrity structure may provide the best analogy for human structure.

when applied to chair design implies a preference for firm platforms and an avoidance of designs, like beanbag chairs, that encourage the body to collapse into itself.

Another thing we can say about the structure of our bodies is that mechanical stability is not built in. The human body is a dynamic system, which cannot find stasis, so somatic practitioners reject the idea that we can find any point of complete rest, short of lying down. Because we have ball-and-socket joints, we have no flat places in our joints that can be lined up against each other to lock into place, which might free muscles from having to do any work. We are always having to do small amounts of muscular work for any obvious movement like sitting up, standing, walking, or crawling. But we are also doing small amounts of muscular work when just standing or sitting still. For chair design, this means rejecting the ergonomic search for a position of "no work." Since there is no seated position of perfect rest for which to design, the idea of total support loses significance.

Another proposition about human structure leads full circle back to ideas about comfort and consciousness. Because somatic practitioners help people's bodies find their natural form and then observe that painful symptoms disappear, many conclude that our backs are perfectly designed and that back trouble is not evidence of an evolutionary "flaw," but rather of incorrect use. Yet, how many times have you heard someone comment that our skeletons never adjusted completely to walking upright? Here is one example from an ergonomic researcher extrapolating from evolutionary concepts: "In terms of adaptation of the process of Darwin's evolution theory, the spine has been required to adjust in too short a space of time; this is why . . . *homo erectus* . . . so often suffers from pathological disorders of the lumbar region in particular."[16] If, instead, incorrect use is the problem, then physical design should promote an active awareness of posture and good use rather than the passive belief that imperfect posture and pain are a part of life. Promoting active awareness challenges our preference not to have to think about either seating or our bodies.

The most wide-ranging philosophical insight from the Alexander Technique and the somatic perspective generally is that human beings are designed for movement, and that more important than any single given posture is the *quality* of our movement, our overall coordination. Desirable as this might be physiologically, such movement may be at odds with the workplace. Employers often worry that they may not get the best out of their employees if they allow unfettered movement, but studies on physiological research show that learning is improved with physical activity.[17] Not all kinds of work involve learning, of course; some are repetitive to the point of boredom, which only underscores the need for movement. Changing positions is essential for the health of our spinal discs. They don't have veins, so must get their nutrition via a process of diffusion, which depends on a pump or sponge mechanism. This requires alternately overloading and underloading the spine through movement. (This means that external disc pressure, which you will recall some ergonomic researchers used as a negative indicator of spinal stress, is actually a necessary and good thing *in the right rhythm.*) Practically speaking, the worker should sit and stand alternately.[18] The irony is that employers ordinarily view such activity as "counterproductive." Employees are expected to be virtually immobile all day and then make up for this on their own time by a short burst in the gym or by jogging.

Another set of somatic principles continues to focus specifically on anatomical ideas. One key insight is that the environment, including chairs, should not disturb the capacity of the person to organize and maintain the proper dynamic between the head and neck. The most important practice a person learns in setting out to study the Alexander Technique is to "let the neck be free so that the head can go forward and up and the back lengthen and widen."[19] Called "primary control," this concept provides the focal point of the technique. The idea is to organize the head and neck first; and then corrections in pelvic balance or hip, knee, and ankle joints will follow. Conversely, disorganization at the head-neck joint will ricochet through the rest of the body.

Any chair design that puts people in a posture that distorts the head-neck joint upsets the equilibrium of the entire body. Too many chairs interfere with "primary control," especially when they follow the ergonomic dictum of opening the angle between backrest and seat to 110 degrees. The idea is to take stress off the spine, but the stress is only transferred to the neck and head, where it may be even more harmful. Somatic logic says that the back should be upright. A chair that is angled at more than a few (3–5) degrees off vertical sends the entire spine in a backward trajectory. Even if people could hold their heads back behind the support of the spinal column, they would then be looking up toward the ceiling. Naturally, they bring their heads forward. If the spine continues to go backward while the head and neck go forward, the neck is forced into a swan-like configuration. This stresses the neck in a variety of different ways and contributes to the myriad problems imposed by bad use generally.

The obvious implication for chair design overlooked by most ergonomic researchers is that if the chair has a back (and that is what makes a chair a chair), it should be high enough to support the shoulders and head. Too often, designers reserve this characteristic only for lounge chairs like the Corbusier-Perriand chaise or the Rietveld lounge. Some fully upright chairs accomplish the same effect; the wing chair is one. (Be careful, though, because large headrests that thrust the head forward are consid-

erably worse than no support whatsoever.) As a consumer, you will certainly want to think twice about selecting club chairs (like Corbusier's *grand* and *petit confort*) that stop midback. *(Fig. 43)*

Another anatomical idea is that the spine as a whole should

Figure 43. In the Confort (1929), Le Corbusier inverted the conventional relationship between structure and upholstery when he used his frame as a decorative exterior.

retain its elongated S-shape. Our spines accommodate flux, but generally the two forward curves at the neck and lumbar should both be maintained, as should the two convex curves of the thoracic and sacral regions. This means that there should be a space hollowed out at the lower part of the chairback to accommodate the lower curve that is amplified by the pelvis, hips, and gluteus maximus. Without the "butt space," your body forms the unfortunate C-shape slump. These distortions put stress on the musculature, internal organs, and spinal discs.

With the addition of lumbar support, spinal imbalance can be worsened. On the whole, lumbar support contradicts the logic of the Alexander Technique. Lumbar support is used by ergonomic theorists in order to keep people's lower backs from rounding. For those with swayback or lordosis, of course, lumbar support is an obvious disservice, but even for others it reduces the overall muscle tone of the spinal muscles and usually interferes with overall balance between the two sets of curves. The reason for this lies in physiology. In the right-angle seated posture, the hamstring muscles that wrap around the back of the thighs and buttocks to insert along the pelvis pull it and the lumbar spine backwards, forming the C-shape. Forcing the lumbar spine forward again by some kind of mechanical support does not change the disproportionate pull that the thigh muscles are exerting on it, nor correct the imbalance between abdominal (front) and erector spinae (back) muscles.

The optimal solution is not a better design of the components of the chair, but rather reconfiguration of the chair itself to allow a fundamental change in posture. In classical chair sitting, the upper leg is at a right angle to the spine; but when this angle is opened wider (in other words, when the thighs slope down toward the floor), the muscular work of sitting upright is distributed most evenly throughout the spine, front to back and top to bottom. (*Fig. 44*) To take advantage of this anatomical observation, a group of Scandinavians invented the balance chair (*see Fig. 36*). This particular chair has been called the most significant design of the twentieth century, even though an earlier chair by Mandal was actually the first to use a forward-sloping seat and create an open angle between trunk and thigh. The balance attracted attention because it reconfigured the basic elements of the chair, eliminating the back altogether, tilting the seat so radically that a knee rest is necessary to support the sitter. (The social acceptability of this chair is another issue, to be taken up in the next chapter.)

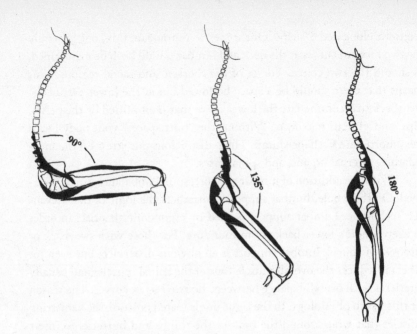

Figure 44. Right-angle seating produces a C-shaped spine. Perching is halfway between sitting and standing, but retains the postural advantages of standing—the S-shaped spine.

A few somatic principles share insights from ergonomic research, and here is one: feeling the sit bones and the transfer of weight down to them is desirable. This indicates that the seat should be planar, but also that it should be only lightly padded. Although a quarter- to half-inch of extremely firm foam is adequate, it eventually "bottoms out," so wool felt (or any other renewable resource) is both anatomically and ecologically preferable.

While Alexander principles give primacy to the freedom between head and neck, all somatic practices emphasize the importance of our feet yielding to gravity (as our backs stay back and up). Whether sitting or standing, we should have our feet on the floor.

The somatic point of view underscores the ergonomic insight that the standard 18-inch chair height with a conventional horizontal seat is appropriate only for tall adults.[20] For conventional seating where the whole thigh rests on the seat, much more attention should be given to height than is routine. Thankfully, almost all contemporary office chairs are now adjustable in height; but what about the less expensive, ordinary chairs in our lives? We might consider having all chairs come in multiple sizes and we might consider reintroducing footstools and footrests as standard equipment to help people make up the difference between the height of a chair and the length of their own shinbones, as discussed in the next chapter.

Somatics addresses the psycho-physical processes of assessing and reporting on sensation. People who try out somatically preferred chairs can find them awkward to sit in. Years of faulty alignment mean that our *idea* of what feels right can take precedence over our direct bodily sensation of what feels right. To the average person, this means that anatomically efficient posture no longer feels "right" or "comfortable," so often we reject it in favor of a collapsed slump. It is tempting to think that the body could be an authoritative touchstone if only we could just tap into it.[21] And so we can. But first we have to *unlearn* the cultural conditioning that teaches us to ignore internal sensory experience in favor of abstract thought. The phenomenon of faulty sensory awareness explains at least in part why ergonomic researchers have tried to measure comfort without relying on people's subjective experience. Since they found people's own reports unreliable from trial to trial and from person to person, they sought objective measures instead—albeit without success. They have observed that people cannot consistently describe what is comfortable, but they don't know why; they just chalk it up to the annoying unreliability or variability of human subjects, rather than asking *why* such profound variation should exist. This much variation points to a profound disturbance in our relationship to our bodies. Rather than try to restore that relationship, as somatic practitioners do, ergonomic science has ignored the realm of kinesthetic reeducation. For designers, somatics creates an unsettling demand to make chairs that might feel uncomfortable until people's bodies and minds unlearn the poor sitting posture learned from conventional chairs.

The intellectual, philosophic, and scientific principles embedded in somatic disciplines have addressed all the significant issues in chair design—seat height, shape of front rail, slope of the seat, angle of back to seat, contour and upholstery, lumbar support, movement, and evaluation of comfort. From a somatic point of view, chairs pose many different problems. They are usually either badly designed or overdesigned—or both. For large sectors of the population, they are badly designed because they are too high, the seat is too deep, or the back tips too far back. Some chairs are designed to make one part of the body comfortable at the expense of other parts. Many conform to a no-work ideal and are too soft, too unstructured, too padded, too "easy." *(Fig. 45)* Others interpret "organic" to mean mimicking human form so that they are overly curved and not planar enough.

The Norwegian balance chairs were designed to eliminate rounding the back to read or write. But when they are not conceived as part of a person's entire furniture system, table heights may be too low, and so the person has to stoop to reach his or her work surface. Overdesigned chairs hold or cradle the body, which promotes stasis rather than movement. Static postures may be the most generic and troubling of all since stasis reduces variation in muscular work, circulation of the blood, motility (the inherent movement of fluids), and, thereby, energy. The chair might be better conceived and designed with the understanding that tonus, an equal distribution of effort, is better than no work at all. The chair could be understood as an athletic device for promoting movement—not just external, but also internal. The chair could even become a way to tune in to the vast interior universe of the body.

SOME FAMOUS CHAIRS EVALUATED

We now have the tools to examine a half dozen of the more famous icons of the twentieth century from the viewpoint of ergonomics and somatics. As we saw earlier, architects have been fascinated with chairs as a design problem throughout the twentieth century. Mies van der Rohe reputedly claimed that the successful design of a chair was as much a challenge as that of a building. But human bodies still receive little atten-

Figure 45. Beanbag chairs are too unstructured, allowing the human frame to collapse inward.

tion. As the New York design consultant Ralph Caplan wryly observed: "Designers who will go to any investigative length to learn about materials neglect such elementary material as flesh and blood—although the flesh is weak and the flow of blood has been greatly impeded by a succession of prize-winning chairs."[22] Reyner Banham, the British historian of modern architecture who taught at the University of California at Santa Cruz, was even blunter about the contradiction between high design and body awareness, maintaining: "All 'well-designed' chairs are both uncomfortable and inconvenient."[23] Rybczynski wrote of this contradiction that there is "something charmingly naive about this belief in the power of art to overcome physical reality."[24]

How do some of the most significant designer chairs rate from a body-conscious point of view? One of the first architects to produce a modern chair was the German, Marcel Breuer. His *Cesca* (1928), according to Cara McCarty, associate curator of the department of architecture and design at the Museum of Modern Art, ranks "among the 10 most important chairs of the 20th century," and it is also among the ten most common (*see Fig. 23*).[25] At first only numbered B32, it was eventually named for Breuer's daughter, Francesca, by the Italian manufacturer who started reproducing the chair in the 1950s. The radical design was inspired by Breuer's insight that he could use bent bicycle tubing to create a continuous cantilevered frame on which he could suspend the wood and woven cane chair seat in midair. Look, Ma, no legs! Well, almost. Two legs instead of four made small modern apartments appear less cluttered and more spacious. This construction was cheap to reproduce—and because never patented, even cheaper to knock off.

Ideologically, this product exemplified early Modernist ideals of simple but sophisticated forms without surface ornament, suitable for mass production. The visual rhetoric of the chair appealed to Modernists not only because it was machine-made but also because it *looked* machine-made. Decoratively, the combination of machine-made and traditional materials has rendered the chair extremely adaptable, allowing it to fit into both traditional and modern decors. The combined effects of economy and adaptability have made the chair so ubiquitous in homes and restaurants that it's probably safe to say we have all sat in one of them.

And what have our bodies experienced? The front of the seat, technically called the rail, is wood, while the center of the seat is cane, which inevitably—and rapidly—sags. That dip creates two problems simultaneously: the sit bones do not receive substantial support; and they slip below the hard front rail, which pushes up into the flesh of the sitter's thighs. This feels uncomfortable and cuts off circulation. Furthermore, when the sit bones sink below the thighs, the pelvis rotates backward and the lower back flattens, becoming rounded. At the same time the thoracic curve increases in angle of curvature, so that the infamous C-shaped spine is generated. Even the original and later versions designed by Breuer himself, let alone all the cheaper copies, have this problem, because it is intrinsic to the marriage of cane and wood.

This combination was well established fifty years earlier in the ubiquitous Viennese café chair, manufactured by Thonet, who also manufactured the first Cesca chair in 1928. Woven cane, no matter how tautly stretched, does not provide adequate resistance to receive the weight transferred down to the sit bones. It captures and holds the sitter's weight at the wrong places—thigh muscles instead of sit bones.

Some of the chair's other problems might be attributed to the shortcuts which diminish the quality of the knockoffs. For example, some unauthorized copies extend the seat too far forward so that the chair is stiff rather than springy; in others, the seat rises at the back instead of remaining parallel to the floor. (Lampoons showing these chairs pitching diners face forward into their soup may, in fact, have confused the knockoffs with the originals.)

Before the Cesca, Breuer had already designed another famous chair, the *Wassily* (1925), named after his painter friend Wassily Kandinsky. *(Fig. 46)* This was a first experiment with a bent metal frame, again joined

with a natural material, stiff leather bands, wrapped tightly from one side of the frame to another to form the seat and back, which look as if they are floating "within a network of lines and planes." The tension provides a slight spring to the chair overall, but the

Figure 46. Marcel Breuer named this chair after his painter friend Wassily Kandinsky in 1925.

leather is so tough that even in chairs that are many decades old, it does not sag. Breuer wrote, "It is my most extreme work both in its outward appearance and in the use of materials; it is the least artistic, the most logical, the least 'cosy' and the most mechanical."[26]

The architectural critic, Rybczynski, also believes this chair is uncomfortable because "it looks more like an exercise machine than an armchair" and because in use it is too rigid: "the flat back and seat discourage movement."[27] Yet my observations lead me to conclude that physiologically it is not as troublesome as the Cesca. The flat surfaces actually *encourage* movement, as opposed to curved or padded ones, which hold the body and discourage movement. Second, in my graduate seminars, the Wassily chair has fit a wider range of body types than most other modern chairs. Finally, the placement of the bands of leather is the secret of the Wassily's success. The occupant slides back to a band that supports the lumbar region, and, importantly, to a second band that also supports the thoracic region. The first band is well placed, because it does not go all the way to the seat, thus leaving room for the sitter's gluteus maximus to round out into space. The second band is also well placed because it supports the reverse curve of the thoracic region, so that the sitter does not get pressure on the lumbar spine exclusively, which would otherwise have increased swayback (lordosis). The wide band that forms the seat of this chair works for both long-legged and short-legged people. It is narrow enough that the very shortest students in my classes do not get cut under the thighs.

The chair's major flaw is that the configuration between the back and the seat angles backward over 15 degrees, which creates problems for the neck and head. Without neck or head support, the sitter bends his head forward, compressing his breast bone and rib cage. It also means the occupant is thrown so far back in space that to get out of the chair many people have to gather momentum and lunge out of it. At this point, the arms—also narrow strips of leather attached to the steel frame—are useful in hauling yourself out of the chair.

If the weakness of the Wassily is the effort it takes to get out of it, it is nothing like the effort required to hurl oneself out of the *Barcelona (see Fig. 6)*. This chair was designed by Mies van der Rohe in 1929 for the German pavilion for a World's Fair in Barcelona. It is essentially an elegant X created by the intersection of two polished steel bars. The seat and the back of the chair are upholstered in leather. The Barcelona has become a symbol of corporate power and refinement, and it is often found bolted to lobby floors in corporate headquarters throughout America. "It is not just, as some would say, the greatest chair of the twentieth century," Vincent Scully dramatizes; "it is the great Platonic image of chair itself."[28] It is the kind of chair, as Tom Wolfe says in one of his satires, *From Bauhaus to Our House,* that architecture students in the late forties and early fifties would scrimp and save for.[29] So what's the problem with this chair, if it is so widespread and revered?

Opinion varies about its comfort. Reyner Banham thought it "un-anatomical" but nevertheless comfortable, because it is big enough for people to fidget and un-designed enough to accommodate "vast tolerances of dimension" and "non-standard anatomies." Another essayist in the same catalogue observes that it is "by no means the most comfortable chair in the world," but then this very same person turns around and cites Philip Johnson's remark that the Barcelona looks comfortable, people sitting in it look comfortable, so it has become comfortable in people's minds.[30] A body-conscious perspective can bring some clarity to this muddle.

It turns out that the X is concave at the back and the seat, so that it reverses the natural curve of the spine: instead of the lumbar region dipping slightly forward toward the belly button when you are seated in the chair, it falls back away from the belly. That, you will remember from the ergonomic research, is one of the great sources of "slipped discs." The seat is concave under the sit bones, and the edge of the seat lifts up slightly and pushes up under the thighs and knees—two more ergonomic problems. The seat depth is so great that very short people cannot even bend their knees over the edge of the front. So they are forced to scoot toward the front, which pulls their pelvis away from the back; the lumbar curve reverses itself even more to reach the back, putting undue stress on the fronts of the big lumbar vertebrae and pushing disks backward. This chair was clearly designed for—and by—a man well over six feet tall, with long legs. Like the Wassily chair, the whole thing is rotated in space so that the sitter has to lean back into the chair. But of course that approach creates the same need for neck and head support that we've seen before.

Getting out of this chair becomes a real issue because you are thrust so far back into it. Many people try to tighten their abdominal muscles and throw their torsos forward over their knees, simultaneously pressing down against the floor with their feet in order to lever themselves up—a particularly difficult feat for people shorter than six feet. So, one of the tricks of the trade becomes swinging your legs over to the side and escaping over the low point of the X.

Not to be outdone by his German colleagues, Le Corbusier designed a chair, also still in production today (*see Fig. 43*). Called the *Grand Confort* (1928), it is another experiment combining metal with leather upholstery. This time, metal rods create a kind of cage, considered elegant because it is a perfect cubic meter, into which five fine leather seat and back cushions fit. This arrangement reverses the traditional order in which the wooden frame is hidden by upholstery; here the frame is external and used decoratively. The Grand Confort is meant to be a modern version of a traditional club chair—masculine, simple, and comfortable. Today, a commonplace remark is that it "looks like a great chair to sink into." Accordingly, a contemporary television commercial for Kodak chose to show Bill Cosby sitting in one.[31]

Corbusier made two versions of this chair, a Petit and a Grand; the latter has a seat 10 inches wider than the Petit so that, according to his notes and drawings, it could accommodate spreading out and slouching. Translations of his own verbal description of the larger chair include "very easy" and "incredibly comfortable." The sitter's weight shapes the cushions, denting them more under the sit bones, which keeps the sitter from slipping forward, so that the exterior frame can get away with being perfectly level to the floor without the tilted seat usually required to stabilize the body. In a contemporary art installation, the Austrian deconstructivist architecture group Coop Himmelblau criticized the excessive rationality of this perfectly right-angled construction by wedging a blue steel beam under the chair.[32] Others note the contradiction between Corbusier's hope to mass-produce his chairs and the reality that each of his designs required a large number of hand-welded, finely finished joints— eighteen in the case of the Grand Confort. Few, however, challenge the premise of comfort that is built into the chair's name.

Yet this chair too violates ergonomic and somatic principles. It forces the spine to round forward, because the chair stops at midback. When the sitter leans back and finds support only halfway up the back, he or she experiences the problem of having to hunch forward with the upper body to compensate for the lack of structural support in the shoulders, neck, and head. Perching upright on the edge of this chair is impossible; one is compelled to sit back into the cushions and be drawn into the chair's structural logic. Once you participate in that logic, your back, trying to compensate for the lack of support, curves forward more. A vicious cycle! Those who call this chair comfortable obviously are defining comfort as some combination of yielding softness and sensuous surface, not postural or structural comfort over the long run. The interior decorator who selected chairs for Kodak's new headquarters insisted on the Grand Confort because "comfortable seating is a 'must,' especially in corporate environments." Here is her definition of comfort: "The leather was soft as a glove, and the seat of each chair was more than 10 inches thick." In contrast, a different definition of comfort is in the mind of the rare critic who wrote that despite the appearance of comfort, "when you sit in it, it slowly slides you forward onto the floor with your knees up, and breaks your spine by reverse flexure in the process."[33]

Another experiment with materials, this time plastic resins, was conducted by Charles Eames in the 1940s. He and Eero Saarinen won an important "organic" design competition sponsored by New York's Museum of Modern Art in 1940 for a chair of molded plywood and aluminum. This chair was never manufactured, but his fiberglass shell chair was by 1946. During World War II, he and his wife Ray worked with medical casts and splints using plastic resins, which gave them the idea of using free-form plastic to produce an "organic" shape with complex curves (see Fig. 24b). Revolutionary in 1950 because it did away with traditional springs and cushions, today the so-called *Eames* chair has become a retro-fashion in the window displays of Urban Outfitters. For the forty-five years in between, it made its way into Laundromats, bowling alleys, airports, auditoriums, stadiums, schools, libraries, and even buses, subways, and other forms of mass transit, because it is easy to produce, move, clean, and pay for. Its most distinctive characteristic is the continuous form running from the back to the seat, stamped from a single sheet of plastic. The metal legs were appreciated for their dramatic visual contrast, although a pedestal version of this chair by Saarinen was meant to get rid of the "slum" of legs.

While the chair may look modern, it offers little comfort for anyone. The eggshell shape usually does not provide adequate space for the gluteus maximus. Because the back and seat are continuous in a rounded curve, when you lean back into it your buttocks are pushed forward; the chair has drawn the spine into a C-shaped slump. After you have slid your sit bones all the way forward, your back is either hunched forward or supported over the rigid edge that knifes you somewhere in the back of your rib cage. In either case, you tire, so you sit up and start the whole process over again. Another difficulty with this chair is its molded back and sides; if anyone has any irregularity in the shape of their back or rib cage—scoliosis sufferers like me, for instance—these chairs are torture chambers. Even for the most symmetrical of body shapes, the seats are harmful in the long run because they turn the pelvis in on itself, rather than offering a plane on which the sit bones can open to help widen the pelvic bowl.

How about the famous *butterfly (Hardoy)* chair, with canvas slung over a metal frame? *(Fig. 47)* Three Argentinian architects (one named Jorge Ferrari-Hardoy) designed it in 1938 and at least five million copies have been sold since. It became one of the conventional symbols of Modernism. The industrial designer George Nelson used it in a story about an architect who was able to get his projects published because he sent his pho-

Figure 47. The butterfly chair, attributed to the Argentine designer Jorge Ferrari-Hardoy, became popular after World War II for its modern, amoeba-like shape.

tographer to every site with the same props: a Noguchi lamp, a large potted rubber plant, a kidney-shaped coffee table, a few pieces of prehistoric pottery, Aalto stools, and butterfly chairs. Certainly modern artists, designers, and architecture patrons like Georgia O'Keeffe, Russell Wright, and the Kaufman family included these chairs in their famous modern residences. Its amoeba shape connotes modern sensibilities; practically speaking, it is relatively lightweight, some versions can fold, and it can be bought in any number of festive colors or in natural canvas or sophisticated black at a relatively low price.

Some people call them comfortable because they invite the sitter to slump and imply that bad posture is not only acceptable but also desirable. Because the chair is basically a sling, the torso is treated like a bag. The thighs and the torso are weighted to drop toward the same center point, so in adults the internal organs collapse and the hip joints are jammed. This is true no matter how you sit in it. If the sitter rotates and sits on this chair on the diagonal, it at least offers support for the head and the neck. But if you sit on it centered, your head has no support, so you bring it forward and exacerbate the collapse already promoted by the sling structure. The architectural critic Joseph Rykwert, of the University of Pennsylvania, has commented on the irrationality of this chair from the viewpoint of the physical body, and has argued that its real purposes are powerfully psychological, because of a simultaneously primeval womblike protection and a visual allusion to modernity.[34] In the 1950s, Lucille Ball turned irrationality into television comedy by struggling to get out of the butterfly chair while pregnant. For babies, these chairs may serve informally as cribs because they can't get out of them either. Today, Sarah Booth Conroy, a self-confessed modernist who has believed in the "Quest for the Perfect Life by Design" ever since her marriage in 1949, admits that at her age neither she, her husband, nor her contemporaries can get in and out of them.[35]

This look at chair history of the early twentieth century has not been very promising so far. Unexpectedly, I see hope for the body in one of the most radical chairs of the twentieth century, the *Red and Blue Rietveld* chair. *(Fig. 48)* Designed by Gerrit Rietveld of Holland in 1919, it is famous not so much as something to sit in but as an ideological statement. As craft, the chair is deliberately crude.[36] Constructed out of ordinary milled lumber, a long sheet of plywood makes up the back and seat, which are strictly planar. Here the chair is presented abstractly, as two systems—one composed of planes for the body and the other a separate structure for supporting those planes. None of the various joints has been hidden, but rather each element bluntly overlaps. Each end of the structural members is painted a different primary color, but their lengths are painted black so that when shown against a black wall, the support structure seems to disappear and the seating elements seem to float in space. Typically, no one calls this a comfortable chair. Designers, artists, critics, and historians admire it, instead, for its conceptual clarity—the separation of structure from seating, its boldly expressed construction, and use of color. How ironic, then, that I find it one of the more comfortable modern chairs.

But let me tell you why. The Rietveld has no padding. In order to keep the sitter from sliding out of the chair, it is tipped back. The designer then accepts the consequence of being rotated back in space by extending the back support all the way up past the shoulders and head. Thus, it does not require you to bring your head forward, increase the thoracic curve of the spine, and thereby collapse your rib cage. This is its great virtue. However, it may be hard on the heads and necks of people whose heads jut forward through years of "misuse." Nevertheless, by being more planar than all the other chairs discussed, it gives the rib cage and the pelvic bowl an opportunity to open out against these planes. Of course, without any padding it will become tiring after some time. But your escape from it is assisted by arms that help you push yourself forward.

Although this chair was designed, apparently, to be expository, it ends up providing longer-term comfort than any of the others in this section. I

Figure 48. Gerrit Rietveld was trained as a cabinetmaker by his father, but in the Red and Blue chair (1918) he deliberately broke the conventions of fine cabinetry by expressing each joint.

was gratified to learn that Rietveld himself "thought of his chairs as a kind of 'equipment'—a means of physically 'toning up' bodies that were neglected during taxing intellectual or professional work. He often said that the verb zitten (to sit) in Dutch was an active and not a passive verb."[37] Therefore, he thought chairs should offer a form of active, playful relaxation, especially for middle-class professionals who had sedentary occupations. Perhaps he qualifies as an early body-conscious designer.

Once you have started tipping the body backward in space and giving it support along its full length, including the head, legs, and feet, you end up creating a chaise longue, where the whole body is supported in a semi-reclining position. During Le Corbusier's collaboration with Charlotte Perriand and Pierre Jeanneret from 1927 to 1937, they created the *Chaise-longue Basculante* in 1928, which is still recommended by orthopedists today. *(Fig. 49)* It is planar, not trying to imitate the shape of the body. It supports the entire back, including the shoulders, neck, and head, and puts the legs at an angle to the torso that opens the joints at the hips, the knees, and the ankles. The entire supportive apparatus sits inside another portion of the metal frame, which allows it to slide along an arc so that the sitter can move along a continuum between upright and semi-supine. One can change the way gravity works on the body, or adjust the relation of the eyes to reading material. Corbusier wrote: "I thought of the cowboy in the Wild West, smoking his pipe, his feet in the air higher than his head against the chimney piece. This is the real machine for rest."[38]

Amazingly, this chaise accommodates a wide range of body types, from very short to very tall people. It has only one place without an open-ended quality—one fixed length, which is from the hips to the knees. But since, anthropometrically, more people are alike from hip to knee than in any other way, the one functionally fixed dimension in this chaise longue works for almost anyone. I doubt that

Figure 49. A true lounge chair like this is far superior to the club chairs that are sometimes called lounge chairs. By Le Corbusier, Pierre Jeanneret, and Charlotte Perriand.

Corbusier and Perriand had that fact in mind; but even if unconscious, their design was probably based on experience. In any case, it works, and we might consider having more true lounges in our lives rather than trying to relax without adequate postural support in club chairs, which, like Corbusier's Confort, are often confusingly called "lounge" (as opposed to task) chairs.

The pioneering somatic thinker F. M. Alexander found all chairs problematic, not just the modern ones being produced by his contemporaries. When asked about chairs for schools, he rejected the possibility of perfecting them, saying: "Let us waste no valuable time, thought or invention in designing furniture, when by a smaller expenditure of those three gifts we may train the child to win its own conscious control, and rise superior to any probable limitations imposed by ordinary school fittings."[39] He was willing to leave chairs as they are, but his assumption that children could be taught to rise above the physical world was mistaken in at least two different ways. First, people suffer physiologically in chairs; and second, chairs communicate messages that have another kind of power over us. Unlike Alexander, but like all scholars of design, I believe in the power of design to "speak" to people. Alexander wanted to stimulate deliberate, conscious control by the individual.[40] But the fact is that the physical world manifests information in a silent way that reaches and influences us unconsciously as well as consciously. Hence the particular potency of the designed world. Messages are encoded into the built world by its designers, and they are decoded (although not always identically to how they were encoded) by consumers. Getting chairs to convey the message that physical welfare counts would be a step in the direction of compassion and empathy. Most people get the message of soft, cushy "comfort" that is built into deeply upholstered armchairs for the home. They also get most of the messages claiming special status for their owners and users. Therefore, I am confident that designers could find a way to communicate regard for human well-being using symbolism other than softness or exclusiveness. The extra challenge is to do so for settings outside the home.

PART III

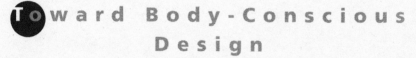
Toward Body-Conscious
Design

Revolutionary changes in living habits won't come overnight, because they entail deep and widespread cultural change. How can the benefits of what we might call "postural pluralism" be experienced by individuals, shared culturally, and established in the major institutions of work, education, and recreation? Part III explores what positive actions we might take, individually and collectively, as consumers and designers, in the face of the intractable problems of chair design. Even if we succeed in changing the way we think about ourselves, and learn new habits of mind and body, the physical environment will not change automatically, of course. The professional designers who design products, interiors, buildings, and cities must be enlisted to translate new ways of living into new forms. Consumers, too, are designers of sorts who make, buy, or otherwise obtain and then assemble all the products in our everyday environments. They too will seek ways to translate sensual rationality into material reality.*

Chapter 5 looks at the physical changes in seating which would be the heart of any transformation in body-conscious design, while the last chapter explores the interior design of domestic and institutional settings—offices, schools, and even public places—before returning to consider how social changes might stimulate these physical changes. Part III comes the closest to being a how-to book, but expands that designation by couching the problem in terms of social and cultural change. Put another way, I want to challenge the conventional distinction between intellectuality and self-help. Ideas should help people in their desires to think about, understand, and potentially change their lives.

---

*Body-conscious design is synonymous with sensuous rationality. Reason and sensation, cognition and perception, are often set up as opposites, but an underlying theme of this book is that it is reasonable to honor both: our sensual wisdom. On its own, rationality runs amok. Freud worried that modern man had become a prosthesis god—powerful, mechanized, and artificial through the use of painful, ill-fitting prosthetic devices, such as buildings and chairs. I assume that we can improve the environment through reason informed by our senses.

Chapter 5

The Chair Reformed

The satirical character Father Guido Sarducci (of *Saturday Night Live*) recently tried to account for the mysterious origin and spread of resin chairs in backyards and public places; he has been "working on a theory that white plastic chairs are alien beings."[1] By now, of course, you may be wondering with me if all chairs are not alien to our being. Compassion for them, but mostly for us, demands that we try to reform them.

Improving the basic configuration of the conventional chair involves aligning and supporting the torso properly. Then the other points of contact and interaction with the immediate environment—head and eyes, hands and feet—automatically require corresponding support from additional pieces of equipment and furniture. Thus, one cannot improve chairs without thinking about footstools, reading stands, and their close cousin, the lounge. Of course, alternatives to the chair seem like a serious option, because the conventional seated posture is so problematic. In this light, modified chairs, specifically kneeling chairs and perches, are especially appealing. But no posture is perfect. Human beings are not designed to hold any single posture for long periods of time, so postural variation is desirable. It is logical to design for movement and a variety of postures; but this requires the most fundamental and far-reaching rethinking of the body-design connection.

The two most unusual criteria for improving chairs are a planar seat and back, and butt space in lieu of lumbar support; both have implications for wheelchairs and baby carriages. I have already explained why seat and back surfaces should err in the direction of flatness. Because this is where I depart most significantly from ergonomic recommendations, the point bears further elaboration. Chair design has the contradictory twin goals of stability and movement. By and large, the people who favor stability favor contouring seatbacks. Contouring the seat helps the thighs and the gluteus maximus stay in place. Similarly, curving a chairback—making it concave around the rib cage—prevents side-to-side movement. By contrast, those who want to make sure that muscles do no load bearing, appreciate motility, and want to make sure that movement is never constricted or restrained favor planar seat and back construction. *(Figs. 50 and 51)*

A simple flat surface when lying down gives the rib cage an opportunity to open; a flat seat gives the sit bones support and organizes

Figure 50. Artist Scott Burton's stone furniture in New York City is structurally better for our bodies than an easy chair.

Figure 51. Architect Robert Venturi's collection of flat chairs strike some as parody, but their planar construction is intelligent for our physical well-being.

the upward drive of the spine. Of course, these criteria—not compressing flesh and not inhibiting movement—could be filled by other types of furniture, such as wide platforms on the floor, or wide benches, or the deep Chinese and Indian low chairs. One of the first efficiency experts in America, Frank Gilbreth, who is better known for the charming account of raising twelve children efficiently (with his wife) in *Cheaper by the Dozen,* relied on a planar church pew, "the only chair which fitted him comfortably. . . ."[2] For those designers who want to work with chairs proper *and* with curves, I suggest that they consider curving the *legs* of the chairs and leaving the human rib cage and pelvic bowl with planes that they can open out against.[3]

The most controversial implication of this pro-planar guideline is that designers as well as users should avoid specialized lumbar support. Additionally, this guideline throws a new, harsh light on chairs designed like slings, such as baby strollers and car seats. My advice to avoid slings probably comes as a surprise to people who remember the change from the flat car seats of the 1950s and 1960s to the enveloping seats of new cars as "progress." I feel sorry for myself and other adults who suffer in car seats, but my heart goes out to the poor babies in sling-style strollers who are forced into a C-shaped slump. Most of us get to at least age two before we begin distorting our postures. *(Fig. 52)* What will happen to babies who are forced into this slump/sling so early? Just because adults enjoy hammocks does not mean that young infants, with their weaker torsos, want

Figure 52. Unstructured strollers cause children to slump into a C-shape posture.

to be forced into a miniature version. Happily, I have seen recently that more baby carriages are now available with relatively rigid flat seats and backs. Parents of young children should be sure to buy these new, improved versions.

The foldable Everett and Jones wheelchair was a tremendous advance over bulky modified chairs-on-wheels that preceded it. However, wheelchair users often develop bad posture while using these chairs, not just because of their disability but because of the yielding foldable seat. A sling instead of a plane, it allows the sitter's pelvic bowl to fold in on itself, which allows the entire spine and rib cage to drive down and collapse inward. Those confined to chairs—more than anyone else—need a firm plane for the sit bones to anchor on so that the pelvic wings can open out. This firm structure should of course be padded with sheepskin or some other similar material, but the underlying structure must be firm. The industrial designer Susan Farricielli is creating just such a new wheelchair.[4] *(Fig. 53)*

The other guideline that I want to call attention to again, because it is so seldom acknowledged in standard ergonomic literature, concerns "butt space." Chair designers should provide a space, a dent, or softer padding between the seat and the back for the gluteus maximus and the back of the pelvis. Instead, seating engineers often widen the angle between the seat and the back. But this approach takes us off our center of balance. It would be better to have a more upright relationship between the seat and the back, and to carve out a space between the seat and the back for this natural protuberance. Traditionally, many designers have done this, but just as many bring the back all the way down in a solid piece to the seat. The need for butt space may be why lumbar support is so popular. Inadvertently, the forward curve creates a space for the

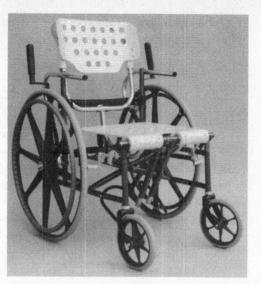

Figure 53. Industrial designer Susan Farricielli is creating a new wheelchair following the principles of planar support.

gluteus maximus, but at the expense of throwing the lower (lumbar) and upper (thoracic) curves of the back out of balance.

In order to maintain both of the major curves in the spine in balance with one another, back support that crosses or brackets the lumbar-thoracic curve is logically more efficient than lumbar support alone. The structural balance between the two curves is part of what keeps the spine erect, so supporting either one in isolation is bound to create problems in the long run. One example of Italian-German collaboration does offer a stylish example of supporting precisely the transition from lumbar to thoracic curves. *(Fig. 54)*

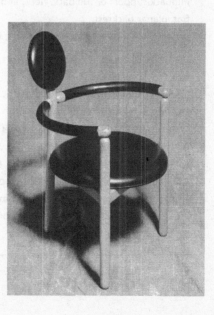

Figure 54. Vico Magistretti designed this chair with back support at just the right spot, supporting both the lumbar and the thoracic curves of the spine.

The following considerations, listed in Box 2, are the most important in selecting a suitable chair:

Chair Recommendations

Specifications:

for conventional right-angled sitting, seat height no greater than the top of your knee minus 2 in.

forward-tilt seat (the more the task takes you forward, the more the seat should tilt forward); you will also require a forward slope for the work surface, and a computer at eye-level; the logic of forward-tilt seats argues for raising seat height significantly (4–6 in.), which creates a perching chair rather than a conventional chair

firm-textured surface, upholstered but not more than ½–1-in. depth

flat, uncontoured seat

butt space between seat and backrest

midback support *or* full back, neck, and head support excepting butt space

flat, planar backrest

armrests for support if reading, typing, keyboarding, painting, or other similar activities

Use:

both feet should be flat on floor (helps organize the spine upward)

legs not crossed (helps protect pelvis)

knees should be lower than hip sockets (takes strain off lower back)

pelvis should not be rolled back

spine should retain natural curves, but appear straight overall

chest should be open rather than collapsed

head should be balanced on top of spine, not resting back and down on it

eyes should be able to look at work or people within a 15-degree cone, not forced to look too far up or down

---

Consumers may feel discouraged about ever finding a chair that meets all these criteria. Consequently, having a chair built to one's own measurements may seem tempting. The argument for customizing chairs is similar to the one we make for shoes and clothing: they should fit individual bodies. But it is obviously expensive to have custom-tailored shoes, clothes, or chairs. Our economy has created, happily, a middle ground between a gunnysack that fits all and handmade clothing. The clothing industry has institutionalized sizing, so that although you buy something not individually adjusted to your body, it is within an acceptable range. Thousands of products in our society are provided in varying sizes. Even then, minor alterations at hem or waistband are sometimes necessary. Surely our most frequently used chairs merit equivalent adjustments with pillows, backboards, and footstools.

The strategy of sizing combines the economic benefits of mass marketing with some of the old virtues of handmade and hand-fitted items. Chairs should probably come in sizes, too. *(Figs. 55 and 56)* In 1969, an English ergonomic researcher suggested that easy chairs "for use by the general population should be available in at least two models, differing in shape as well as in size."[5] In 1994, the Herman

Figure 55. Steven Narcissian designed this chair as a student project to show that Modernist concerns for the way materials like wood and steel come together can be expressed in a chair scaled in size to a short person.

Figure 56. Wharton Esherick built a choice of leg length into this couch.

Miller Company produced the Aeron office chair in three sizes, and in 1997, Haworth followed suit by offering their new chair for "active sitting" in three sizes.[6]

Instead of producing two to five sizes, most of the furniture industry has grappled with making an adjustable chair. The industry still hopes to produce one chair that fits us all, and since few chairs outside the home are used by only one person, their focus on designing adjustable chairs has a compelling logic. Much energy and research has been devoted to this enterprise. However, in the 1960s, anthropometric data (differing sizes of human frames, etc.) were used to support an argument *against* chairs that could be adjusted to different sizes:

> It has been shown that if more than two dimensions are adjustable, a person may not be able to remember enough about previous settings to decide which of a large number of resulting adjustments fits him [and her] best. . . . [W]hen one is fresh it is much easier and quicker to adapt one's posture to inconveniently dimensioned equipment than to set about undoing clamps, winding handles, etc. Later, when one is tired by the effect of maintaining an uncomfortable posture, there is even less motivation and energy available for the effort of adjusting the equipment.[7]

A generation later, the same problem of too much gadgetry prompted Vernon Mays to report in *Progressive Architecture* that people end up "more uncomfortable than they might have been with a simple, straight-back chair."[8] Of course I hear in this statement an unconscious longing for the planar qualities of a "simple, straightback chair." But the furniture industry has moved, instead, through several stages of thought. First, the industry believed that adjustable chairs were not worth the extra expense involved; then proponents decided that all adjustments must be made by the sitter while sitting in the chair; and third, they have currently concluded that since users still are not making the adjustments, the chair itself should make the adjustments in response to the sitter's routine movement.

The more sophisticated office chair designers today have built potential ergonomic adjustments into the structure of the chair, such as knee-tilt mechanisms and synchronous movement. The knee-tilt mechanism moves the pivot point from the center of the chair to a point just behind the sitter's knee, allowing people to lean back while keeping their heels on the floor, and synchronous movement allows the sitter to move both the chair's seat and its back at different, but proportional rates. For instance, you might press the back of the chair five inches, but doing so would only move the seat three inches forward. (Remember that when leaning backward, the pelvis scoots forward.) These adjustments might be especially useful in rooms like theaters and auditoriums where people cannot select their own seat size.

For the places where we use the same chair regularly—at home and work—buying a chair just for ourselves is logical. You can search for the right chair in the mass-produced market, or go so far as to choose a customized one. One couple has designed an adjustable rig with which they measure individuals for personal chairs. First, they establish the optimal seat depth, height, and angle to the floor—in that order. Then, if the chair is going to have arms, they establish the height of the armrest, and next the angle of the back of the seat. Finally, they adjust a series of back supports, working from the bottom to the top. Aesthetically, they point out that one still has a lot of artistic freedom because of the many different ways to assemble all these dimensions.[9] The problem with this method is that they make adjustments until the sitter *feels* (that is, *thinks* he or she feels) fine. This raises again the old problem of whether to rely on objective or subjective measures of comfort. In contrast, another craftsman fits the chair to the individual by taking objective measurements of the client. He makes as many as twelve adjustments to the basic design, ranging from the position of the headboard to the length of the arm to the angle between the seat and the chair back.[10]

Whether you customize to your perceived notion of comfort or to your objective body dimensions, or even to some normative notion of comfort, children would outgrow a customized chair, and adults might too if they change in size or attitude. As you progress through life, just as you outgrow your shoes, you would outgrow chairs and produce hand-me-down chairs. One consequence is that you might not have chairs in matching sets. That would challenge the Victorian practice, thereby fighting against tradition, manufacturers, and advertisers. Peter Opsvik invented a children's chair that makes an end run around this outcome by having the chair adjust to the child's growth. *(Fig. 57)* Yet a business advantage of adults periodically wanting a new, better-fitting chair is that it would stimulate the furniture market, turning it from an "inelastic" to an "elastic" one.

The seating industry has produced many adjustable chairs over the last two or three decades to address the problem that no chair is able to serve all body types.[11] However, even adjustable chairs can't serve everyone, so the size extremes could indulge in customizing. For public settings that must accommodate many people without the money for adjustable chairs, we should expect and demand different sizes of chairs.

The workplace is a more complex issue. Who should pay for the chairs at work, especially since people change jobs frequently? People could bring their chairs with them just as they bring other personal effects to a job; but the employer would have to tolerate all the chairs looking different from one another, or be willing to pay for look-alike adjustable

Figure 57. Peter Opsvik designed the Tripp-Trapp chair to accommodate children's growth.

chairs that could accommodate each new employee—which is what most places are doing. Getting people to make the adjustments is another issue (discussed in the next chapter), related to employee education.

"GUERRILLA ERGONOMICS"

Since most chairs we encounter are not adjustable, carrying our own portable backboards, footrests, and seat cushions is our best alternative. With these, almost any chair can be made workable on the spot. Similarly, if you as an individual cannot buy a new chair for yourself, you can modify what you have in many different ways, or an organization that cannot afford new chairs can use some "guerrilla ergonomics" to "customize" each employee's immediate work environment. Marvin Dainoff, director of the Center for Ergonomic Research at Miami University in Oxford, Ohio, uses this term to describe ergonomic improvements made from materials that are free, cheap, or regularly available.[12] Taped phone books provide cheap footstools; a book wrapped in a towel can take the swale out of a car seat and make a long journey less fatiguing. I have helped people cut foam or fold wool blankets to fill in typing chairs, executive chairs, and armchairs that let the front of people's rib cages slide down over the diaphragm and belly. Scott Donkin, the chiropractor who wrote *Sitting on the Job,* offers many such survival tips for the office worker, although he accepts the scenario of seated work as a given.[13]

Many commercial products are available to aid the hapless sitter. Entrepreneurs have invented body-conscious products, like neck pillows, footstools, foot cushions, Recaro car seats, and chairs that give a massage mechanically. One particularly odd-looking device is a seat cushion with a cut-out space for the tailbone. Perhaps more important, the overall shape is a forward-sloping wedge. It is this forward slope that maintains the natural lumbar curve, preferable to traditional lumbar support.[14] If anyone still thinks chairs are healthful, the number of backboards on the market alone should dispel that illusion. Most backboards feature some form of lumbar support, which advertisers point to with pride. But as I have said before, if you are going to support the spine, do so for both curves—the lumbar and the thoracic.[15] Often something is needed to help people fill in concave curves in plastic molded seats, as well as upholstered airplane and car seats. Ideally, one would want a planar backboard that would fill in the whole surface without being too bulky to carry around. Thus, it would fold or telescope down to briefcase size. Unfortunately, I know of no such product on the market, so this is a call to designers: Make it fold or hinge, strong when opened, lightweight but costing less than $100! In the meantime, a planar back support put out by Posture Education Products retails for about $85.[16] In order to keep down costs, it does not fold to briefcase size, but it is lightweight and comfortable to carry under one arm. I rely on it constantly to help me cope with sagging theater seats, trains, planes, and other people's cars.

What about your own car? Make sure you have a backboard to help you take those concave curves out of your car seat. Often car seats have excessive upper lumbar push that makes your chest collapse and thrusts your neck forward. It is frequently claimed that a Recaro seat is the best you can find, but I find all car seats to be overly contoured. Volvo has a reputation for good seats, yet even they are a little bit too concave for my body. I know one body-conscious M.D. in Milan who keeps a firm, wedge-shaped piece of foam in a cotton cover in her Volvo seat at all times to fill in the seat pan and raise the hip sockets above the knees. Even very expensive, leather-upholstered cars like Mercedes and Infiniti may need some modifications, such as foam pads to fill in concave backs on their seats.

Marketing departments usually design car seats by assembling a panel of judges to sit in a range of seats for 8.5 minutes and then rank them to find the "best." Why 8.5 minutes? Because this, my industry informant tells me, is the average time a customer sits on a seat when buying a new car. So much for body-conscious design. Car seat design lags behind the sophistication otherwise lavished on vehicle design and research.[17]

For the sporty set, there are the car seats with side-to-side rolls on either side of the rib cage to counter high-speed turns around curves. Those also tend to turn the rib cage in on itself. For the even sportier, there are the cars that have you virtually lying down as you drive. Lying down is usually desirable, but as you have to see the road when driving, you end up being goose-necked. The best available car seats are the 1950s bench-like seats you still find in Volkswagen campers, in the old, nearly extinct Checker taxicabs, and in pickup trucks. But even many pickups these days have the bucket seats of race-car imagery. The tragedy of progress.

COMPLEMENTING CHAIRS: FOOTSTOOLS AND
READING STANDS

The effort to make chairs less hazardous to our health continuously extends our concerns beyond the chair proper. Our feet affect our structural organization fairly obviously, so footstools should be involved in chair design, and can be a literal part of the chair, as they are in many lounge chairs like the infamous La-Z-Boy. Matched chair and ottoman sets separate the two elements only slightly further. Separate footstools, when not in use for our feet, can sometimes do double duty as side tables or stools.

Sitting on a chair that is too tall, so that your thighs are pressed from underneath, is surprisingly debilitating. Footstools really are essential if you cannot find an appropriately scaled chair at your workplace or for your dining-room table. They were used in Pompeii, and I have seen them in nineteenth-century Swedish farmhouses; but in contemporary America, footstools have somehow become old-fashioned. *(Fig. 58a and b)* I have very

Figure 58. Footstools in *(a)* a reconstruction of a Roman bedroom and *(b)* a nineteenth-century Swedish farmhouse.

few chairs in my house, though I have left two at the dining-room table. When I sit in one of these, I use an inch-thick cookbook on the floor to ensure that my heels meet the ground firmly—another example of guerrilla ergonomics. Similarly, yoga teachers recommend telephone books as footrests (or as seats to elevate the pelvis for those who cannot otherwise kneel comfortably).

Our eyes interact with the environment in ways that also require special equipment. In order to mitigate the stresses imposed by working in chairs—especially reading and writing—many products on the market provide appropriately elevated and slanted surfaces. One is an ungainly plastic device that moves in many different angles, called the Able Table, priced at about $45. A catalogue from Levenger offers more elegant wooden versions of reading stands "for the serious reader." Not even these more expensive wooden ones, however, would meet a designer's criteria for elegance or artistry. In the language of furniture connoisseurship, the reading stands available today lack visual integration. The pieces are assembled, not composed, lacking a sense of either deliberate constructivism or organic harmony. They have an uninspired look about them. *(Fig. 59)*

This is another area where designers could make a significant contribution by producing objects that integrate beauty and ease.

REPLACING CHAIRS: STOOLS

Stools offer a middle ground between right-angle sitting and other postures like perching, standing, or squatting that

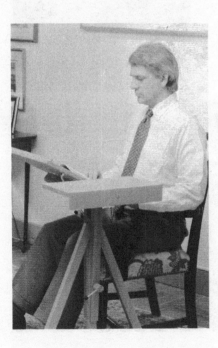

Figure 59. Reading stands should be marketed in a wider variety of styles in order to fit into traditional, modern, and other decors.

Figure 60. Stools can look like backless chairs, like the ones in this nineteenth-century Swedish farmhouse.

make more active use of the whole body. They could be introduced into contemporary life as a compromise for those who are not ready for a seating revolution, but who are still interested in either social or physical improvement. Sitting without a backrest promotes autonomous seating, thereby rebuilding torso strength. Because many stools are the same height as chairs (17 and 18 inches tall), the two can be mixed together around a dining-room or conference table without having to replace the existing ones. In the nineteenth-century Swedish farmhouse, I saw a dining-room suite that included both regular chairs and backless chairs. These seats were upholstered in exactly the same way, so calling them backless chairs seems as accurate as calling them stools. *(Fig. 60)* Culturally, they had been assimilated into the category of chair even though physiologically they functioned differently.

Perhaps the most unusual stool I have seen is the European pivoting stool. I first learned about this from photographs of the office of Barbara Tietze, the Berlin ergonomics professor who has gone beyond conventional ergonomics. These pivoting stools are particularly useful for talking on the telephone; a pedestal rests on a pivoting semi-sphere, so that a person perched on the seat rocks around.[18] Stability is created by forming a tripod between pivot and feet, allowing the seat to move in any direction the user wishes. In a similar spirit—but with a very different look—some somatic practitioners have started to advocate using large inflated

Figure 61. (a) An inflatable therapy ball being used as a chair. *(b)* An Alexander teacher designed this chair to capture the benefits of sitting on therapy balls.

balls as seats. *(Fig. 61a and b)* Sitting on a relatively unstable surface requires the person to use the legs and torso actively and to use slightly different muscles continuously, which overcomes some of the circulation and muscle fatigue problems associated with sedentary work, and has the additional benefit of keeping the mind alert. Such a "stool" no longer conforms to conventional chair seat height, but rather approaches the height of a perch, halfway between sitting and standing.

Stylistically, stools can be treated in a wide variety of ways. In order to convince my students of their functional and artistic versatility, I have started to collect images of high-style stools. This attention to high style emphasizes the communication function of furniture, which can be expressed even without the emblematic chairback. For example, for centuries the Chinese have used formal lacquered dining-room sets consisting of tables and stools, often square in shape. They also have utilized ceramic stools, usually round, in outdoor garden settings. The Finnish

Figure 62. Movement is built into the spring feet of these "543 Broadway" chairs and stool by Gaetano Pesce.

Modernist Alvar Aalto created three-legged stools that can be stacked for storage into a sculptural display that might be viewed as a giant DNA-like molecule. Contemporary Italian, American, and Swedish examples abound in metal, leather, and wood. *(Fig. 62)*

A commonly held idea is that stools are very simple things and are therefore stylistically and functionally limited; in fact, they exhibit great variety. *(Fig. 63)* In Stockholm, I saw conventional circular stool seats set atop many different kinds of supports. One restaurant had stools of two different heights, to accompany two slightly different bar heights. *(Fig. 64)* In another upscale restaurant, I saw tall stools at a bar and low stools

Figure 63. Stools can be high-tech, as in this proposal for high-fashion stools with adjustable heights.

Figure 64. Stools and bars of slightly different heights in an outdoor bar in Stockholm (1989).

with elegant maroon leather tops that matched the leather on the eating banquette—but not one single conventional chair.

KNEELING CHAIRS

Until the introduction of the Norwegian Balans (balance) chair, the multi-billion-dollar international chair industry had been surprisingly homogeneous. This chair is certainly the most radical of the twentieth century and probably since the invention of the chair-throne itself *(see Fig. 36).* It directly challenges habits that have been in our culture for millennia. As a type, it is ambiguous because the sitter is between sitting and standing, and does not have a back to lean against. It is not a stool, but it does not look like a chair.

The Balans chair was engineered in the late 1970s in Norway by Hans Christian Menghoel, and then designed by Svein Gusrud and Peter Opsvik, who were influenced by Mandal's 1967 chair design and by his 1970 publication advocating forward-tilt seats.[19] The Norwegian design team presented their prototypes to the public in Copenhagen at the 1979 Scandinavian Furniture Fair. Exports to the United States began in 1981, and over the last seventeen years this chair has slowly diffused into American culture. Many copies have been produced in Asia, but in order to cut costs, and possibly to avoid patent infringements, the expensive laminated wooden rockers have been replaced by flat wood or metal supports.

The chair's justification lies in its having solved the problem of stressing the lower back (the flattening or even rounding of the natural lumbar curve) which is associated with conventional right-angled sitting—by dropping the legs. When our thighs are at an oblique angle in relation to our spines (somewhere between 120 and 135 degrees), the muscular work of sitting upright is balanced between the front and back of the spine. This makes sitting upright feel almost effortless. The Balans chair opens the possibility of doing away with the chairback and all those related problems described in Chapter 3. But since this chair is one of the few that avoids the intrinsic problems of right-angle chair sitting, why hasn't it been adopted wholesale?

The first source of resistance is that it doesn't fit into established cultural patterns. But that doesn't entirely explain its current status, because many successful innovations have required cultural accommodation. To take one example, Americans learned to drink orange juice for breakfast because of nutritional campaigns in the 1940s; previously, they thought orange juice too acidic for breakfast. In order to understand how the kneeling chair is being received in the United States, graduate students and I conducted a study of attitudes toward the chair. In 1984, my seminar on research methods designed and administered a one-page questionnaire to seventy-three design students, about half of them at San Jose State College and the other half at the University of California at Berkeley. Ten years later, I conducted a similar study with another group of graduate students, distributing the same questionnaire to seventy-nine architecture students, this time all from the University of California at Berkeley. In both years, filling out the questionnaire while seated at a table in exactly the same kneeling chair—an inexpensive copy with flat supports and no adjustable components—took each respondent five to ten minutes. *(Fig. 65a and b)* (Using a cheap copy is not an accurate way to evaluate the Norwegian Balans chair, because it eliminates the important quality of movement that is built into the original Balans Variable with its curved rockers. Instead, using the copy

Figure 65. *(a)* Cheap copy of the Norwegian Balans chair directed to the American market (1980s). *(b)* The rockers on the Balans Variable add to the cost but add greatly to the comfort.

evaluates only the open angle between spine and thigh.)

We learned that the kneeling chair has clearly become known to a greater part of the population. In 1984, one-third of the seventy-three respondents had never seen a kneeling chair before sitting in the one used in the study, and they marked "yes" when asked if they needed instruction to figure out how to sit in it. By 1994, the percentage of those who had never seen one dropped to less than one-tenth (8%).[20]

Since personal computers have become widespread, the balance chair—now viewed commonly as a "computer chair"—has become more easily recognized. In 1984, when asked, "Where might you expect to see this chair being used?" only five respondents (7%) said the chair was used with computers; whereas in 1994, the percentage more than doubled, to 18 percent. But even in 1984 it was predominantly linked to the world of work: thirty-one people (42%) thought it was used in an office, while only twelve (14%) saw it as a chair for the home.

Yet when asked, "Where would you go to buy one?" few in the 1984 sample replied at a computer store (only three) or an office supply store (six). Instead, most would turn to a furniture store or department store, and surprisingly, the picture is not much different today, with most mentioning a furniture or department store and a few (five) specifying a Scandinavian furniture store. The only shift in perception of where to go is that twenty-one people would turn to an office supply store. This change points to an association between the chair and office work that became stronger over the decade. In fact, office supply stores today do sell these and other kinds of office chairs; but computer stores still don't sell any chairs whatsoever, let alone "computer" chairs. I conclude that the balance chair is still viewed most generally as a piece of furniture, more specifically as office furniture, but not yet as a piece of equipment. This means the kneeling chair will continue to be judged by the standards and expectations for furniture, both residential and office.

Furniture helps define the social situation and expectations for behavior, so people are sensitive to what kind of furniture belongs where. Asking about their perception of where the chair would be appropriate reveals what kind of furniture they think it is. The 1984 survey queried the appropriateness of the chair for different situations—office, bedroom, dining room, living room—and some of the results were surprising. While it is no surprise that the greatest number judged it appropriate in a work environment, why did the next-largest number indicate that the bedroom was okay? Was that because many students study in their bedrooms, or because they wanted to avoid it being seen by others? When considering the living room, ambivalence emerged: the sample was neatly divided fifty-fifty between those who thought it appropriate for a living room and those who did not. In the dining room, ambivalence gave way to clear disapproval. The formal rooms of a house are where its occupants seek to communicate their identity and aspirations to themselves and to visitors. Since a dining room is the most formal of the four choices, this disapproval suggests that the kneeling chair is viewed as useful but not prestigious.

By 1994, this divergence between practicality and prestige had become wider. Over 80 percent thought the chair was appropriate for a working environment, but over half said it was *not* appropriate for their bedroom; even more did not want it in a social environment; over two-thirds did not think it appropriate for their living room; and over three-quarters did not want it in their dining room. Apparently, ambivalence and confusion about how to categorize this chair have been resolved so that it is now clearly perceived as *utilitarian.* The perceived purpose of the chair has become narrowed and fixed as technical—not social or leisure.

To find out what activities would be pursued within the setting, we asked, "Would you use this chair while reading for pleasure? Studying? Writing? Watching TV? Playing a musical instrument? Relaxing or talking? Drawing? Working at the computer? Eating?"[21] The most preferred activities were work-related—working at the computer (86%), writing (72%), studying and drawing (both 67%). Most people said they would avoid the chair for eating, reading for pleasure, relaxing or talking, and watching TV. Due to the spread of personal computing, the kneeling chair has become increasingly associated with work. Having had less experience with it, our 1984 sample was more open to imagining its use in a wide variety of settings and for a wide variety of activities. Since then, people have come to associate the chair with task-focused activities.

We wanted to know if consumers understood the reason for its unusual shape. When we asked, "Why do you think it is shaped the way it is?" a clear majority (over three-quarters) perceived the designers' intention to be to promote greater health and comfort, not innovation for its own sake.

We also asked, "Are you comfortable now in the chair?" You might be surprised, if you yourself haven't sat in one, that a sizable majority (fifty-five) said yes, while only sixteen said no.[22] We pressed the point about comfort, asking in another way: "Does the chair seem to fit your body's size and proportions?" and responses overwhelmingly confirmed its physical support (sixty-three said yes, and eight said no). Not to be too easily convinced, we tried yet another angle, asking, "Are there any points where your contact with the chair causes discomfort?" This time we received twenty-nine "yes" responses (about 40% both years). Given that this chair is designed to translate weight to the shins, the complaints were about pressure on the knees or legs. This is one reason that Mandal prefers perching to kneeling chairs.

What about gender? Scandinavian advertisers in the eighties "bent over backwards" to present the Balans chair as usable by both sexes. Ads show both men and women using it together socially, say for coffee breaks, or families eating together. Computer programmers have been by and large male, but computers are now used equally by men and women; if they eventually take on the association of primarily female work, as happened historically with typing, the kneeling chair could become associated primarily with women.[23]

Although 75 percent of the respondents were comfortable sitting in the chair, and 64 percent had used one before, the students were unlikely to buy one. The survey results did not indicate that price was a deterrent. Our student sample was not a furniture-buying population because of limited funds and temporary residences, but they do buy other tools, revealing in yet another way that the kneeling chair is in the mental category of "furniture" rather than "tool." If that were changed, would students everywhere buy them more frequently?

A promotion strategy might be to define the balance chair as part of an entire complex of computer-related furniture. Marketing could make it seem essential by bracketing the chair with the personal computer and rendering it demountable for easy packing. Surprisingly, the current advertising and retailing has not tried to capitalize on its sharper definition as a computer chair. Because computer use has led to back pain and repetitive stress syndromes, the balance chair could be touted as being indispensable for one's health.

Another strategy would be to provide more opportunities for direct experience. Although awareness of the chair is high by now, the number of people who have actually tried one for a period of time is considerably lower. Given the importance of direct experience if an innovation is to become known, suppliers might consider offering the chair at a discount to architectural studios and computer rooms in universities, thereby tapping into a large market. The original version, with curved rockers that allow for movement and continuous adjustment, is ergonomically superior, but about eight to ten times more expensive than the copies; retailers might consider displaying both in their showrooms, so that customers can directly experience these differences for themselves.[24] Gifts to waiting rooms in public places might also be cost-effective.

Paradoxically, the biggest impediment to the balance chair's popularity is probably what Siegfried Giedion observed about the fate of patent furniture one hundred years ago: that it may be too utilitarian, and not enough about style and image.[25] Modest, pragmatic appliances don't communicate enough about an owner's attitudes, preferences, and values.[26] To find greater acceptance, the designers and retailers might take a closer look at the marketing history of the butterfly chair, which is physiologically dysfunctional but psychologically and culturally effective at expressing an image of modernity along with womblike nurturance.[27] The distinctive shape of the kneeling chair might perhaps be exploited by exaggeration and selective emphasis to address postmodern anxieties and resolve modern conflicts, such as work versus play, license versus restraint, and conformity versus rebellion.[28]

PERCHES

The physiological observation that led to the kneeling chair is that muscular effort is most evenly balanced front to back and top to bottom of the torso when the legs are at an oblique, not a right, angle to the spine.[29] Another vision of seating reform has been developed around perching that offers similar biomechanical advantages. *(Box 3)* Many researchers agree that the least harmful solution for the lower back when seated is to assume the position that naturally occurs when seated on a high stool or lying down on one's side in bed.[30] Mary Plumb Blade, a retired mechanical engineering professor at Cooper Union in New York City, and a researcher into the problem of sitting, is not an advocate of the chair. She says that if you must sit, perching is the best way to do it. Perhaps not coincidentally, the 135-degree relationship between spine and legs is the one used in the martial arts for greatest stamina and flexibility. Called "the horse," the position is difficult for an opponent to uproot and, at the same time, readies the actor to move in any direction.

Mini-Exercise in Experiencing Difference Between Right-Angled Seating and Perching

1. Place a conventional chair or stool (17–18 in. high) next to a 24-in. stool.
2. Sit on the chair with your feet on the floor and pay attention to your lower back, noting the amount of muscular effort required to sit upright.
3. Move to the higher seat, sit at its edge with your feet on the floor, and again tune in to your lower back, noting the amount of effort needed to sit upright.
4. Did you notice a difference between the two? You might want to move back and forth between the two seats once again. You may notice that sitting up straight on the higher stool requires less effort.

F. M. Alexander called it "the position of mechanical advantage." Personally, I was intrigued to learn that this 135-degree relationship is the same position the body assumes when floating through space in conditions of zero gravity. It is reassuring to note that strength and readiness are embedded in the ease of being in this "neutral" position.

This insight goes much further back in Western civilization than is ordinarily recognized. Sometimes furniture historians mention the choir stalls in medieval churches as a forerunner of the chair, but they downplay the true significance of a key feature, the *misericord*. *(Fig. 66)* This device offered the singer a choice between sitting and perching. When not singing, choir members could rest by pulling down a seat on a hinge to sit conventionally. But they usually had to sing for long periods of time, and singing cannot be done properly when seated because lung capacity is reduced. Therefore, carved into the underside of the seat was a flange, just big enough to catch a person's sit bones. When the seat was flipped up, the singer could perch on this little seat. Perching allows the lungs and torso to remain fully extended so that one can still sing properly while resting one's legs. The literal meaning of the Latin *misericordia* is telling: "sympathy from the heart." Those in charge of Christian religious ritual showed that they cared about the physical well-being of the choir by providing such a special seat.

Many experts consider horseback riding healthy because the legs drop away from the spine while the pelvis is widened. Mandal, as well as other physicians, physical therapists, and Alexander teachers, recommends the saddle as therapy for some back problems. Some physical therapists are using large physio-balls to simulate the motion as well as the biomechanics of riding *(see Fig. 61a)*. Mary F. Gale, a physiotherapist from Australia, has invented a *Bambach Saddle Seat;* June Ekman, an Alexander teacher in New York City

Figure 66. The medieval misericord offers a choice between perching and right-angle seating.

has patented a Pneumatic Ball Chair; *(see Fig. 61b);* and Peter Opsvik has also designed a saddle chair, *the Capisco,* manufactured by HAG, the best ergonomic office chair I have ever experienced. It doesn't have a forward-tilt seat, but the sitter's legs drop away because of the saddle shape of the seat. *(Fig. 67)* Forward-tilt is not an end in itself, just one means for getting the legs to drop away from the spine at an angle greater than 90 degrees.

Because the angle between spine and legs in perching is similar to horseback riding, several experts recommend it as a reasonable facsimile. Dr. Mandal wants seats in schools that put children's legs into the same relation to the spine as when mounted on a horse.[31] He reasoned that since sitting is hard on the back, and standing hard on the legs, the compromise position of perching averages out the strain of the two extremes.[32] He has designed school chairs with seats that tilt forward and are higher than the conventional 17–18 inches, so that a person can sit with legs dropping away from the spine but the feet still planted flat on the floor. (He thinks very tall pupils have a special need for perches because they suffer most from conventional-height chairs and desks.) Mandal's chairs, halfway between sitting and standing, do not require threading the feet and ankles behind knee supports as in the balance chair. According to Mandal, people prefer his chair because they do not feel locked into it the way some feel in the kneeling chair.[33] Some people find this position precarious because once they have threaded their feet into the chair they feel they cannot get them out fast enough. Moreover, from an Alexander point of view, being able to sense our weight through the feet is preferable because the reflexes that allow us to act without having to go all the way to the brain are activated.[34] I note that with forward-tilt perching seats even short people can sit without compressing their thighs and

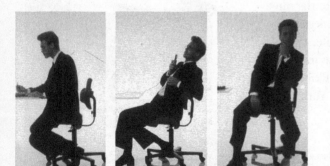

Figure 67. The Capisco saddle chair by Peter Opsvik offers support from the front, back, or side.

still have their feet flat on the floor with all the attendant benefits. The perch has another advantage over the balance chair. Sitters don't rest on their knees in the perch, so that source of pressure is missing.

Scandinavian occupational therapists have learned that perching is the best position to use when they are administering physical therapy, because it spares the therapist's back. At least two Americans have designed and marketed office chairs with forward-tilt seats that support the body in the natural, zero-gravity posture that I call perching: ergonomicist Jerome Congleton, who produced the Pos-chair, and Dr. Stephen Brooks, a neurologist who collaborated with BodyBilt, a manufacturer in Texas.[35] Another American manufacturer has developed a sit-stand stool, and targets workers, such as assembly-line employees and check-out counter workers, who cannot sit down on the job.[36] A California chair designer of a perch with a pivoting seat calls his a "continuous-balance" seat.[37] A student in one of my classes, Justin Irons, has made a proposal for a forward-tilt seat on a swing. *(Fig. 68)* But even without a movable seat, perching is superior to classical right-angle sitting. (If perching is not possible, at least make sure the cant of the seat slopes forward, not backward.)

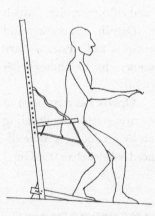

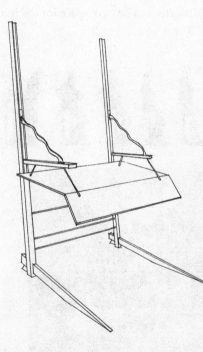

Figure 68. A student proposal for a forward-tilt seat on a swing.

Figure 69. The Gravity converts from lounge to conventional chair to kneeling chair.

The problem with perches is that they require raising the heights of work surfaces. While this argues for adjustable surfaces to go with adjustable seat heights, most offices have not yet found such flexibility acceptable. The Aeron chair is caught in this tension; it tries to introduce the benefits of forward-tilt seating, but does so within the limits of standard desk and chair heights, and therefore cannot create a true perch. (I have an additional problem with the Aeron: the back is overly shaped; the lumbar support, while adjustable, isn't adjustable enough to be eliminated altogether in favor of space for the buttocks.) In contrast, Mandal's higher

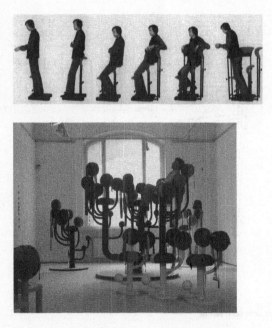

seats require higher table and desk surfaces than the standard 24–27 inches, so he has raised desk height and sloped it forward toward the sitter. This represents a substantial material and cultural change, which the Danish, Swedish, and French school systems have been willing to undergo (*see Fig. 38*).

Opsvik has responded to the criticisms of the kneeling chair by producing a more advanced balance chair (the Grav-

Figure 70. (a and b) Peter Opsvik has specialized in designing for movement.

Figure 71. (a and b) Both these chair styles fit under a conventional dining table, desk, or conference table. They look conventional but offer a forward-tilt seat.

ity), which offers three different poses. *(Fig. 69)* You can rock the seat forward and tuck your feet behind your knees in the Balans chair-kneeling posture, but you can also place your feet on the ground in a conventional right-angle way. Moreover, as a rocker, it allows you to rock back on the runners and extend your feet, as you would in any type of recliner. He has gone on to develop the principles of choice and movement, building them into his individual chairs, his seating clusters, and most recently into two different types of dining-room chairs. *(Fig. 70a and b and 71a and b)* They offer a choice of sitting conventionally or in a modified perch. One, the "Actulum," works like a modified rocker with only two positions, flat and forward. The other, called the "Flysit," uses a combination of spring mechanisms and stops to provide three choices between classical right-angled posture, leaning back, or forward in a modified perch, meaning that the knees are substantially lower than the hip sockets, but nowhere near halfway between sitting and standing.

RECLINERS

Just as perching is halfway between sitting and standing, lounging is halfway between sitting and lying down. In fact, one can think of lounging and perching as the same beneficial posture, rotated differently in space. *(Fig. 72)* The advantage of lounge chairs is that they take load off the spine like any other backrest, but, also, just as importantly, they take the load off the neck and head, otherwise forced into a swanlike configuration. People raise the objection that you can't work in a semi-reclined seat. However, many like to drive that way; so why not keyboard that way? Progressive offices in Finland, Silicon Valley in California, and elsewhere have set up workstations in lounge chairs with the height and angle of computer monitors adjusted accordingly. (I currently use such an arrangement without a problem.)

Recently, an engineer inspired by NASA data about neutral body posture designed a chair that puts all muscular forces into "biomechanical equilibrium" with the knees level with the chest—a recliner by any other name.[38] (The doctor who invented the BarcaLounger used a similar rationale about the position of a body when "floating on water" for the design of his recliner in the thirties.)[39] The science and technology writer Edward Tenner, who has helped us imagine recumbent automobiles, truck cabs, aircraft controls, computer monitors, and keyboards, believes recliners may come into use despite what he recognizes as a "cultural prejudice against reclining."[40] This prejudice may be the heart of the problem; as the authors of *The Encyclopedia of Bad Taste* observe, "etiquette demands that polite people sit upright while in the company of others. Lying flat on one's back in the living room, or even tilted forty-five degrees with one's feet raised in the direction of everyone else present, is good form only for invalids or babies."[41] Such social disapproval is exactly what needs to change.

Perhaps the most important recliner, from a Modernist point of view, is the Corbusier and Charlotte Perriand chaise-longue of 1928, discussed in Chapter 4. It still is recommended by back surgeons as good for people suffering from back problems. From a somatic point of view, there are

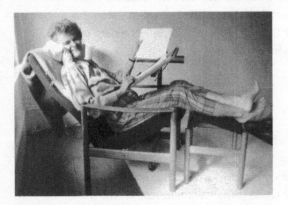

Figure 72. If you rotate the perch position, it becomes a lounge chair. This Danish modern recliner got me through graduate school.

good reasons for this recommendation. The chaise is planar, and it supports the entire back all the way up—including the shoulders, neck, and head—instead of the ribcage only. However, the cylindrical neck roll is too thick for many people, requiring adjustment by taking out some of the stuffing (*see Fig. 49*). In 1947, two designers, *Ba*rtolucci and *Wa*ldheim, put out another lounge chair, the Barwa chair, which took its inspiration from a recliner from 1893—in those days called an invalid chair.[42] Today, many mass-market designers are trying to get a share of the La-Z-Boy market, previously mocked as lowbrow. The Japanese designer Toshiyuki Kita, who studied in Italy, designed an animated chair called "WINK" for Cassina that unfolds to become a lounge. Selected for the permanent collection of New York's Museum of Modern Art in 1981, it shows enormous charm (with its rounded shapes, bright color palette, natural fabrics, Mickey Mouse–like ears), but it is too concave to outshine the Corbusier and Perriand lounge. A radically different Scandinavian version of the recliner flips you over onto your stomach. This allows you to lie prone on your chest, with your head supported and your face peeking through an opening for reading material on the floor. Physiologically, it is undoubtedly more stressful than lying on one's back; but for variety and for reading it could be useful.

Recliners come in all kinds of materials—leather, canvas, and so on—but they all involve some sort of mechanism that makes them adjustable, one of their several virtues from a body-conscious point of view. Most often today lounges rely on adjustable joints, but the Corbusier and Perriand has no hinge. Instead, a convex body fits into a concave support, moving on an arc, so that the head height is adjustable. Peter Opsvik's Gravity chair involves movement not so much through a mechanism as through careful engineering that allows you to move the chair into a different position by shifting your body weight. Moreover, the Gravity provides a space for the shoulder girdle to rotate independently of the head and spine (*see Fig. 69*).

ROCKERS

A 1997 advertisement for retirement planning assures active sixty-five-year-olds that they are not ready for the rocking chair. It is a pity that rockers are associated with inactivity, because they provide one of the more active ways to sit. Their chief virtue, from a somatic point of view, is that they move the ankle, knees, and hip sockets directly, and the head-neck joint and the entire spine only slightly less directly. In addition, rockers usually offer appropriate support to the shoulder, neck, and head because they often have high backs.[43] Seat height does not go up and down so much as it pivots around an invisible axis, part of how rockers allow for internal adjustments kinesthetically. How gratifying to find that rocking chairs exemplify a kind of comfort that accommodates the body, yet is not so enervating as to induce slumping and drowsing. Everyone should have one. The historian David Hanks says rocking chairs were the most comfortable chair of their time when they were introduced around 1774.[44] They still are, so don't overlook rockers just because you might think they are old-fashioned. They can be styled in contemporary ways, even winning design awards: in 1984, Knoll International's rocker, designed by Carlos Riart of Barcelona, received the Roscoe Award for "outstanding creative achievement and for significant contribution to the total environment."[45]

Perhaps movement has its limits. I would avoid wasting money on mechanical massage chairs, for fear that they would jiggle and massage me into the contours of a chair that is, in all likelihood, not body-conscious in its design.[46] Besides, vibration is tiring, and in other contexts considered an occupational hazard.

Chair reform has its limits. No chair is perfect, partly because no posture is perfect. As Peter Opsvik quips, "The best posture is always the next one." Designing for movement takes us beyond a single object into the realm of interior design and planning. Rooms—complete ensembles of objects, furniture, and the floors and walls of rooms themselves—are just as much, if not more, in need of body-conscious design as are single objects.

Chapter 6

Beyond Interior Design

Probably the single most important principle of body-conscious design is to use design to keep posture varied and the body moving. We need to consider not just different ways to sit, but also ways to incorporate a variety of postures—including lying and standing—into our lives. This means that one of the most important aspects of a designer's role is to help change social perception. People will generally use what is made available to them. Designers can help legitimize people's need to change positions simply by providing furniture for a variety of postures. If we provide places for people to lie down, stand up, squat, or crawl, then we acknowledge those postures as a part of normal living.

THE HOME: CHANGING POSTURE MEANS CHANGING LIFESTYLE

Changing cultural attitudes and environments in public institutions may take a lot of advocacy and a long time. In contrast, changing your own home environment may be easier and faster. Actually, changing one's home can be almost as challenging because we see ourselves as others—those proverbial Joneses—see us. But, technically, you only have to convince yourself and those who live with you to try to live differently. (And success here might later give you the confidence to take these postural attitudes with you into more public places.) Here are a few suggestions:

Practice autonomous sitting and perching. One of the things we as individuals can do to improve our posture is to practice sitting without chairbacks—what Rudofsky called "autonomous seating." One of the easiest ways to wean oneself from chairs is to start using stools more often. Once I realized that leaning back in a chair was weakening my torso, I started using stools a lot more in my own home. They are at conventional chair height, which means they fit with existing tables and desks. (Unfortunately, if your experience is like mine, you may discover that continuing to use the traditional table height tempts you to round your back as much as chairs do; but at least on a stool you may also be strengthening your back and stomach muscles.)

I view stools as a kind of halfway house, a sort of stopping-off place before the great decline of chair sitting proper, or, alternatively, the first step away from chair dependence. Stool sitting is an intermediate posture, because it has some but not all of the detriments associated with chair sitting. On the positive side, the sitter practices autonomous sitting, which rebuilds musculature, and by virtue of not being able to lean back, does not easily slide into the C-shaped slump.

However, stools can be tiring because they strain the lower back. So, what next? A taller stool makes perching come naturally. What I call a three-quarter-height stool, technically 24–26 inches high, approximates the perching position. But even conventional-height stools of 17–18 inches offer the possibility of autonomous seating, so they should not be disregarded. The balance chair would be an even more useful addition to your life, not only because it is backless but also because it opens up the angle between the thighs and the back significantly more than 90 degrees. This may make you more—dare I say it?—comfortable because the posture distributes muscle work evenly between front and back and top and bottom muscles.

If you start evaluating your environment in terms of building bodily strength, these new chairs begin to look good. But can you imagine an American advertisement for a chair that says it would be "good training for the back and stomach muscles," as one Scandinavian company advertises routinely? Another European magazine ad touts the benefits of a chair that needs "a little practice." This ad campaign is surprising to us because we conceptualize chairs as a place to relax. Presumably, we too could think of chairs as athletic training devices, not just support. But American retailers have a long way to go before they succeed in so positioning the balance chair in the American marketplace.

To practice autonomous sitting at my dining-room table, I use a combination of pieces: 17- and 18-inch stools along the sides, two straight-backed conventional chairs at one end, and a balance chair for me at the other end. The look is a little "mix and match," but even stylistically this could be justified by invoking the idea that each chair around a dining-room table should be different to give people choices that express their different personalities.[1] Or it could be justified artistically as postmodern, since matching is currently outmoded in clothing.

I first experienced the advantages of perching at the island in my kitchen, which accommodates two 24-inch-high stools at a 36-inch-high work surface. For years I found myself preferring to eat there and not knowing why, until I learned about the biomechanical advantages of perching and of appropriately raised work surfaces (just below the elbows). Sitting at high stools at kitchen bars, islands, and counters is already an established convention that doesn't look new or unusual, so I recommend that others take full advantage of it.

Use a variety of postures, including lying down, standing, squatting, and crawling. A 1984 study of lower back pain is telling. The most common aggravating factor was stooping, which increased the pain of 65 percent of the subjects. Next was sitting, which increased the pain of 30 percent of the subjects. But let's focus on what gave the subjects relief from lower back problems: lying down (52–54%), and walking around (34–39%).[2]

Let's discuss lying down first. Theoretically, one could lie down anywhere from the floor all the way up to the ceiling if there were shelflike supports available. But because of the dominance of the chair, very few such places have been designed. Instead, at home most people use the couch in the living room as a de facto bed. Unfortunately, "couch potato" accurately captures what happens to our bodies' internal structure when we sink into its soft upholstery: we collapse inwardly into a relatively undifferentiated lump. Instead, we might be better served by creating special places for lying down.

But what about relaxing? People do get tired, so how can they rest when sitting on a stool, bench, or platform? Rather than letting the spine sag in a slump when tired, decide to rest it by lying down in the *constructive rest position. (Fig. 73)*

Here's how: lie down on a firm surface so that the spine can extend itself and the rib cage can open out against this resistant plane. The surface should be firm enough to keep the body from sinking down, which means firmer than most beds. Avoid any surface that curves. At the same time, bring the knees up. This helps the lower back release, thereby easing lower back strain. Bend the elbows and bring both hands over the midriff in order to let the shoulders slide back and the joints open at shoulder, elbow, and wrists. (Somatic disciplines differ over the position of the head in constructive rest position. Alexander teachers prefer a book thick enough to take the head slightly forward to the spine, while others advocate a pillow or roll under the neck to promote the cervical [neck] curve, and yet others advocate nothing at all.) The rest position is useful for fifteen minutes once a day; more if fatigue tempts you to slump.

One design implication of the idea of the rest position is that we need to lie down more, but this does not mean that we have to go to bed all the time. In fact, for rest position to be effective, it requires a firm surface, not a bed or couch. This means we need surfaces as firm as a carpeted floor to lie on, but the floor itself may be too drafty. Radiant heat in floors is one design implication for new construction or major remodeling, but in most cases a raised platform would be more immediately practical. Such platforms could be in a special place like a meditation room; but generally

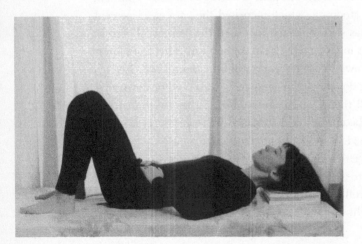

Figure 73. Constructive rest position.

speaking, removing oneself from the flow of social and work life in the home could be perceived as sickness, which is obviously undesirable. Instead, they could be incorporated into the living room, the dining room, the study, family room, or TV room—any place where it is easy to take a break that does not require removing oneself from the normal flow of activity.

We need surfaces that are comfortable enough to lie down on but look tailored enough to be appropriate in shared spaces. Here platforms and benches are particularly useful. First, they can be used for sitting in a variety of postures; moreover, they can be carpeted to give a tailored look. Visual continuity between the floor and the platform can be created by using the same color carpet for both; obviously, postmodern contrast is just as easily attained. Eileen Gray and Adolph Loos are two early twentieth-century high-style designers who used platforms and vertical planes to advantage in the design of domestic interiors. Eileen Gray is known for her austere planes, with sensuous surfaces: wall and screen, floor and bed executed in satin, leather, fur, labor-intensive Japanese-style lacquer. The Austrian Adolph Loos is also known for planes, usually connected by stairs, which create intersecting volumes within a room.[3]

A bench, basically, is just a narrow platform. *(Fig. 74a, b, and c)* It is so narrow that it does not look like a bed, but you can take a five- to fifteen-minute break on it and it will do wonders for your spine. The essence of the idea is that as you go through the work day, rather than slumping more and more as you get more and more tired, you can give your spine a few minutes of rest and reverse the desire to slump. The design of the bench is important. If it is narrow, it doesn't support arms and shoulders, so that lying down on it doesn't work for long. I have a related problem in my office. I have installed a bench wide enough to lie on for rest, about 20 inches across. When I want to perch on the edge of the bench for conferences with visitors, it is just fine; but if I want to indulge myself by sitting on the bench and leaning back at the same time, 20 inches is too deep for my upper legs, so I am forced to use a block of foam as a chairback. This need for a bolster introduces an extra, slightly annoying step in the process of taking a seat.

Lying down on the floor is not always comfortable, of course, especially if there are drafts or it is dirty. But in some contexts it can be very useful. If you have small children, it helps you directly to experience the environment they are experiencing, so that you can make any necessary ad-

Figure 74. Benches are useful indoors and out—(a) Oakland urban plaza; (b) Venice railroad station; (c) Swedish farmhouse.

justments either in temperature or in sharp objects. Children should be on the floor, from a developmental point of view. The psychologist Arnold Gesell described the floor as "the athletic field of the well child."[4] Crawling occasionally is even good for adults, and is part of the general ideal that bodies are designed for movement and that, therefore, we should move them in as many different ways as possible in order to activate our full neurological and muscular potential. *(Fig. 75)* I notice that when adults regress, as they do when they become lovers, they are willing to lie around in public spaces, as socially astute photographers like Henri Cartier-Bresson have documented. In Japan, tatami mats offer springiness and texture for babies and adults alike to move on. If floors are so important environmentally, we need to increase our sensitivity to floor surfaces so that they are comfortable for the knees. We might want rugs or matting that would make working occasionally on or near the floor attractive. An architectural implication in northern climates is to heat them from below, as Frank Lloyd Wright did when he introduced radiant heating beneath the tile floors in his Usonian houses in the American Midwest.

Figure 75. A social advantage to crawling and squatting is relating to infants at their level.

Alan Watts, best known as the leader of the American Zen move-ment, radically rethought the relationship between culture, body, and do-mestic design. Simple pads on the floor were enough for him. As he ex-plains:

> I have very little furniture. I don't have any overstuffed arm-chairs or overstuffed couches. I don't have any bedsteads. I have pads. Bedsteads with headboards and glass balls on them and all that kind of thing strike me as utterly depressing sleep-ing machines. I don't even have a bedroom. I have always just curled up on the pad in the living room, or in my library, and I usually sleep under a Mexican blanket. All those bedrooms have struck me as a total waste of space. . . . I always look upon chairs as surgical appliances. They are sort of ungainly perches for people who are not related to the earth.[5]

As the building shell itself became more differentiated from the me-dieval to the modern period, so, too, furniture has become more differen-tiated and people more separated. One way to get back to earth is for peo-ple to get back in touch with one another. The therapeutic effects of touch are enormous.[6] If the house were designed as a sensory haven, a place of restoration and balance, one would expect people—whether family or friends—to be able to lie down in each other's presence and be touched in a therapeutic way. One implication is that surfaces for rest position should allow approach from all sides. This would allow another person to touch the head of the person resting, massage the feet, even pick up a shoulder or an arm or a leg on either side. These surfaces could be designed to swing out from a wall or be freestanding in the middle of a room as space and furniture conventions allow. *(Fig. 76)*

The floor itself is a possibility if it's warm enough, but until people get good at squatting, it's harder for them to reach one another on the floor than at table height. The floor is even more open-ended than a back-less stool as a setting for social life. A wider range of communication is possible due to the range of physical movements. Designs like the 1960s "conversation pit" that encouraged people to sit touching each other would also facilitate this kind of exchange. Images like these

Figure 76. This living room includes a multipurpose table for rest or massage.

challenge the strict segregation of functions so characteristic of modern times.

Perhaps because the floor is "the playground of the child," staying off it is considered a sign of maturity. Certainly by the time students reach college, they are well socialized to learn in the classic right-angled seated posture. Students in my lectures still resist using the carpeted floor in the Wurster Hall auditorium, even when given the option. And I have experienced my own resistance. When I moved into the world of body-centered education, I can recall how embarrassed I sometimes felt if I saw myself, a tenured professor, as others from my university life might see me, crawling or lying on the floor. But I also learned the importance of actually experiencing the physical and cultural implications of moving away from sitting in a chair. Peter Smithson, a well known British modernist architect, on a recent visit to Berkeley described one of those implications: designers should plan to light floors adequately for use as living and working surfaces.

Lying down should be easy in the privacy of your own bath. Why are American bathtubs usually designed so that lying down is impossible? Their size and shape forces one to stoop while bathing—no wonder so many people, especially tall ones, prefer to shower. If one tries to recline, the head and neck hit an awkward edge. Why not lie flat, fully extending the spine to float on the water? Even elaborate and expensive whirlpool tubs have not solved this problem. Little inflatable plastic pillows are as close as anyone has come to body consciousness in bathing.[7] The institution of bathing could easily be revolutionized in the United States.

Westerners are often shocked by the ability of those from other countries, especially non-industrialized or Third World countries, to squat. Those of us in the West lose this ability—along with good posture in general—at differential rates, depending on our parents' posture and movement, whether we are male or female, and a variety of other social and psychological circumstances. In American culture, men—except for baseball catchers—lose the ability to squat especially quickly. The good news is that this ability can be regained by practice. (To help with the stiff hips that make squatting difficult, one can practice with support wedges under the heels.)

Squatting is important because it saves the spine from collapsing into the questionmark form that is too common among us; it stretches the spine pleasurably, opens the hip joints, widens the lower back, and activates the ankles and feet.[8] It is a comfortable position for waiting, and even eating, in other cultures. It is also said to be the preferred anatomical position for birthing and elimination, and it is still used those ways in many non-industrialized cultures. One design implication, then, is to adopt the "Italian" or "Turkish" porcelain flush, squat toilets. As a compromise, some immigrants and visitors from abroad use flanged lids on Western chair-type toilets in order to squat on the seat!

All this postural variety involves designing for movement. Mandal's perch chairs facilitate shifting easily between leaning forward, backward, or standing. Another way to introduce movement is by setting up different furniture configurations and then orchestrating a path through them so that we can move from one relatively static pose to another and the entire process exercises different sets of muscles, moves various bodily fluids, stresses different bones, and exercises different internal organs and sheets of fascia. In homes, a simple version of this is at work already. People often serve pre-dinner drinks on the patio, then sit at the table for dinner. Then the hostess may suggest moving to the living room for dessert or coffee.

For tasks that require bending over, use the position of mechanical advantage. Obviously, we can accomplish only so much when sitting and perching or lying down. We also have to stand for many activities and we often have to bend over as part of the activity. What isn't so obvious is how to bend over properly. Most of us share a misconception about the anatomy of the spine that allows us to think that bending at the waist is appropriate, when in fact it is anatomically harmful.

The waist is not a hinge. When a person needs to bend over, he or she should instead flex the knees, ankles, and hip joints. The position of mechanical advantage keeps the entire spine as a single unit, which allows it to maintain its double concave and convex curves. This position is very similar to perching, with the difference that one is not seated, but rather standing and pivoted slightly forward to reach or look at something.[9] This is the neutral position to which the body reverts in outer space in zero gravity ("the horse" in the martial arts, nicknamed "the monkey" by Alexander students). To use this position, one has to have space for the knees to move forward. This means that one needs knee space under kitchen and bathroom sinks and other work surfaces. As an intermediate, remodeling measure, one can remove the doors that often cover the cupboards beneath sinks. *(Fig. 77)*

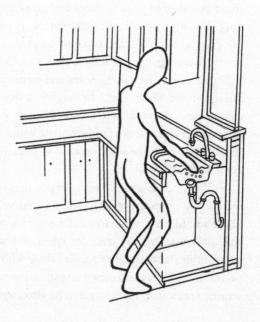

Use reading and writing stands. The eyes

Figure 77. Remove cupboard doors from under kitchen and bathroom sinks in order to use a position of mechanical advantage.

extend our perceptual abilities and indirectly affect the structure of the upper body as much as the feet affect the physical organization of the legs and pelvis. In the case of slanted work surfaces, ergonomic and somatic paradigms converge. Reading and writing stands are key components of the fight against physical stress. Copy stands bring material up to eye-level, not only for speed of reading, but also to avoid stressing the joint between head and top vertebra (called the "atlas" because it holds up the world). Ordinarily, reading on a flat surface requires that we tip our heads forward more than the top joint can sustain for long; more often, we pull the entire neck forward, which compresses the front of the rib cage and rounds the spine. Even worse would be using a laptop computer on your lap: your head has to lean too far down and your spine loses the S-shape, moving into the C-shape. The extra force of note taking, writing, or keyboarding while so bent forward is a recipe for disaster. An American massage therapist, Verla Ubert, who wrote a master's degree thesis on the mechanics of sitting on stools, recommends using a slanted desk to prevent upper back pain.[10]

Adequately angled work surfaces mean that the designer, manufacturer, retailer, and user have to think about the chair and the desk, table, or stand in relationship to one another.[11] The height of the work surface should be derived from the height of the seat surface. This means that you could buy slanted work surfaces with appropriate seating from the beginning. But for immediate improvement, if you cannot change your table height, you can put a desktop reading stand on top of a stack of books on the table and change the height that way. Don't forget the importance of a slanted surface for taking notes and writing. For reading for pleasure in a living-room chair, consider buying a freestanding reading stand. Of course, you can try to hold a book up with your hands, but this position is tiring, so you will tend to be resting your elbows on the chair arms, and thereby lowering the book enough to force your neck and upper spine to curve forward and down.

If we pursue a wide variety of postures in the home, we can move toward a more sensory, sensual, and restorative idea of domestic space. The home would become an arena of retreat. A special chamber designed for the kinds of activities I have described, a cross between a gymnasium and a meditation room, might appeal to those who want separation, but I would prefer to see the *entire* home reorganized around these concepts. They do require continued, regular use to be effective.

Redesigning our entire home setting as a place for creature comfort has several implications. The most important one, over and above the actual physical changes, is the challenge to the notion of the home as a place for status display.[12] Typically, people decorate their homes to show their educational level, taste, class, and where they have traveled. Instead, the home could become a retreat for recharging and rejuvenation. In the long run, those who have the new "creature comfort" home might accrue high status; but in the short run, it might mean abandoning old forms of status.

The aesthetic of the new ensemble created by this new use of surfaces, platforms, stools, benches, kneeling chairs, perches, and the like could take many forms. The look is stylistically open and unlimited, neither necessarily eccentric nor dull. These new forms and arrangements could draw on vernacular traditions, such as the Turkish raised platforms, the Indian divan, the Japanese floor-oriented tatami, the Chinese heated *k'ang* for sleeping and social life, or even the firm beds that serve as sleeping spaces and "seating" by day in contemporary Chinese mass housing.

Another aesthetic possibility is high-tech. Body-conscious design could harmonize with the high-tech emphasis on smooth surfaces and planes. Alternatively, a rich and lush treatment of the same platforms and planes could draw upon embroideries, vibrant colors, and numerous textures to create an atmosphere of sumptuous pleasure. These forms, just like Western furniture, can be used in an austere and intellectual way, a sensual or erotic way, or a comfortable and cozy way.

A final implication is that if people get used to this kind of sensual ease and pleasure in the home, they might begin to demand it in the workplace, in public transportation, in places of public assembly, in doctors' waiting rooms, airports, libraries, and the like. Unfortunately, today the influence is often the reverse. We get used to institutional stiffness and then accept it, if not aspire to it, in our homes.

THE SCHOOL

The most vocal advocate for children's physical welfare in relation to furniture is the Danish doctor A. C. Mandal, who has built a strong case for the anatomical vulnerability of children. However, Mandal does not think that conventional posture training is the solution to the problem of the poor fit between children and their furniture. He studied Danish schoolchildren who had received ninety brief lessons on correct posture over a period of five years. Photographs were taken of those pupils, age fourteen to sixteen, at twenty-four-minute intervals during a four-hour exam. Despite their posture training, their backs were bent over their desks during the entire exam.[13] I might interject that there is a world of difference between posture training and the Alexander Technique.[14] However, my Alexander training has made me more, not less, sensitive to stresses imposed by an inadequately designed environment. Because we cannot train our way out of these problems, the quality of the built environment deserves our conscious attention.

Dr. Colin James Alexander argues that chair sitting is responsible for varicose veins, and that the damage is done primarily in childhood, specifically by school furniture. If varicose veins are a preventable disease, then, according to Alexander, we are obliged to liberate children from the right-angle seat in schools. Dr. Mandal has gone so far as to state that children should be allowed to determine what is best for them. But before they start designing anything, adults have to decide to let them. Attitudinal change sometimes has to precede physical change. Anthony S. Jones, a new breed of learning environment consultant, despairs at adult resistance:

> Most educators are reluctant to ask students what they prefer. That reluctance is the reason any changes we have made have been merely tokenistic. The mistrust of student opinion is based primarily on the knowledge that suggestions from students will be bizarre in comparison with what the current classroom exhibits. That "bizarreness" in itself signifies the disparity between what is and what could be, and is even more reason to consider the students' suggestions.

Further, he says, "Adults feel that children are not practical, therefore, anything they have to say is 'cute' but relatively useless."[15]

One might wonder what such freedom for schoolchildren would look like, environmentally speaking. As a graduate student in architecture at the University of California at Berkeley, environmental design researcher Carolyn Frances concluded that schoolrooms should offer choice, control, and change (with constancy). For instance, virtually every activity engaged in in the primary classroom could be done either sitting or standing, and several could be done lying down. Therefore, classroom environments should allow that full range of possibilities. The sociologist Donna Huse reports that the educational restructuring movement of the eighties and nineties agrees. These reformers have challenged the model of assembly-line control in disciplinary mass schooling, seeking freedom of body movement, community through conversation and laughter in informal groups, and physical comfort, including eating, resting, and places to lie down.[16] Such variety need not necessarily look cluttered, because simple forms usually facilitate more choice than complex ones. According to Professor Roger Hart, co-director of a center on children's environments at the New York City University Program in Environmental Psychology, who has worked with children to design schoolrooms and schoolyards, children usually design multipurpose platforms as their preferred form of furniture.[17]

A former city planner for Philadelphia, the author of *The Design of Cities,* Edmund Bacon, has proposed that every classroom be an environmental laboratory, with movable walls and ceilings, and a variety of objects for sitting or reclining.[18] Each week a different student would be assigned to create a distinctive configuration for the class meeting. Someone would observe the social interactions, in an attempt to judge the effect of spatial and postural configuration on the learning process. Bacon gave the keynote address to celebrate the appointment of the new dean of architecture at the University of Michigan in 1987, where he made the same proposal again: that environmental design education, in particular, treat the classroom as a laboratory.[19] These proposals still await enactment.

In Wurster Hall, which houses the College of Environmental Design on the campus of the University of California at Berkeley, where I teach, we have an auditorium that was empty for over fifteen years awaiting funds to finish the interior. When it was finally finished, the university could not afford fixed, auditorium-style seating, so stacking metal chairs designed by David Rowland in 1964 were bought. They look elegant when stacked, but they are cold and uncomfortable to sit on, violating many ergonomic and somatic principles. *(Fig. 78a and b)* It almost doesn't matter that the chairs are not body-friendly, because the virtue of not having the fixed seating is that we are able to stack the chairs to the side and sit

Figure 78. David Rowland's stacking metal chairs violate several ergonomic rules. *(a)* The auditorium at Berkelely's College of Environmental Design is equipped with these chairs, while *(b)* the auditorium at Harvard's Graduate School of Design uses carpeted planes for seating.

on the carpeted floor. However, this rarely happens until I have given an hour's lecture on the subject. Only after such discussion will students feel comfortable in going against propriety.

For the last several years, I have studied the choices students make when given the option of sitting on chairs or on the carpeted floor. Here is what I learned: the class divided 50-50. Practical factors justified their decisions: chair sitters cited note taking, the desire to stay awake, or the need for back support. Those who chose the floor said they had more room and freedom. Neither my teaching assistants nor I observed any obvious sex difference, probably because female architecture students are just as likely to wear pants as the males.

The most interesting difference was a personality issue, having to do with the *symbolism* of students' choice between chair and floor. There was a radical-conservative split. The conservatives thought sitting on the floor was unseemly and the radicals thought it was cool to do so. The choice doesn't seem to have anything to do with "comfort" or body health. Rather, it shows where they stand socially—status once again. One person wrote, "I am a conservative and I don't like doing what the cool people are doing." The switchers—those who moved back and forth on different days— tended to be females. Are women more open-minded and flexible, or uncertain and fickle? Some of the floor sitters did lie down to listen to lectures and explicitly appreciated having the option to do so. This experiment led me to conclude that more auditoriums should provide the *option* of sitting or reclining without the benefit of chairs.

However, the cultural pressure is so strong that in some years the professors who use the auditorium after my class have complained to the dean's office about the chairs not being in place. I have contacted them to explain and suggest that some of their students might like the option of sitting on the floor. I found resistance, particularly from one professor who felt that students couldn't master serious material while sitting or lying on the floor. Even though I told her about research on study habits showing no difference between those who studied on their beds and those who sat at desks, she would not be dissuaded. Social constructs are many times just too hard to break.

PUBLIC PLACES

If standards for deportment remain conservative in schools, perhaps a new attitude to chairs and body-conscious design might find receptivity in other public environments. *(Fig. 79a and b)* A new twist on seating appeared in Berkeley in the late summer of 1997, when organizers of an outdoor film festival held in a parking lot asked patrons to "B.Y.O. Seating and Sofas," promising prizes for the most original. A student in one of my seminars has experimented with designing theaters where people could semi-recline while watching the screen, which would be placed at a diagonal between wall and ceiling. Another student explored the possibility of changing church seating, looking to Buddhism and Islam for models that use

Figure 79. Artist Lloyd
Hamrol designed viewing
platforms at the ocean
edge in Santa Barbara to
protect the cliff from
erosion. One allows
picknicking, while the
other allows semi-reclined
sunset viewing.

floor seating. Yet a third explored semi-reclined positions for reading rooms, with the reading material projected onto a screen somewhat like the movie theater's. I have often thought that waiting rooms in doctors' offices could be designed to accommodate the rest position. Since people are there for health-related reasons, they might as well wait in a posture that promotes well-being.

Certainly when giving birth, being able to assume comfortable postures is vital. Bianca Lepori, a psychologically oriented architect in practice in Rome, has described a new kind of birth environment for hospitals. Based on what she learned from home births about the range of body postures to be supported, she has designed rooms with an empty center for the spiral path women follow, a pool of water, bars for hanging, and—once again—a platform, low and broad, where mothers "can sit, kneel, rest, lie down, stand again, or kneel on the floor with their elbows over it."[20]

Public transit is certainly in need of reform. Buses and airplanes provide disastrous options. Ironically, while seats for the elderly and handicapped in public buses are up front near the driver, they are also the highest seats, raised to house the bus wheels, and so are the least comfortable for short people, who sit there with their feet dangling. The seats themselves are overly concave, leading to the C-shaped slump. For the present, many regular airplane travelers fill in that concave space with pillows in order to get through a long flight.[21] But transit designers need to rethink the whole process of waiting in lounges, as well as the actual travel seat itself. For instance, some Japanese airports are said to offer sleeping berths, along with small hotel rooms for business travelers, rented by the hour. A few such accommodations are available in Canadian airports as well. Why not redesign the airplane cabin itself for lying down in transit? We Americans could at least start with the waiting areas in the airports. *(Fig. 80)*

And how about restaurant reviews based on not only food and ambiance but also on chair quality? I maintain a (short) list of restaurants with body-friendly seating in San Francisco and in other cities that I visit frequently. One restaurant reviewer has evaluated restaurants from the point

Figure 80. Airport design might accommodate people who want to lengthen the spine before compressing it in those merciless airplane seats.

of view of physical comfort—a woman after my own heart. She revealed that restaurateurs sometimes purchase "fifteen-minute" chairs, deliberately uncomfortable to encourage people to make their space available to the next customer. The experts she interviewed added that without intending to do so, even luxury restaurants may end up with such chairs because they were chosen by the interior designer solely for their aesthetic appeal.[22]

We also need to retrofit libraries, where slanted reading surfaces (with lips to keep books from falling off) could be manufactured to meet the aesthetic standards of whatever style is already in place. Historically, libraries gave up slanted reading tables when law books became so big and heavy that they kept sliding off the angled surfaces. Flat tops became a necessity, and rather than have two types of tables, the one type prevailed. A return to angled tops is long overdue. For children, the work surface should be brought up to within 12 inches of their eyes, the focal length up to age ten or twelve, so that they can see without having to slump over. On the job, employers should provide seated workers with adequately angled work surfaces.

THE OFFICE

How can office environments be adapted to somatic principles? We need to begin with the question of sitting at length. William Stumpf, a major office chair designer, says that "You shouldn't sit in even the best-designed chair for more than thirty or forty minutes at a stretch."[23] Designers who assume that people are going to sit still in a chair all day permit the chair to become a harness rather than a platform. Remember that chairs only became common in offices after 1900. In the previous century, office workers sat on high stools or stood, which made postural adjustment comparatively easy.

A 1991 brochure from a major manufacturer, Steelcase, entitled *The Healthy Office,* acknowledges the desirability of adjusting all equipment to the worker using it: seating "should have height, swivel and tilt adjustments, with optional arms" in proportion to the amount of time they spend at one task. The less variation you have in your job itself, the more adjustability you should have in your seating and other equipment. Another

Steelcase brochure in the same series, *Healthy and Effective Offices: Some Ergonomic Tips,* recommends varying tasks, paying special attention to movement, and taking periodic breaks from the computer.

Why do we assume that our human need to move disappears in adulthood? Remember that walking around came right after lying down as a way to get relief from back pain. Moreover, logic, movement, and memory are located in the same part of the brain.[24] That is probably why, when medieval monks had to memorize texts, they would walk through a space while doing so. Many people report anecdotally that pacing helps them organize thought logically—as well as remember it. For these reasons, walking should be integrated into office life. From a design point of view, this means that circulation systems could be designed not just to get from the lobby entry to your work station, but also to form a circuit for taking a walk when you want to think through a problem. Landscape architects, take note: when designing a rooftop garden, balcony, or courtyard for employee use, plan it with the idea of walking circuits in mind. That space should not simply be a center area for gathering, with plantings around the perimeter. It should provide a path.

If you are going to design expecting people to move at regular intervals, what further implications does this have for the office? One option is workstations that offer everyone a place to lie down, stand up, squat, kneel, and sit cross-legged. Haworth, number two in the office furniture industry, has responded only partially to the need for "continuous movement," by introducing a new chair, not a complete workstation.[25] Their competitors criticize this chair for "active sitting," a cross between a saddle chair on a stool and a pogo stick, by asking how it will fit in with the rest of the office furniture. Good question, but not a useful criticism because we don't want to stop introducing new types of chairs, but rather to begin to rethink the entire office complex. Here is one idea: You may want to think of your work environment as a par course. You probably have a par course on your local college campus or park, where you run from point A to point B and stop there to exercise a different part of your body. Why not apply the same concept to offices or schools? The office "par" course would include different ways to work: workstations at which one stands, perches, sits without back support, sits conventionally with back support, reclines with full back and head support, and even lies down in the fully horizontal position. This proposal has little to do with the ill-fated "office landscaping" movement from Germany of the 1960s and 1970s, which arranged furniture according to work flow and communication patterns, without adequate separation for privacy.

A few ergonomic researchers have recognized that not only work-station design, but also job design and health education would be required to make sure that everybody gets to change positions regularly.[26] I would go further than they have in advocating alternating between sitting and standing, although that is a good start. Their larger point is well taken that those in charge of describing jobs need to plan with postural variety in mind, and employees need education to understand the physical and mental importance of posture.

Walking is closely related to standing. A designer once told me about creating exclusively stand-up desks and work surfaces in an office for an attorney suffering from bursitis in the hip sockets. He and his client considered that they were designing around a disability. But I'd like to suggest that we design for standing workstations simply because, as Po Bronson's hero argued, they are rational. When Frank Gilbreth turned his expertise to chairs in 1914, he recommended extending chair legs to make them tall enough to enable workers to move easily between sitting and standing. These modified chairs proved "so comfortable that the worker who has . . . one" refuses to give it up.[27] It has been a commonplace for a long time that brass rails, as in bars, are good because by propping one foot on them while standing, alternate sides of the back are rested. When I recently visited Professor Barbara Tietze in her country home in Germany, I saw that she has such railings built into her kitchen for use when standing to stir or chop. Peter Opsvik has designed for sequences of movement even during office meetings. He has created a cluster of supports on pedestals, reminiscent of a ring of mushrooms. In order to accommodate various forms of standing, each support is at a different height, and all have different kinds of resting pads. As an environment it allows you to stand and lean to the right, to the left—and backward; to lean forward on your elbows on one of the front pedestals; or to perch at a three-quarter height. A cluster of these rings would form a "conferring" environment in which people could pace backward and forward, shift weight back and forth, perch, kneel, and stand, all the while maintaining eye contact when speaking and listening. His approach is radical, yet rational, because he combines two needs: the anatomical need for postural variety and movement and the social need of people doing business to have eye contact at meetings (see Fig. 70a).

Industry can readily produce the necessary new equipment if our culture decides to take adjustability seriously. Consider, for example, an advertising brochure from McDowell-Craig, a California company that produces personal computer workstations. Their workstation is adjustable to any height or tilt, and the keyboard can be angled as well, as demonstrated by photos of a woman both sitting and standing at the same computer and another of a model working from a wheelchair.

If chair heights adjust to the average five foot three woman, so that her heels can rest on the ground, she may have to contend with a desk or other work surface that is too high for her, unless she uses something like the adjustable workstation just mentioned. Some employers are amenable to outlays for updating computer technology and even chairs, but adjustable desks might be seen as too expensive. Actually, in setting up an office from scratch, adjustable work surfaces cost almost the same as regular ones. While money is a real issue, could control issues be just as basic? After all, a money-saving guerrilla ergonomics approach would propose using concrete blocks to change table and desk heights; but I wonder how many office managers would resist this tactic as incompatible with office image. A consistent look communicates organizational control.

Few think the unthinkable and challenge the chair-desk complex radically—even if they go so far as to admit that working while reclining may be appropriate to some personal styles. One *Progressive Architecture* article touted the benefits of reclining while working in adjustable chairs and predicted that new models might "begin to recline a bit more or come up with coordinated foot pillows."[28] They did not quite have the nerve to say lounge chair, let alone an E-Z-Boy! Not to worry: industrial designer Niels Diffrient has already responded to the fact that many executives like to tip their chairs all the way back onto the two rear legs while talking on the phone or conducting other office business. He designed a lounge chair named the *Jefferson* because the early president liked to work while lying on a chaise lounge, as did Mark Twain and Winston Churchill. *(Fig. 81)* "Diffrient's chair prompts visionary speculations about the office of

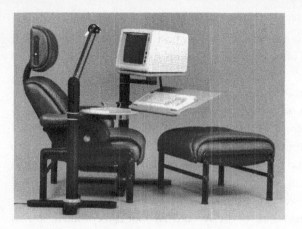

Figure 81. Niels Diffrient's Jefferson lounge chair.

the future," says one reviewer. "How about a congenial grouping of Jefferson lounge chairs, their occupants all watching the displays presented on their individual monitors?"[29]

If the office worker really were to be liberated from the tyranny of the chair, fundamental and tumultuous job redesign on a large scale would be necessary.[30] *(Fig. 82)* When we begin adjusting the height of tabletops, we are asking to change Western culture itself. Consider one example: Luigi Colani, an Italian designer, has argued for a body-conscious secretary's seat. In that seat, the secretary (shown as a woman, of course) reclines into a set of Mickey Mouse–like earphones from which she takes dictation, and she types in that nearly horizontal position, which means that she "may no longer be able to get up as casually as she used to." She would literally be lying down on the job! But I note that the prototype remains in the designer's office, and the Museum of Modern Art in Houston has only photographs of it on display. Is it coincidence that the Jefferson chair—for the executive—has been produced, whereas Colani's secretary seat has not? Would lounging secretaries be a threat to hierarchy or propriety?

As individuals, we first have to become aware that such changes would be helpful, and then we have to believe that we have the right to make these changes without feeling foolish, disrespectful of others, or just plain wrong. The underlying social-psychological changes are more important than any particular physical change. First and foremost, we must acknowledge and respect other people's needs for personal control.[31]

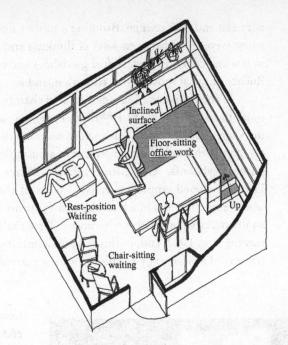

Figure 82. This proposal for a small architectural office accommodates both floor and chair sitters.

Inclined surface

Floor-sitting office work

Rest-position Waiting

Chair-sitting waiting

Up

POSSIBILITIES FOR CULTURAL CHANGE

In considering how to reduce our dependence on chairs in rooms and even outdoor spaces, larger questions about cultural, social, and psychological change emerge: how does it happen, when, how difficult is it, what opportunities lie ahead?

Can we really change the practice of sitting in chairs? It is embedded so deeply in our culture that it seems natural, meaning virtually biological, and therefore not susceptible to change. But rather than being natural, chair sitting exemplifies what the anthropologist Edward Hall calls "formal" knowledge that we learn at our mother's knee primarily through observation of behavior without even knowing that we know it. This is in fact unconscious knowledge, which is harder to change than either the rational/technical knowledge we learn in schools or the informal knowledge that people tell us in the process of living.[32] The difficulty of changing an unconscious practice like chair sitting includes resistance to the subject by dismissing it as absurd or trivial.[33] Nevertheless, even formal knowledge can and does change. Bringing a subject into conscious awareness is a first step; after that, new ways of thinking and acting can be instituted in law and codes, in professional guidelines and standards, and by the influence of social movements, education, and art. *(Fig. 83)*

In theory, mandating a new kind of chair by fiat could be the fastest route to social change. In 1990, San Francisco passed a new law regulating visual display terminal use, which was intended to protect office workers' bodies through the requirement of adjustable chairs, desks, and computer keyboards, and fifteen-minute breaks. However, some San Francisco–based employers resisted parts of that ordinance because it would cost them too much to buy new furniture and make San Francisco an unattractive business environment. They challenged it in court, overturning it in 1992, and, in this case, undermining law as a speedy path to reform.[34] Laws are only as effective as the cultural consensus that underlies them.

Other avenues to reform include bureaucratic codes and agency policies, such as those of the Occupational Safety and Health Administration (OSHA) and state agencies on rest breaks for typists and keyboarders to combat carpal tunnel syndrome and other repetitive stress syndromes. Since designers rely on published guidelines and standards, a way to influence them is through argument

Figure 83. Artist Don Jacot converted a chair into a fantasy of cultural transformation: chair showrooms go out of business, while shops offering alternative seating prosper. "Chair Today, Gone Tomorrow" (1995).

and research that shows the genuine need for new design codes. Entrepreneurs can also stimulate social change by setting up businesses that promote body-conscious products, such as neck pillows, balance chairs, and Recaro car seats. Advertising contributes to social change by promoting such new products.

Social movements are leaderless groups in some insurgent relation to established institutions, and by this definition I am not sure that the cause of freeing oneself from the tyranny of chair sitting will ever become a real social movement. Yet "holistic" or "natural," "alternative" or "complementary" health practices do fulfill this definition, and the issue of finding alternatives to chairs could easily be included in those movements. Alexander teachers and other somatic practitioners are part of this general social movement, which does have the potential to resist and criticize the environments that harm our bodies.[35]

Cultural categories are important to those who want to promote social change because such categories influence inventions and their diffusion. To give just one example, the steam engine was invented by the ancient Greeks, but conceptually viewed as a toy and therefore never applied to work in their civilization.[36] In modern life, too, if an invention falls into an undesirable category, we might reject it, as Siegfried Giedion explained for mechanical (adjustable) chairs.

Taken literally, consciousness raising is no different from scholarship that brings unconscious practices to our conscious attention; but as a social practice, consciousness raising is a politically motivated use of ideas, specifically aimed to stimulate social change.[37] Feminist consciousness raising comes to mind. Certainly, the kinds of changes I envision in schools and the workplace cannot be achieved by individuals alone, so groups of like-minded individuals will need to get together to institute more body-oriented seating in public places.

But broad acceptance will require at least two things: an educational approach, and a change in the physical objects around us. Usually an either-or trade-off between bodily training and physical invention has been acceptable in the West.[38] However, we need both. We need better objects *and* we need to take responsibility for how we use ourselves while using them.[39] Both designers and consumers need to be educated about how chairs affect our bodies.

Yet our cultural training so far is fairly inept and inadequate. What does it mean, for instance, to "stand up straight" or "sit up straight," as we were told to do as children? Someone might have suggested that you imagine yourself suspended from a string attached to the center of your head. (Poor advice because this flattens the face rather than letting it lead.) I was told to command my shoulders to go "up, back, and relax." Girls in the 1950s were offered the information that fashion models and the women of their grandmothers' generation improved their posture by balancing a book on top of their heads. If you were a male in teenage athletics, you were probably told to stand up with your shoulders back and your stomach tucked in. Most of that advice was on the indifferent to bad side.

Another way to change our cultural seating practices is to make sure that the best ergonomic criteria get institutionalized in manufacturing practice. How likely is that to happen? The manufacturers in Germany have adopted the strictest ergonomic standards for chair design, but their codes threw the Italian chair design and manufacturing industry into a tizzy. Italian design is famous for looks and formal invention rather than physical comfort. Americans have never agreed on a codified list like the German one, although we have experimented with standards from the point of view of occupational health and safety. The standards could come from the manufacturers themselves rather than from government agencies, and manufacturers would probably prefer that. But the question remains: to whom are they going to listen in order to determine what is reasonable? I would hope both business and government include among their consultants experts in the somatic disciplines, not just ergonomic science. The fusion of the two perspectives is important because, as you remember, some ergonomic criteria contradict one another, and the integrated body-mind perspective provides intelligent criteria for setting priorities.

Highly specialized systems of posture and movement like the Alexander Technique, Feldenkrais, tai chi, and yoga take a lifetime to perfect. Happily, more immediately applicable lifestyle improvements are available. Information sheets put out by doctors, chiropractors, and occupational therapists tell people how to sit, stand, shovel snow, and lift heavy packages without harm; for example, they will say to make sure your heels touch the ground when sitting and not to lift heavy objects above your head. Even airlines such as British Airways, Lufthansa, and Northwest offer in-seat aerobics instruction for their cramped and cranky fliers trying to overcome the muscle stiffness of long flights. Such pragmatic advice pops up in a wide array of publications. In *Smithsonian magazine,* for instance, the seating engineer Mary Plumb Blade offers the following good advice: "When I have to drive a long way, I put a board on the seat so I don't sink into the upholstery."[40]

Not that such advice is common throughout American society. It is much more widespread in Sweden, where student newspapers provide photographic examples and verbal descriptions of how to keep yourself fit even though you are studying almost constantly.[41] I have never seen a campus newspaper in the United States give advice about how to study from a physical point of view. In Sweden, such advice continues into work life. Swedish occupational therapists offer advice, illustrations, and demonstrations to different types of workers: bricklayers are taught not to lift bricks with one hand, crane operators are taught how to lean back to maneuver overhead loads, construction workers are taught to lift by bending at the knees. On one visit to Sweden, I saw possibly the best use of a regular right-angle chair: a photograph of a construction worker on a rest break showed him lying on the floor with his legs up at right angles, the calves resting on a chair seat. *(Fig. 84)*

A body-conscious attitude offers new criteria by which to evaluate the environment. In interior architecture and planning, a research specialty called "post-occupancy evaluation" tries to determine to what extent the environment has served people the way it was intended. The ultimate purpose of such research is to improve a specific type of environment—a hospital, school, or housing project—the next time one like it is built. These evaluations will eventually improve the quality of what is known as architectural programming. Programming means that the architect or a staff member works with the client and so-

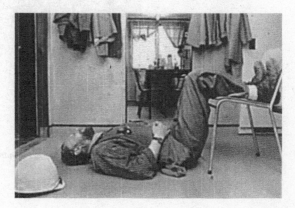

Figure 84. In Sweden, occupational therapists encourage workers to rest their backs like this.

cial scientists, bankers, planners, and so on to conceive and execute an environment that will meet the needs of all the building's users. The human body's needs are implicitly included in the standards issued for thermal comfort and air quality, and those who love materials might already be thinking about how textures of doorknobs, railings, and switches feel to the touch. But I would also like to see the need for movement explicitly incorporated into criteria for a healthy environment. Surprisingly, discussion of planning and design both inside and outside buildings seldom mentions movement except when describing processions and pedestrian flow, and even then it is done in rather abstract, bird's-eye terms. Design evaluation would be improved if critics routinely asked how postural variation is accommodated in every setting. *(Fig. 85)*

Are users locked into only one body posture in this environment, or are more options provided? Is there a place to do stand-up clerical work? Is there a place to lie down? Is it possible to sit cross-legged? Or to kneel or squat? Different types of buildings must accommodate different reper-

Figure 85. Here, body-conscious design not only affects furniture, but architecture as well. Le Corbusier's Master Bath Chaise in Villa Savoye (1928–30).

toires of postures. In a nursery for small children, an especially wide range of movements and postures should be accommodated. In the more formal areas of corporate offices, the current range of acceptable postures is generally too limited, and perhaps especially for women where dress codes are most constraining. Is it all right for both men and women to lie down? Previously, of course, women's restrooms have included (in a separate area) cots, platforms, or other spaces for them to use when suffering from menstrual symptoms. But generally, women cannot lie down anywhere in public—indoors or out—without arousing comment from passersby (except at a swimming pool). Would women lying down be viewed as offering a sexual invitation? Would they be viewed as lying down on the job? There are certain tasks such as talking on the phone that could be accomplished productively in an office while lying down. Why not?

Another way to improve chairs and liberate interiors is through the curricula of design departments in colleges and universities. The best criteria from ergonomics should be included in design school curricula, along with a broader view of the body. Although the body has become fashionable in all sorts of academic discourses, it is usually treated as a metaphor rather than as a physical entity, so I doubt that including that kind of body consciousness will affect design students' work effectively. Architecture schools rarely get down to the scale of the near environment or of interior design. Many schools think that is not their concern, and interior design schools think of the body as a set of measurements at best. Neither the interior design programs nor the architecture programs yet offer an integrated view of the person as a psycho-physical entity grounded in somatic disciplines. Instead, a lot of attention is directed to the emotional appeal of one environment versus another—the attitude or feeling that some decoration will evoke. At the other extreme, some design faculties may include behaviorists or ergonomically oriented designers who pay attention merely to people's physical dimensions and the dimensions of their reach, rather than their psychological experience of movement.

Students in my classes have found that thinking about designing from the body outward has proved rich in generating designs not only for interiors but also for the relation between rooms, the relation between public and private spaces, and the relationship between various urban design elements (bus stops, phone booths, hydrants, etc.) with consequences for cityscape. The reason they find this approach so rewarding is, I think, that it provides an authentic criterion for evaluating what is good and what is bad. It's authentic because it is grounded in their own experience and does not reduce the body to a machine. The concept of the self as an integrated psycho-physical entity honors both mind and body.[42]

Americans could learn from the rest of the world about how to accommodate the body's needs for a variety of postures. Gordon Hewes, the anthropologist who studied posture, agrees that the so-called First World has much to learn from the Third:

> At present nearly all our complex tools, instrument panels, control boards, benches, lathes, etc., have been planned for the use of people accustomed to the postural traditions of Western cultures. Human engineers might profitably consider a wider range of postures in planning for working or resting space requirements, not only because some of our traditional postures may be less efficient than those employed by Asians or Africans, but also because it might be easier to train our people to use a wider range of postures than to keep on trying to fit furniture designed for drawing rooms, throne rooms or banquet halls into crowded quarters. . . .

Hewes continues, "We ought to go much further and explore the possible usefulness to us of the various cross-legged, squatting, kneeling and other postures which so many millions of people outside the orbit of Western civilization have found convenient for their daily work."[43] By looking at the diversity of culture, we reinforce the idea that chair design is a cultural product and not a biological given, find inspiration for change, and offer physical models to give people options within an environment.

Sometimes blends of cultures will be appropriate, as in the example of a Berkeley architecture student, now a practicing architect in India, who incorporates traditional Indian divans into her contemporary interior design practice. She has designed platforms that are lower to the ground than Western chairs and can be used for a variety of postures—you can perch at the edge with one leg folded and the other dropped to the floor, or sit cross-legged without back support but with the option of using firm bolsters at the back to facilitate lounging. Historically, the Chinese experience with Western chairs offers an example of living with a range of options. Specialists in Chinese furniture disagree about whether the Western chair was first a seat of formality or informality, but in either case they agree that the Chinese remained at ease with both Western and Eastern sitting.[44] Even after the chair was introduced, their *k'ang* platforms often had small stands on them so people could shift their bodies, and for dining the Chinese retained the use of stools around low dining tables rather than chairs.[45] In other words, many alternatives existed in that culture. We could do well to follow their example.

As a byproduct, this proposal might serve to halt the adoption of Western chairs in Japanese homes and in other countries that are "modernizing." Rather than adopt chairs, a prized symbol of Westernization, they might look to these more advanced Western ideas from somatic practices as a warning. Already Japanese people who work in Western-style offices have grown so accustomed to sitting on chairs that the floor is becoming uncomfortable for younger generations.[46]

MY IDEAL WORKPLACE

After many years of researching and thinking about body-conscious design, I had a chance encounter at a conference with someone who runs creativity workshops for corporations and government bureaucracies. Our conversation turned to the office environment and its effect on creativity and invention. He is convinced that a person cannot be creative in a windowless, tiny box, and he asked me if I had any ideas about the ideal environmental aspects for creativity.

My vision is an aggregation of details from my own house in Oakland, my office in Berkeley, photographs I have seen of Professor Barbara Tietze's office in Berlin, and visits I have made to offices in New York City that follow ecological principles—the architect Randy Croxton's work for the National Resources Defense Council and his highly praised Audubon Society building retrofit and Bill McDonough's work for the Environmental Defense Fund. The ecological housekeeping and maintenance practiced on the grounds of the Tassajara Zen Mountain Center in the Los

Padres National Forest in California, and my mother's and grandmother's own households, also contributed to my understanding of environmental quality. It is promising that body-conscious design and ecologically sensitive design interlock so beautifully.[47] Both philosophies demonstrate respect for the organism—ours and Gaia's.

Here is what my ideal workplace, an office where others would work too, would look and feel like.[48] As you approach the door, you notice a lever, not a doorknob, which allows for less stress on the wrist since one is pushing down and not rotating. It's locked, though, so as you fiddle for your key, you are able to set your books and files on a package shelf located next to the door.

When you open the door, a Mozart violin concerto comes over the sound system. (The reason it is Mozart, and the reason it is a violin, is that Alfred Tomatis, a French ear doctor and brain researcher, has found that this is the most uplifting music for the human brain because it stimulates the neocortex, which is responsible for reasoning and higher-order problem solving.)[49] You know that in the most intimate work spaces you are going to be shoeless—the equivalent of a massage, good for the feet and the rest of your body—so you decide whether to leave your shoes here or keep them on until you reach the carpeted zone.

What you see before you is a spacious office, with natural light streaming in through the windows on three sides. You have walked on hardwood flooring outside and over the threshold; after you begin moving into various sectors of the room, the flooring changes to carpet. The carpet is natural, undyed wool that is tacked down, not glued down with toxic chemicals. The water-based paints used on the room—shades of white and pastels that reflect light—were applied to the walls within three weeks of manufacture, so the paint contains no formaldehyde or fungicides. Since there is no off-gassing from walls, carpet, or furniture, and because the windows are operable, a fresh smell pervades the place. Assuming this is California, a lot of the fresh scent comes from the vegetation outside. If this were New York or Chicago, it would come from the potted plants inside. (And of course since I work with architects, the potted plants would be deployed in a pattern that accents workstations or architectural rhythms within the structure of the space.)

In order to minimize the difference between the temperature indoors and out, the office temperature will be 68 degrees in the winter and 75 degrees in summer. Air conditioning contributes to ozone depletion (and I live in the temperate Bay Area), so there will be none. This approach will be good news for sufferers from arthritis, rheumatism, and plain old stiff backs. (After all, that is why people move to warm climates when they retire.) If I transplanted this office to a tropical climate, I would follow the example of the military, which simply cancels activity when the heat/humidity index exceeds a predetermined level. (In New York City, the Gaia Institute estimated five to ten such days per summer.) Alternative technologies are available for air conditioning without the use of ozone-depleting freon if I were to live in Florida or anywhere else where the temperature stays above 90 degrees for three months.

You have a lot of postural options for working in this office. You can stand to lay out research data, articles, or slides. You can stand or squat in front of files to use them. Floor-to-ceiling bookshelves allow you to stretch up or squat down. You can prop books open on an eye-level-slanted shelf before you decide to move it to your workstation. As you survey the room, you experience a sense of being invited to work here because so many different work spaces have been designed to accommodate different activities.

A feature of the office that strikes you immediately is a series of three-sided, U-shaped alcoves. Each is composed of three adjustable-height surfaces devoted to a single project. When you want to do some word processing, you can recline in a lounge chair with the keyboard on your lap and the screen mounted at an angle, like a hospital-room television set on an expandable arm. You could also choose to dictate to your computer standing or perched on a high stool.

When the phone rings, you have a choice of stretching out on a carpeted platform, which is 17 inches off the ground; sitting on its edge as if it were a conventional seat; or leaping to your feet if you get really excited. When standing, a chest-high surface within arm's reach allows you to take notes without bending your spine. While you like to have all these options, you find the most frequently used position that allows you to dictate into a tape recorder, talk on the phone, or take notes is a lounge chair. It is accompanied by a galaxy of tables in the air: a slanted reading surface, another for writing, and a disc to hold the phone, with another for a computer monitor. I see a cross between Niels Diffrient's high-tech version with its many "planets" to hold various accessories on the one hand, and Opsvik's and Corbusier and Perriand's leaner, more articulated lounges on the other.

All your associates in the office wear soft clothes in the natural fibers of silk, cotton, and wool, so they do not bind or restrict if the person wants to sit cross-legged on the padded platforms while discussing business. These yielding clothes also enable anyone who has a kink in the back to lengthen his or her spine by stretching out on the platforms for a few minutes. The platforms and various bolsters and wedge-shaped pillows, which can be used to create the equivalent of lounger chairs on a flat surface, are also covered with sensuous textiles—mohair, silk, sheepskin, linen, or down.

If you have to examine documents, you move to one of the U-shaped surfaces devoted to a single project. You gather around it on three-quarter-height perching stools. A light table is built into one end. This is as close as you are likely to get to a formal meeting with note taking and document perusing because there is no traditional boardroom table. If you were a newcomer, the thing in the office that might make you most curious is related to exercise: a large inflated ball over which staff members occasionally drape themselves to promote flexibility of the spine. Some sit on it in lieu of a stool. It also keeps children entertained when they visit. You might be equally intrigued by a cluster of three rings of Opsvik pedestals that support a variety of standing postures. An overhead bar for hanging and an inverter offer other opportunities to stretch your spine.

Without a conference table, you might wonder where people eat lunch. A countertop has been designed to allow people to eat while perched on bar stools. Typically, meals are eaten from bowls that can be lifted Chinese-style; I have observed that flat plates at conventional table height condition people to hunch over their food rather than bring the food to their mouth. Recycling is easy in this office: containers are labeled for colored paper, white paper, and in the kitchenette, for wet garbage to be taken away for composting. Instead of paper towels, each person has his or her own napkin ring for a cloth napkin; cloth dish towels are used in the kitchen. Of course, the restroom uses squat toilets.

You notice a set of French doors that lead onto a wooden deck or balcony, vine-covered. Down the steps is a pool or fountain. Sometimes people assume the rest position on the deck or exercise or eat or talk on the phone. Inside and outside are not that different—a Modernist's dream.

But this vision need not remain a dream. Running throughout this study of the chair has been a call to action. First, honor your body; learn how to attend to it, and educate it to communicate with our culture. From this, develop your own ideal environments. Identify what forces keep such visions of sensual rationality from becoming our cultural standard. And become your own advocate for body-conscious design.

N o t e s

INTRODUCTION

1. Theodore Roethke, "The Chair," *The Collected Poems of Theodore Roethke* (Garden City, NY: Doubleday, 1966), p. 178. Thanks to colleague Jill Stoner for bringing this poem to my attention.

2. Bill Morris, "Khakis: A Perennial Fashion Favorite," *News and Record* (Greensboro, NC), March 26, 1995, p. 8, and "Arts," *The Independent,* April 6, 1995, p. 26.

3. A sizable number of the paintings in the museums of America and Europe include at least part of a chair. Even though the depicted seating is usually fairly unobtrusive, it conveys information about the historical period, the type of situation, the social role of the people, and their individual characteristics. Some examples, ordered chrono-logically, of paintings from the 1400s to the 1900s include Masaccio's *The Virgin and Child* (on a throne), Raphael's *The Madonna and Child with St. John the Baptist and St. Nicholas of Bari* (on a throne), Leonardo da Vinci's *The Last Supper,* Rubens's *Hélène Four-ment and Her Children,* LeNain's *Peasant Interiors with an Old Flute Player,* Vermeer's *Woman Reading a Letter,* Steen's *Her Toilet,* Champaigne's *Ex-voto de 1662,* Hogarth's *The Marriage Contract,* Chardin's *Le Bénédicité,* David's *Portrait de Juliette Récamier* (after whom this lounge was named), Toulouse-Lautrec's *At the Moulin Rouge,* Degas's *Hélène Rouart in Her Father's Study,* Whistler's *Whistler's Mother,* Monet's *The Luncheon,* Van Gogh's *The Chair,* Dali's *Partial Hallucination: Six Pictures of Lenin,* and Bacon's *Seated Figure.*

4. Leora Auslander, a contemporary historian at the University of Chicago and a furniture maker, has spelled out the complex symbolic interplay between self and others that occurs when buying a chair, even when one is not anxious: "When I go into a store to buy a chair, I carry . . . my family and digested and undigested childhood experiences . . . what certain styles signify, in terms of social and political position. . . . Over the next months and years guests respond to me and to my chair, some seeing in it one thing, some another. . . . They respond with their interpretations of my chair and me; I respond and am changed by their responses. . . . The chair was full of meanings over which I had no control, and of which I had only partial knowledge when I acquired it. In my home it acquired new meanings. My guests have a certain understanding of me when they arrive in my home; as a result of viewing my chair they have somebody different. In their eyes I become different—perhaps also in my own." *Taste and Power: Furnishing Modern France* (Berkeley, CA: University of California Press, 1996), pp. 18–19.

5. Annette Page, "Ballet Faux Pas," *The Times* (London), July 7, 1993, Feature section.

6. John Pierson, *Wall Street Journal,* Sept. 12, 1995, pp. B1–B7. The National Institute for Occupational Safety and Health alone estimates compensation claims for lower back injuries at $11 billion per year—Corey Takahashi, "Office Chair Encourages 'Active Sitting,' " *Wall Street Journal,* July 21, 1997, p. B1. Low back pain has been the most frequent cause of diminished capacity to work, according to ergonomic researchers for several decades—G. B. J. Andersson, "Epidemiologic Aspects on Low Back Pain in Industry," *Spine,* 6 (1981), pp. 53–60.

7. Much contemporary scholarship has acknowledged the body, but as metaphor, symbol, cipher. In contrast, this investigation draws attention to the body as we experience it physically and psychically.

CHAPTER 1: HOW CHAIRS EVOLVED

1. *Camber's Edinburgh Journal,* vol. 15 (May 31, 1851), p. 3. Thanks to Swati Chattopadhay for bringing this article to my attention.

2. Gordon W. Hewes, "The Anthropology of Posture," *Scientific American,* vol. 196, no. 2 (February 1957), pp. 122–32.

3. British artists in India during its long colonial rule showed Indians sitting on the ground in a variety of attitudes for many different tasks and social occasions—Pratapaditya Pal and Vidya Dehejia, *From Merchants to Emperors: British Artists and India, 1757–1930* (Ithaca, NY: Cornell University Press, 1986).

4. Jagjit Kaur Dhesi and Francille M. Firebaugh, "The Effects of Stages of Chapati Making and Angles of Body Position on Heart Rate," *Ergonomics,* vol. 16, no. 6 (November 1973), pp. 11–15.

5. Roy Sieber, *African Furniture and Household Objects* (Bloomington, IN: Indiana University Press, 1980), pp. 125, 159.

6. Omar Michael Burke, *Among the Dervishes* (New York: Dutton, 1975), p. 192.

7. Andrew Pollack, "In a Painful Situation, Japanese Choose Chairs," *New York Times International,* August 25, 1995, p. A2.

8. C. P. FitzGerald, *Barbarian Beds: The Origin of the Chair in China* (London: Cresset, 1965), pp. 71–72.

9. Bodil Kjaier, "Everyday Furniture of the People of China," *Mobilia,* 291 (1980), pp. 41–45.

10. George N. Kates, *Chinese Household Furniture* (New York: Harper & Brothers, 1948), p. 38.

11. James Hillman, *A Blue Fire* (New York: HarperPerennial, 1991), p. 71.

12. Siegfried. Giedion, *Mechanization Takes Command* (London: Oxford University Press, 1948), p. 259.

13. Professor Anne Kilmer, Department of Near Eastern Studies, University of California at Berkeley, personal telephone communication, February 7, 1995, and A. Salonen, *De Mobel des Alten Mesopotamians* (Annals of the Academy of Finnish Science, Helsinki, 1963).

14. Professor Margaret Conkey, Department of Anthropology, University of California at Berkeley, personal telephone communication, February 8, 1995.

15. Some of the rare photographs and drawings are in books and publications from Russia, in Russian, with no ISBNs. My thanks to Mirjana Stevanovic at U.C. Berkeley for sharing this material with me. Marija Gimbutas has published some of this evidence in her extensive collections, *The Language of the Goddess* (San Francisco: Harper, 1989) and *The Civilization of the Goddess* (San Francisco: Harper, 1991).

16. See Henry Petroski, *The Evolution of Everyday Things* (New York: Knopf, 1992).

17. Alex Bavelas, "Communication Patterns in Task-Oriented Groups," *J. Acoustical Soc. Amer.,* 22 (1950), pp. 725–30.

18. Jerome Carcopino, *Daily Life in Ancient Rome* (New Haven: Yale University Press, 1940), pp. 30–35.

19. Bernard Rudofsky, *Now I Lay Me Down to Eat* (New York: Anchor Books, 1980). Bill Countryman, a Bible scholar at the Graduate Theological Union, Berkeley, confirmed that the verbs used in describing the Last Supper in Matthew, Mark, and John indicate reclining posture; further, the phrase "in Jesus' bosom" only makes sense assuming the reclining posture—Personal telephone communication, July 1997.

20. Giedion, op. cit., p. 261.

21. Carcopino, op. cit., p. 34. The drawings do not indicate that these women lay back because of being pregnant.

22. John Gloag, *A Social History of Furniture Design: From B.C. 1300 to A.D. 1960* (New York: Crown, 1966), p. 74.

23. Carcopino, op. cit., p. 265.

24. Giedion, op. cit., pp. 261–62; see also "Middle Ages," *Encyclopedia Americana International Edition*, Vol. 19 (Danbury, CT: Grolier, 1994).

25. John Gloag, *The Englishman's Chair: Origins, Design, and Social History of Great Furniture in England* (London: Allen & Unwin, 1964), p. 2. See also J. Charles Cox and Alfred Harvey, *English Church Furniture* (New York: Dutton, 1907), pp. 255–61.

26. Phyllis B. Oates, *The Story of Western Furniture* (New York: Harper & Row, 1981), p. 38.

27. Gloag, *A Social History*, p. 75.

28. "Furniture," *Encyclopaedia Britannica*, 11th edition (1911), p. 363.

29. Gloag, *A Social History*, p. 93.

30. Oates, op. cit., p. 43.

31. Giedion, op. cit., p. 268.

32. Edward Lucie-Smith, *Furniture: A Concise History* (New York: Thames & Hudson, 1990), pp. 69–91. John Gloag, *Time, Taste and Furniture* (London: F. A. Stokes, 1955), pp. 70–74.

33. Gloag, *A Social History*, p. 62.

34. Oates, op. cit., pp. 57–64.

35. Giedion, op. cit., p. 309.

36. Oates, op. cit., pp. 141, 106, 112.

37. Allan Greenberg, "Design Paradigms in the Eighteenth and Twentieth Centuries," in *Ornament, Via III: The Journal of the Graduate School of Fine Arts* (University of Pennsylvania, 1977), pp. 64–81.

38. Gloag, *A Social History*, p. 171.

39. Oates, op. cit., p. 150; Giedion, op. cit., pp. 428, 436.

40. Vincent Scully, *New World Visions of Household Gods and Sacred Places: American Art and the Metropolitan Museum, 1650–1914* (Boston: Little, Brown, 1988), p. 27.

41. Jack Larkin, *The Reshaping of Everyday Life, 1790–1840* (New York: Harper & Row, 1988), pp. 137–47.

42. Georges Teyssot, "The Disease of the Domicile," *Assemblage,* 6 (June 1988), pp. 72–97.

43. Gloag, *A Social History,* p. 181. See also Katherine C. Grier, *Culture and Comfort: People, Parlors, and Upholstery, 1850–1930* (Rochester, NY: Strong Museum, 1988), pp. 101–28.

44. Gloag, *The Englishman's Chair,* pp. 209–18.

45. See Gloag, *A Social History,* pp. 171–84. Debora Silverman, *Art Nouveau in Fin-de-Siècle France: Politics, Psychology, and Style* (Berkeley, CA: University of California Press, 1989), and Auslander, op. cit., argue that Art Nouveau actually had ideological roots in rococo.

46. Oates, op. cit., pp. 156–66. Auslander gives more weight to technology (personal communication, Nov. 9, 1997).

47. David A. Hanks, *Innovative Furniture in America from 1800 to the Present* (New York: Horizon Press, 1981).

48. Giedion, op. cit., pp. 390–406.

49. See Adrian Forty, *Objects of Desire: Design and Society from Wedgwood to IBM* (New York: Pantheon, 1986), pp. 94–119; Joan Kron, *Homepsych* (New York: Potter, 1983); Grier, *Culture and Comfort;* and Galen Cranz, "Redesigning the Home in Response to Ideas About Healthy Posture from an Integrated Body-Mind Perspective," Paper presented at the International symposium on Meanings of Home, Alvkarlyby, Sweden, 1989.

50. Walter A. Dyer and Esther S. Fraser, *The Rocking Chair: An American Institution* (New York: Century, 1928), p. 18. Some say Benjamin Franklin may have been the first to attach rockers to chairs, but historians assure me that household inventories show that people in New England and the mid-Atlantic colonies did the same and possibly earlier.

51. Hanks, op. cit., p. 1.

52. Dyer and Fraser, op. cit., pp. 46–47.

53. Greenberg, op. cit., p. 80.

54. Peter Stewart, "A Randomized Trial to Evaluate the Use of a Birth Chair for Delivery," *The Lancet,* 8337 (June 11, 1983), pp. 1296–98.

55. Charles Winick and Herbert Holt, "Seating Posture as a Non-Verbal Communication in Group Analysis," *Psychiatry*, 24 (1961), p. 172.

56. FitzGerald, op. cit., p. 72.

57. Forty, op. cit., Chapter 5, "The Home," pp. 94–119.

58. I first discovered the work of Leora Auslander in *University of Chicago Division of Social Science Reports* (Spring 1990), pp. 10–11, but refer the reader to her more recent, fascinating book, *Taste and Power: Furnishing Modern France*.

59. Susan Brownmiller, "Locked Knees, the Debutante Slouch, Hair Twisting: The Contrived Postures of Femininity," *Ms.* (March 1984), pp. 53–54, 94.

60. E. F. Le Carpentier, "Easy Chair Dimensions for Comfort—A Subjective Approach," *Ergonomics*, vol. 12, no. 2 (1969), pp. 328–37. Everybody needs to keep their knees lower than their hips in order to relieve strain on the lower back, but taller people—usually men—may find this particularly difficult, so two sizes make sense. This interpretation of Le Carpentier's observations will be clearer after Chapters 3 and 4.

61. Georgia Dullea, "What Women Want: Their Own Recliners," *New York Times*, Jan. 14, 1991, pp. C1, C6.

62. Janet L. Fix, "A Bundle of Sticks," *Forbes*, Nov. 18, 1985, pp. 202–04.

63. Dylan Landis, "Dressed to Kill," *Chicago Tribune*, June 12, 1988, Home section, p. 1.

64. Sheila Levrant de Bretteville, "The 'Parlorization' of Our Homes and Ourselves," *Chrysalis*, 9 (Fall 1979), pp. 38–41. I suspect that the couch did not evolve directly from the couches of ancient Egypt and Rome, or even from the continuous seating like the benches around some European peasant rooms. Rather, it may have evolved from the settee, which is a two-person chair. I speculate that the contemporary couch had to work its way through Western individuality, in this context the cultural experience of a single person sitting above ground in a fairly static pose. This kind of sitting may be a "masculine" idea; certainly it does not embody the kind of femininity associated with languorous poses on a Turkish sofa or divan.

65. Mary McCloud, "Furniture and Femininity," *Architectural Review*, 181 (January 1987), pp. 43–47. See also Isabelle Anscombe, *A Woman's Touch: Women in Design from 1860 to the Present Day* (New York: Viking, 1984), pp. 128–30.

66. Eileen Gray designed a number of chairs that were well known in her day, notably the Transat (1924), the Nonconformist (1925), and the Bibendum (1925). See Peter Adam, *Eileen Gray: Architect/Designer* (New York: Abrams, 1987), and Philippe Garner, *Eileen Gray: Designer and Architect* (Cologne: Benedikt Taschen, 1993).

67. Elspeth Thompson, "The Bottom Line," *The Guardian* (U.K.), Nov. 20, 1991, p. 37. Thanks to Professor Helen Mellor of Nottingham University for sending me this review. I note that the furniture designed by the female architect Gai Aulenti, internationally recognized for harmonious, sensitive remodeling of buildings for museums, is neither better nor worse from a body-conscious point of view than that of her male counterparts.

68. Mark Patinkin, "It's My La-Z-Boy Recliner and It's Staying Put," *Providence Journal,* Sept. 22, 1994, p. 2F.

69. See Carol Gilligan, *In a Different Voice* (Cambridge, MA: Harvard University Press, 1982).

70. Po Bronson, *Bombardiers* (New York: Random House, 1995), pp. 187–88.

71. F. Duffy, C. Cave, and J. Worthington, eds., *Planning Office Space* (London: Architectural Press, 1976), pp. 72–73.

72. See Francis Duffy, Andrew Laing, and Vic Crisp, *The Responsible Workplace: The Redesign of Work and Offices* (Oxford and Boston: Butterworth Architecture in association with Estates Gazette, 1993); Liverpool University Department of Building Science Pilkington Research Unit, *Office Design: A Study of Environment* (Peter Manning, editor) (Liverpool, 1965); and Eric D. Sundstrom, *Work Places: The Psychology of the Physical Environment in Offices and Factories* (Cambridge and New York: Cambridge University Press, 1986).

73. David A. Harris, et al., *Planning and Designing the Office Environment* (New York: Van Nostrand, 1981), p. 23.

74. Ellen Konar, et al., "Status Demarcation in the Office," *Environment and Behavior,* vol. 14, no. 5 (September 1982), pp. 563, 570, and Fred I. Steele, *Physical Settings and Organizational Development* (Reading, MA: Addison-Wesley, 1973).

75. "The Steelcase Study of Office Environments, No. II," conducted by Louis Harris and Associates, Inc., Grand Rapids, MI. Cited in Walter B. Kleeman, "The Furniture of the Office," *Environment and Behavior,* vol. 14, no. 5 (September 1982), p. 606.

76. Barbara Flanagan, "The Office That (Almost) Does the Work for You," *Working Woman* (October 1990), p. 113.

77. F. H. A. Bex, "Desk Heights," *Applied Ergonomics,* vol. 2, no. 3 (September 1971), pp. 138–40. See also K. H. Eberhard Kroemer and Joan C. Robinette, "Ergonomics in the Design of Office Furniture: A Review of European Literature," U.S. Air Force Wright-Patterson Air Force Base, Ohio, July 1968.

78. Linda Brown and Deyan Sudjic, *Twentieth Century Chair Design* (London: Institute of Contemporary Arts, 1988), p. A1.

79. Michael Brill, "Productivity: How to Define It and Achieve It in the Office," Presentation at National Exposition of Contract Furnishings, The Merchandise Mart, Chicago, June 1980. Cited in Kleeman, op. cit., p. 607.

80. Birgit Helene Jevnaker, "Make the World a Better Place to Sit In!" *Design Management Journal* (Fall 1991), pp. 48–54. The brochure for the Credo chair reads: "Credo—for any position" (p. 52).

81. The move from switchboards to video display terminals for telephone operators is a case in point. A study of individual changes in movement revealed that "each subject practically halved his or her number of changes in position per hour in the transfer from the old to the new workstation"—A. Grieco, "Sitting Posture: An Old Problem and a New One," *Ergonomics,* vol. 29, no. 3 (1986), pp. 345–62.

82. An interview with Hajo Eickhoff is in Simonetta Carbonaro, "The Chair and Its Sedative Effects," *Ufficiostile* (1991), pp. 55–57. His thesis is developed in German in Hajo Eickhoff, *Himmelsthron und Schaukelstuhl* (Munich: Carl Hanser Verlag, 1993). In 1997, Eickhoff organized an exhibit in Dresden at the Hygienic Museum; the catalogue is in German, but with enough images to be of value to those who cannot read German—Hajo Eickhoff, *Sitzen* (Frankfurt am Main: Anabas-Veri, 1997).

83. Don Johnson, *Body: Recovering Our Sensual Wisdom* (Berkeley, CA: North Atlantic Books, 1992), pp. 66, 183, 194.

84. "Montessori System," *Encyclopaedia Britannica* (Chicago: William Benton, 1986), Vol. 15, p. 787.

85. Susan Brink, "Smart Moves," *U.S. News & World Report,* May 15, 1995, pp. 76–84.

86. See Roger G. Barker and Herbert F. Wright, *One Boy's Day: A Specimen Record of Behavior* (New York: Harper & Row, 1966).

87. Nicolas Andry de Bois-Regard, *Orthopaedia, or, The Art of Correcting and Preventing Deformities in Children.* Classics of Medicine Library Special Edition (Birmingham, AL, 1980), pp. 86, 116.

88. A. C. Mandal, "The Seated Man *(Homo Sedens).* The Seated Work Position—Theory and Practice," *Applied Ergonomics,* vol. 12, no. 1 (March 1981), pp. 19–26. Mandal has drawn on the work of the American orthopedic physician J. J. Keegan in "Alteration of the Lumbar Curve," *Journal of Bone and Joint Surgery,* 35 (1953), pp. 589–603. See also A. C. Mandal, "The Correct Height of School Furniture," *Human Factors,* vol. 24, no. 3 (June 1982), pp. 257–69.

89. Independently, findings from the Noll Laboratory for Human Performance Research at Pennsylvania State University support Mandal's contention that slanted desks are preferable to flat ones because working at a slanted desk produces more erect posture and reduces restlessness, fatigue, and discomfort. They found less EMG (electromyogram) activity in the lower back when subjects were using slanted work surfaces—M. C. Eastman and E. Kamon, "Posture and Subjective Evaluation at Flat and Slanted Desks," *Human Factors,* vol. 18, no. 1 (February 1976), pp. 15–26.

90. Mandal, "The Correct Height of School Furniture," p. 266.

91. A. C. Mandal, "Investigation of the Lumbar Flexion of the Seated Man," *International Journal of Industrial Ergonomics,* 8 (1991), pp. 75–87, and A. C. Mandal, "Changing Standards for School Furniture," *Ergonomics in Design,* (April 1997), pp. 28–31. Only Germany and Austria have dissented, sticking to the old standards.

An Australian team tested the Mandal hypothesis that a forward-tilt seat with a sloping desk is healthier than conventional seats with backward slope and level desktop, and concluded that his type of chair maintains "a more efficient anatomical alignment of young children when sitting and writing"—M. Marschall, et al., "Effect of Work Station Design on Sitting Posture in Young Children," *Ergonomics,* vol. 38, no. 9 (1995), pp. 1932–40.

92. H. W. Oxford, "Anthropometric Data for Educational Chairs," *Ergonomics,* vol. 12, no. 2 (1969), pp. 140–61.

93. Charles Winick, unpublished study cited in Winick and Holt, op. cit., p. 173.

CHAPTER 2: THE ELEMENTS OF STYLE

1. "The Aesthete," trans. Joern Kroll, from *Christian Morganstern's Galgenlieder,* trans. Max Knight (Berkeley, CA: University of California Press, 1963), p. 185.

2. Paula Deitz, "Twenty-Three Best Chairs," *Connoisseur,* 221 (May 1991), pp. 58–63.

3. *Time,* September 18, 1978, p. 21.

4. Four of six particularly useless pieces of furniture by artist-designers were chairs, critiqued by John Miller, "Furniture Without a Cause," *SF Magazine of Design and Style* (November 1989), pp. 78–81.

5. Nigel Whiteley, "Semi-Works of Art (Consumerism, Youth Culture and Chair Design in the 1960's)," *Furniture History,* 23 (1987), p. 119. Another interesting use of furniture as a social indicator is Gerald L. Pocius, "Gossip, Rhetoric, and Objects: A Sociolinguistic Approach to Newfoundland Furniture," in Gerald W. R. Ward, ed., *Perspectives on American Furniture* (New York: W. W. Norton, 1988), who explores the ways that people speak to one another through objects.

6. Edward O. Laumann and James S. House, "Living Room Styles and Social Attributes: The Patterning of Material Artifacts in a Modern Urban Community," *Sociology and Social Research,* vol. 54, no. 3 (April 1970), pp. 321–42.

7. Doug Stewart, "One Man's Private Cache Pays Off for the Rest of Us," *Smithsonian* (February 1995), pp. 103–10.

8. Sarah Booth Conroy, "Design: Keeping the Faith with Modern," *The Washington Post,* June 4, 1992, final edition, p. T14.

9. Mary Beth Sammons, "Sitting Pretty: Busy People Find Comfy and Unique Places to Take It Easy," *Chicago Tribune,* March 27, 1994, Home section, p. 1.

10. Ralph Caplan, "How Chairs Behave," *Psychology Today* (February 1983), pp. 46–52.

11. Jules David Prown, "Style as Evidence," *Winterthur Portfolio,* vol. 15, no. 3 (Autumn 1980), p. 208, emphasizes that our direct sensory experience of objects allows us to empathize with historical events and figuratively speaking "get inside the skins" of the people who commissioned, made, used, or enjoyed them. In his judgment, "chairs are particularly revealing of cultural values because they so easily become human surrogates. . . ." (p. 199).

12. Ellen Lupton and J. Abbott Miller, *The Bathroom, the Kitchen, and the Aesthetics of Waste—A Process of Elimination* (Cambridge, MA: MIT List Visual Arts Center, 1992), p. 2.

13. Sammons, "Sitting Pretty," p. 1.

14. These terms are more encompassing than the names for stylistic periods conventionally used in furniture histories.

15. Lucie-Smith, op. cit., p. 18.

16. Ibid., pp. 53–55.

17. Auslander, *Taste and Power,* pp. 38, 68.

18. Ibid., p. 64.

19. "Furniture," *Encyclopaedia Britannica,* p. 304.

20. According to different sources, Georg Junigl of Vienna created the coil spring in 1822, whereas others attribute it to Samuel Pratt, who patented it in 1828—Dennis Young, "New Developments in Chair Manufacture," *Modern Chairs 1918–1970* (London: Whitechapel Art Gallery, 1970), p. 14.

21. Carol Hogben, Introduction, ibid., p. 9.

22. Marilyn Hoffman, "Danish Designer Hans Wegner," *Christian Science Monitor,* June 20, 1986, pp. 27–28.

23. The sociology of style could take us far afield from the micro issues of line, shape, and decoration to macro issues like "Which kind of chair producer is most satisfied, best paid, and is least objectively alienated with most control over work process and decision to sell?" This approach must await a future study of chairs, but it was used by the sociologist Barbara Rosenberg, who asked about the three different types of photographers (fine art, newspaper, advertising) she identified in *Photographers at Work* (New York: Holmes & Meier, 1978).

24. Charlotte and Peter Fiell, *Modern Chairs* (New York: Perimeter, 1993), covers chair design between 1885 and 1992 in the connoisseur tradition.

25. Paul Overty, "Equipment for Utopia; Gerrit Rietveld's Furniture and Architecture," *Art in America,* vol. 82, no. 1 (January 1994), p. 34.

26. See Ulrich Conrads, *Programs and Manifestoes on 20th Century Architecture* (Cambridge, MA: MIT Press, 1970).

27. Lucie-Smith, op. cit., p. 15.

28. Greenberg, op. cit., p. 78.

29. Deyan Sudjic, "A Survey of the 20th Century Chair," in *Sit: A Catalogue of Modern Chair Design: Chairs from the "Sit" Exhibition, 22–24 March 1982 and the People Who Sat on Them* (London: IBA Magazine, 1982), p. 8.

30. Bruno Taut, *Modern Architecture* (London: The Studio, 1929), p. 8.

31. Sudjic, "A Survey," p. 8.

32. David Morton, "Emilio Ambasz: Poetic Pragmatics," *Progressive Architecture* (September 1978), pp. 98–101. Many other serious ergonomic work chairs have followed. Of the several dozen on the market, Stumpt and Chadwick's may have received the most attention from the design world.

33. Sidney Tillim, "Designer Go Home: 'High Styles' at the Whitney," *Art in America,* (March 1986), p. 17.

34. Fred Davis, *Fashion, Culture, and Identity* (Chicago: University of Chicago Press, 1992).

35. Naomi Gilman, "The Chair and the Contemporary American Artist," in *American Chairs: Form, Function and Fantasy* (Sheboygan, WI: John Michael Kohler Arts Center of the Sheboygan Arts Foundation, 1978), p. 51.

36. Debbie Zike, " 'The Chairs' Will Remain," *Rockridge News,* Dec. 16, 1995, p. 5.

37. Sybaris Gallery, announcement for *"The Chair: Deconstructed/Reconstructed,"* Dec. 9, 1995–Jan. 13, 1996, Royal Oak, Michigan.

38. Sheri Craig, "Interpreting Chairs," *Canadian Interiors,* vol. 34, no. 3 (June 1997), pp. 20–21.

39. Lucie-Smith, op. cit., pp. 14–15.

40. Gilman, op. cit., pp. 51–77.

41. John Pierson, "Sculpted Chairs Offer Solid Support," in "Form + Function" column, *Wall Street Journal,* April 10, 1992, p. B1.

42. J. M. Berthelot, "Sociological Discourse and the Body," in Mike Featherstone, Mike Hepworth, and Bryan S. Turner, eds., *The Body: Social Process and Cultural Theory* (London: Sage, 1991) pp. 390–404.

43. Two of the essayists in *Modern Chairs 1918–70* (London: Victoria and Albert Museum, 1970) comment on the significance of the chair, in contrast to tables, sofas, or the floor, as a representative of the individual.

44. Scully, op. cit., p. 64.

CHAPTER 3: AN ERGONOMIC PERSPECTIVE

1. Roethke, "The Chair," op. cit., p. 178.

2. Doug Stewart, "Modern Designers Still Can't Make the Perfect Chair," *Smithsonian* (April 1986), pp. 97–104.

3. Chair design might be called a wicked problem because no single solution can fulfill all of the desirable criteria. But more than frustrate designers, chairs can actively harm human beings. Horst Rittel and Melvin Webber, "Dilemmas in a General Theory of Planning," *Policy Science* 4 (1973), pp. 155–69, first described wicked problems.

4. Several review articles provide a jump start on the often tedious and dispersed ergonomic studies on chairs: Kroemer and Robinette (1969), Branton (1969), Grandjean (1969), Andersson and Ortengren (1974), Osborne (1982), Lueder (1983), Grieco (1986), and Zacharkow (1988). In addition, I have provided a list of all the ergonomic studies I consulted in the Bibliography at the back of this book.

5. See "Sitting Down on the Job: Not as Easy as It Sounds," *Occupational Health and Safety,* vol. 50, no. 10 (October 1981), pp. 24–26. Another summary of seating is by Dennis Zacharkow, *Posture: Sitting, Standing, Chair Design and Exercise* (Springfield, IL: Charles C. Thomas, 1988). Reviews of the strains imposed on the spine by sitting usually cite a series of six research articles by B. J. G. Andersson, et al., published in the *Scandinavian Journal of Rehabilitation Medicine* in 1974, and followed by additional publications in *Spine, Engineering in Medicine,* and *Human Factors in Transportation Research.* A chiropractor has tried to help people cope with the strains of sedentary work: S. Donkin, *Sitting on the Job* (Boston: Houghton Mifflin, 1986).

6. Lesly Reisbrod and Sander Greenland, "Factors Associated with Self-Reported Back-Pain Prevalence: A Population-Based Study," *Journal of Chronic Diseases,* vol. 38, no. 8 (1985), pp. 691–702.

7. T. Hettinger, "Statistics on Diseases in the Federal Republic of Germany with Particular Reference to Diseases of the Skeletal System," *Ergonomics,* vol. 28, no. 1 (1985), pp. 17–20.

8. W. H. Fahrni, "Conservative Treatment of Lumbar Disc Degeneration," *Orthopedic Clinics of North America,* 6 (1975), p. 93. Cited by T. Hettinger, "Occupational Hazards Associated with Diseases of the Skeletal System," *Ergonomics,* vol. 28, no. 1 (1985), pp. 69–75.

9. George A. Gross, "Preventing Low Back Pain," in Richard B. Goldbloom and Robert S. Lawrence, eds., *Preventing Disease: Beyond the Rhetoric* (New York: Springer-Verlag, 1990), p. 205 and p. 208, citing Adams and Hutton, "The Effect of Posture on the Fluid Content of Lumbar Intervertebral Disks," *Spine,* 8 (1983), pp. 665–71.

10. W. Hunting, T. Läubli, and E. Grandjean, "Postural and Visual Loads at VDT Workplaces," *Ergonomics,* vol. 24, no. 12 (1981), pp. 917–31.

11. Eugene Nordby, M.D., "Epidemiology and Diagnosis in Low Back Injury," *Occupational Health and Safety,* vol. 50, no. 1 (January 1981), pp. 38–42.

12. John Sarno, M.D., *Mind Over Back Pain* (New York: Berkley Books, 1986).

13. More recent research has found that most ulcers are caused by bacteria.

14. Wilfred Barlow, "Psychosomatic Problems in Postural Reeducation," *The Lancet,* Sept. 24, 1955, pp. 661–62, 664.

15. Suzann Roalman, letter to *The New York Times,* Sept. 17, 1991, p. A20.

16. Riesbrod and Greenland, op. cit., p. 694.

17. T. M. Grimsrud, "Humans Were Not Created to Sit—And Why You Have to Refurnish Your Life," *Ergonomics,* vol. 33, no. 3 (1990), p. 291.

18. Susan R. Orenstein, Peter F. Whitington, and David M. Orenstein, "The Infant Seat as Treatment for Gastroesophageal Reflux," *New England Journal of Medicine,* vol. 309, no. 13, Sept. 29, 1983, pp. 760–63.

19. Colin James Alexander, "Chair Sitting and Varicose Veins," *The Lancet,* April 15, 1972, p. 822.

20. Because we have good reason to believe that chair sitting causes anatomical and physiological problems and because we have seen that not everyone practices chair sitting, we could test the assertion that it is detrimental to health by comparing rates of back or other health-related problems in chair-sitting cultures with those in non-chair-sitting cultures. Unfortunately, there is little evidence of such epidemiological research. In the absence of comparative data from different cultures, we could compare occupational groups within the same culture. But even those groups who do non-sedentary work still have the twenty-five to twenty-eight chairs available to them on a daily basis, just like the rest of us. We do know that bus drivers have more problems than any other occupational group. However, their work conditions are compounded by vibration and the stress of driving in traffic, so testing the effects of posture alone has not been possible. I hope that this book may encourage sponsors to commission cross-cultural studies comparing the effects of chair-sitting and non-chair-sitting cultures on health.

21. One of my engineering colleagues—a woman—after hearing this information speculated that the systematic difference in constant compression of women's thighs could contribute to the distinctively female problem of cellulite. Colleagues with a medical education have confirmed that this is a reasonable possibility.

22. A. Shihadeh, e-mail communication, July 16, 1997. A. C. Mandal would err in the direction of shortening seat depth so that it only carries the weight of the torso. Pressure under the thighs will tilt the pelvis backwards, which he says is the key issue, because it forces people to round their backs.

23. This interpretation is based on years of observation as an Alexander teacher. It also stands to reason, although biomechanical researchers might interject that there is "no evidence," meaning that no formal experimental study has been done. Long-term longitudinal studies with control groups would be fine, but until research funders are convinced of the theoretical plausibility of this relationship (and I hope this book will help), such studies will be a long time coming. In the meantime, Alexander training is a minimum of three years and produces people capable of observing with equal accuracy. Thus the community of Alexander teachers constitutes observers capable of "reliable" judgments, in the scientific sense of the word.

24. Grieco, "Sitting Posture: An Old Problem and a New One," pp. 345–62.

25. Rudofsky, op. cit.

26. See Etienne Grandjean, *Fitting the Task to the Man* (London: Taylor & Francis, 1980), pp. 54–55.

27. As an Alexander teacher, I have more direct experience with morphological damage being done by habitually improper movement of the body (and more importantly, being *undone* by correct movement) than ergonomic researchers, and so am more likely to see cause and effect than they are. I was able to see morphological change in myself, in other students of the Alexander Technique, and especially in training classes where people practice the technique three hours a day for three years; I also saw many time-lapse photographic studies showing change and heard dozens of accounts by students and by teachers of morphological re-forms.

28. See Erik Berglund, *Sittsproblers Matt: The Dimensions of Seating Furniture* (Stockholm: Mobilinstitutet, 1988), pp. 32, 34. Mercifully, some designers believe that the chairback should simply follow natural spinal curves, rather than actively reproduce them.

29. Tom Bendix, et al., "What Does a Backrest Actually Do to the Lumbar Spine?" *Ergonomics,* vol. 39, no. 4 (1996), pp. 533–42.

30. Rani Lueder, "Work Station Design," *The Ergonomics Payoff* (New York: Nichols Publishing Co., 1986), p. 163; also Shihadeh, e-mail communication, July 16, 1997. Other references on the relative usefulness of armrests include Ulf P. Arborelius, et al., "The Effects of Armrests and High Seat Heights on Lower-Limb Joint Load and Muscular Activity During Sitting and Rising," *Ergonomics,* vol. 35, no. 11 (1992), pp. 1377–91.

31. Witold Rybczynski, *Home: The Short History of an Idea* (New York: Viking, 1986), p. 6.

32. Rani Karen Lueder, "Seat Comfort: A Review of the Construct in the Office Environment," *Human Factors,* vol. 25, no. 6 (December 1983), p. 701. See also Lueder's *The Ergonomics Payoff.*

33. Mark Bruton, "Comfort," *Design,* 323 (November 1975), pp. 30–35. Despite such research findings, the staff at *Consumer Reports* naively conducted their own test of forty-five ergonomic office chairs over a four-month period and concluded that the first impressions of a chair's comfort corresponds well to week-long impressions, maintaining that if you sit in a chair in a store and like it there, "you will probably find it comfortable after you get it home"—"Make Yourself Comfortable," *Consumer Reports,* vol. 61, no. 9 (September 1996), p. 34. This was not my experience of buying a chair in graduate school. It was not until I got my chair home and sat in it for forty-five minutes that pain set in. I returned to the store with a book so that I could sit for forty-five minutes per chair!

34. D. M. Barkla, "Chair Angles, Duration of Seating, and Comfort Ratings," *Ergonomics,* vol. 7, no. 3 (1964), pp. 297–304. Also cited in Lueder, "Seat Comfort," p. 706.

35. E. N. Corlett and R. P. Bishop, "The Measurement of Spinal Loads Arising from Working Seats," *Proceedings of the Human Factors Society 27th Annual Meeting* (Santa Monica, CA, 1983), pp. 786–89. Cited in Lueder, "Seat Comfort," p. 706.

36. R. A. Wachsler and D. B. Learner, "An Analysis of Some Factors Influencing Seat Comfort," *Ergonomics,* vol. 3, no. 4 (1960), pp. 315–20. Cited in Lueder, "Seat Comfort."

37. P. Branton, "Behavior, Body Mechanics, and Discomfort," in E. Grandjean, ed., *Proceedings of the Symposium on Sitting Posture* (London: Taylor & Francis, 1969), p. 210.

38. Rybczynski, op. cit., pp. 230–31.

39. Lueder, "Seat Comfort," p. 704.

40. Branton, op. cit., p. 210.

41. Ibid.

42. H. W. Jurgens, "Body Movements of the Driver in Relation to Sitting Conditions in the Car: A Methodological Study," in D. J. Oborne and J. A. Levis, eds., *Human Factors in Transport Research* (New York: Academic Press, 1980). Cited in Lueder, "Seat Comfort," p. 707.

43. They include the Danish physician Mandal, the Norwegian designer Opsvik, the German ergonomic professor Barbara Tietze, the American somatics Professor Don Johnson, the German philosopher-historian Eickhoff, several Scandinavian furniture manufacturers who produce school furniture to Mandal's specifications, and others who showcase the designs by Opsvik.

44. Mandal wants to retain the option of using a backrest because it facilitates variation in postures.

45. Simonetta Carbonaro, "The Office Cries and Asks for Freedom," Interview with Barbara Tietze, *Ufficiostile,* vol. 22, no. 6/7 (July–August 1989), pp. 90–93.

CHAPTER 4: A BODY-MIND PERSPECTIVE

1. As a tiny antidote to our cultural emphasis on the mind, I use the term "body-mind" here rather than "mind-body." Additionally, I have been influenced by Bonnie Bainbridge Cohen, who uses the trademark Body-Mind Centering.

As well as offering a new theoretical model of the relationship between body and mind, the somatic perspective gives a general critique of the culture of science. It expands the ergonomic approach by demanding a more complex model of coordinated functioning of the "body-mind" which Alexander called the self; admittedly, the greater complexity makes defining and measuring concepts more difficult. However, this perspective does not reject a scientific approach, but rather demands better science, requiring validity (measurement that means what the researcher claims that it does) in balance with reliability (consistent results) and the ability to predict outcome. Measurement-oriented science (sometimes disparaged as "scientistic" by those more interested in concepts and how they might theoretically interrelate) too often sacrifices validity for reliability, which is the sacrifice ergonomicists have made by and large. Using objective measurements that increase the chances that two or more researchers will observe similar results has proved easier than finding measures that capture the actual complexity of the human body in action. Ideally, since classical science seeks to balance both validity and reliability, both somatic and ergonomic science should contribute to this synthesis.

2. For more details on the field, see: Thomas Hanna, *The Body of Life* (New York: Knopf, 1980); Michael Murphy, *The Future of the Body: Explorations into the Further Evolution of Human Nature* (Los Angeles: J. P. Tarcher, 1992); and Don Johnson, ed., *Groundworks: Narratives of Embodiment* (Berkeley, CA: North Atlantic Books, 1997).

3. Paul Linden, "Somatic Literacy: Bringing Somatic Education into Physical Education," *JOPERD* (September 1994), p. 16.

4. Ibid., pp. 15–21, emphasis in the original.

5. For a fuller account of my personal reasons for studying chairs, see Galen Cranz, "The Chair Is Where the Body Meets the Environment," in Jerry Sontag, ed., *Curiosity Recaptured* (San Francisco: Mornum Time Press, 1996). For those interested in scoliosis in particular, I can report that when I started studying the Alexander Technique full time as a teacher trainee at age forty, my spinal curvature straightened substantially. Such improvement is not medically expected, but I have X-rays, as well as other measures, to demonstrate the changes.

6. Perhaps this is more than an unavoidable bias, but rather a theoretical necessity, since Linden has written that "the only way to discuss somatic education with any degree of concreteness is to refer to one particular approach"—Linden, "Somatic Literacy," p. 16.

7. Murphy, *Future of the Body*.

8. In 1993, the U.S. Department of Labor classified Alexander teachers as "teachers, other." The North American Society of Teachers of the Alexander Technique has repeatedly reaffirmed its intention of remaining educators, rather than allying with other bodyworkers seeking recognition as alternative or complementary healing practitioners.

9. The spiritual side of somatic practices frees the psyche to care about the whole world or even the universe.

10. Laban movement analysis and Body-Mind Centering both argue that the arm initiates locomotion, while the head establishes direction. Thanks to Martha Eddy for this clarification.

11. Bernard Rudofsky, *The Unfashionable Human Body* (Garden City, NY: Doubleday, 1971).

12. The difference between East and West may be diminishing, as evidenced by a recent report that Japanese now find traditional kneeling postures painful—Andrew Pollack, "In a Painful Situation, Japanese Choose Chairs," *New York Times,* Aug. 25, 1995, p. A2.

13. Duane Juhan, *Job's Body: A Handbook for Bodywork* (Tarrytown, NY: Station Hill Press, 1987).

14. An example of a traditional M.D. and past chair of the department of physical medicine and rehabilitation at UCLA who recognizes that the relationship between bones, e.g., the curve of the neck, is supported by soft tissue is Rene Cailliet, *Neck and Arm Pain* (Philadelphia: F. A. Davis, 1990).

15. Ron Kirby, *The Probable Reality Behind Structural Integration: How Gravity Supports the Body* (Boulder, CO: Designpress, undated, 1980s). Rolfers now consider the tensegrity model provocative, but not literal because it does not correlate with anatomy—Michael Salveson, Rolfing practitioner and instructor, personal correspondence, August 22, 1997.

16. Grieco, "Sitting Posture: An Old Problem and a New One," pp. 345–62. A more popular example of someone assuming an evolutionary flaw comes from the front page of the *East Bay* [Berkeley] *Express* in 1992: "What is the source of this ping, this crunch, this collapse, this malfunctioning, this error in design and construction, this catastrophe, this PAIN? Without warning, your back has suddenly, as they say, GONE OUT." Fred Setterberg, *Ouch!* vol. 14, no. 43, Aug. 7, 1992.

17. Brink, "Smart Moves," pp. 76–84.

18. Grieco, "Sitting Posture," p. 347.

19. Edward Maisel, *The Alexander Technique: The Essential Writings of F. Matthias Alexander* (New York: Carol Publishing Group, 1990), p. xxiii.

20. For years the early Swedish chair researcher Bengt Akerblom argued for a lower seat height in conventional right-angle chairs. Liberal reformers have sought the same in order to accommodate the shorter half of the population. However, the radical reformer Mandal has argued just the opposite in order to promote perching.

21. The body is not a simple biological entity; it is instead a complex social reality, both a product and a producer of physical conditions. Values are translated into roles, which in turn shape our organism. I say this to avoid biological reductionism, but at the same time I want to acknowledge that the body is the matrix within which consciousness develops, and therefore a reliable source of information. See J. M. Berthelot, "Sociological Discourse and the Body," in Featherstone, Hepworth, and Turner, eds., *The Body: Social Process and Cultural Theory,* pp. 390–404.

22. Caplan, "How Chairs Behave," p. 51.

23. Reyner Banham, "The Chair As Art," *Modern Chairs 1918–1970,* p. 21.

24. Rybczynski, op. cit., p. 211.

25. Elaine Louie, "The Many Lives of a Very Common Chair," *New York Times,* Feb. 7, 1991, p. B5.

26. Sarah Booth Conroy, "Modern View of Marcel Breuer," *The Washington Post,* Oct. 11, 1981, Living section, p. L1.

27. Rybcynzski describes a gift of the Wassily from his wife, who was surprised to learn that although he had admired the chair, he had never sat in it—Witold Rybcynzski, lecture at the International Design Conference in Aspen, Colorado, June 16, 1994.

28. Quoted in Paula Deitz, "Twenty-Three Best Chairs," pp. 50–63.

29. Tom Wolfe, *From Bauhaus to Our House* (New York: Farrar, Straus and Giroux, 1981), p. 55.

30. Sherban Cantacuzino, "The Chair: Today and Tomorrow," *Modern Chairs 1918–1970,* p. 25.

31. Patricia Rogers, "Technology, Tradition and Production Today," *The Washington Post,* Oct. 15, 1987; Home section, p. T23, and final edition, Home section, p. T20.

32. Joseph Giovannini, "Gone Ballistic! Austria's Funder Factory," *Harper's Bazaar* (March 1993), p. 258.

33. Stewart, "Modern Designers Still Can't Make the Perfect Chair," p. 96.

34. Joseph Rykwert, "The Sitting Position—A Question of Method," in Charles Jencks and George Baird, eds., *Meaning in Architecture* (New York: George Braziller, 1969), pp. 233–43.

35. Sarah Booth Conroy, "Keeping the Faith with Modern," *The Washington Post,* June 4, 1992, Home section, p. T14.

36. We know that this was deliberate, because Rietveld made his living as an exacting and sophisticated master craftsman who knew how to join pieces of wood so that they would appear to be carved from a single block—Overty, "Equipment for Utopia: Gerrit Rietveld's Furniture and Architecture," p. 34.

37. Ibid.

38. Patricia Dane Rogers, "Grand Comfort by Le Corbusier," *The Washington Post,* Oct. 15, 1987, final edition, Home section, p. T20.

39. F. M. Alexander, *Man's Supreme Inheritance* (London: Dutton, 1918), p. 2. Mandal has commented that school furniture was far better in Alexander's days.

40. The title of one of Alexander's four books, *Constructive Conscious Control,* emphasizes exactly this.

CHAPTER 5: THE CHAIR REFORMED

1. Quoted in Leah Garchik, "Personals," *San Francisco Chronicle,* April 3, 1997.

2. Frank B. Gilbreth, Jr., and Ernestine Gilbreth Carey, *Cheaper by the Dozen* (New York: Thomas Y. Crowell, 1948).

3. I hope to reassure the style-conscious that planar can be chic, so I have collected illustrations of contemporary high-style chairs that are planar. The first is a beech-wood chair designed for Cappellini International that appeared in the *New York Times Magazine*—Carol Vogel, "Modern Conveniences," *New York Times Magazine,* Dec. 6, 1987, pp. 136–37. The Italian designer Achille Castiglioni also provides an example of working with planes in a stylish way. But there is a reason he uses stick figures to illustrate people sitting on his seat-couches; the reclining element does not work by anyone's standards, ergonomic or somatic. They do, however, offer good surfaces for lying down—"Perfectly at Home in Hill Country," *Ottagono,* 104 (September 1992), pp. 174–77. Another Italian designer, Paola Piva, has designed a modular seating system, primarily planar, with a hint of Deconstructionist aesthetic—International Design Convention of New York City Show Daily, Fall 1991, p. 11. At another pole, a mix of Matisse and Morocco employs richly upholstered planar sofas, like the original divans of Turkey, India, and North Africa—Jed Perl, and Andre Leon Talley, "Matisse's Eastern Eden," *Vogue,* vol. 180, no. 3 (March 1990), p. 432.

4. Alvin V. Sizer, "Work Continues on a Better Wheelchair," *New Haven Register,* Sept. 22, 1996, p. D2; Alvin V. Sizer, "Of Course We Can Build a Better Wheelchair," *New Haven Register,* May 7, 1995, p. D2. Farricielli may be contacted by calling her product design business at (203) 488–1751 or through e-mail: Farricielli@CompuServe.com. Her mailing address is P.O. Box 935, Branford, CT 06405.

5. Le Carpentier, op. cit., p. 336.

6. Corey Takahashi, "Office Chair Encourages 'Active Sitting,' " *Wall Street Journal,* July 21, 1997, p. B1.

7. Furniture Industry Research Association, "Anthropometric Data: Limitation in Use," *Architects' Journal Information Library,* Feb. 6, 1963, p. 325.

8. Vernon Mays, "The Ultimate Office Chair," *Progressive Architecture* (May 1988), p. 101.

9. Glenn Gordon, "Design a Chair that Fits Like a Glove," *Fine Woodworking* (September–October 1992), p. 89.

10. "Furniture by Robert Erickson: Chairs That Fit" brochure, Nevada City, California, 1992.

11. This conclusion almost seems a truism, but it was formally studied in a 1968 review of office furniture by Kroemer and Robinette. The proliferation of adjustable chairs since then reinforces this observation that no chair can serve all body types, at least no fixed chair.

Even though there cannot be one perfect chair, the wish to offer a universally useful model has not died easily. In one 1973 investigation, the authors looked at twelve different types of chairs, then did a rank ordering in terms of perceived comfort. They then combined the best features of the top-ranked chairs and ended up offering a diagram of dimensions and proper relationships; that is about as close as ergonomic researchers come to offering a pattern for a single chair. The sad thing is that with its slightly concave seat pan and overly molded back, it is exactly the sort of chair for which you'd need to bring along a pillow to fill in the hollows.

12. See Steve Ditlea, "Ergonomics: Designing to Fit Human Needs," *Hemispheres* (December 1992), p. 46.

13. Scott W. Donkin, *Sitting on the Job: How to Survive the Stresses of Sitting Down to Work—A Practical Handbook* (Boston: Houghton Mifflin, 1989).

14. Advertisement from Handsome Rewards, Perris, California, circa 1985.

15. If you have kyphosis (rounded back), lumbar support might be appropriate; but if you have lordosis (swayback), lumbar support would intensify your problem.

16. Posture Evolution Products, Katona, New York; (914) 232-9668.

17. David Boost, personal communication, October 17, 1995.

18. Sella stool, 1957, Achille and Pier Castiglioni, made by Zanotta.

19. In 1967, Mandal created a prototype of a chair with a forward-sloping seat, followed by mass production in 1968, followed by a 1970 publication in the *Danish Weekly Bulletin* (vol. 132, no. 36, pp. 1699–1703) advocating a 15-degree, forward-tilted seat.

20. In 1984, only 25 percent of those who had seen such a chair before had seen one in a real-life setting—and then only in a store. This means that in 1984 the realm of advertising and retail was more influential on attitudes toward the chair than by 1994, when people were more likely to have formed opinions about the chair based on their own and others' experiences, and, importantly, on the models of use that they saw in real life. Students in 1994 were significantly more likely to have seen one in a setting where it was used: 44 percent in someone's home and 27 percent in an office. This is particularly important because personal communication and direct observation are still the most effective means for the diffusion of innovation.

21. In 1984 among our sample of architecture students, the most frequent response was drawing, but by 1994 even architecture students selected working at a computer first, followed by writing, drawing, and studying. Watching TV and relaxing or talking were selected less often in 1994 than they had been in 1984. This matches the drop in perceived appropriateness of the chair in bedrooms, living rooms, and social environments because those are the sorts of activities one would expect in these environments.

22. Another summary of this research is Galen Cranz, "Managing Design Innovations: A Longitudinal Study of Attitudes Toward the Norwegian Balance Chair," *Managing Design Innovation* (Montreal: Environmental Design Research Association, 1997).

When asked why or why not, the responses included "comfortable and relaxing," and "cushiony." Of those who did not like the balance chair, three called it "precarious," two called it "confining" or "limiting," three described "uncomfortable pressure."

23. The survey brought up the clothing issue to find if the students thought the balance chair would be more difficult to sit in if you were wearing skirts or dresses. It turned out that sixty-five of the seventy-three students were wearing long pants, so the issue was hardly an overwhelmingly important one here. However, in an office where women have to wear skirts it might be an issue.

24. When the balance chair was introduced to the United States in 1981, it was an exotic commodity and sold for about $150; and in 1997 about $250, due to inflation. By the early 1980s, knockdown versions that you assemble yourself were advertised for a mere $69.95, and by the mid-1980s the knockdown price from Asian manufacturers was down to $29.95.

25. See Giedion, *Mechanization Takes Command.*

26. Gerald L. Pocius, "Gossip, Rhetoric and Objects: A Sociolinguistic Approach to Newfoundland Furniture," in Ward, ed., *Perspectives on American Furniture.*

27. Joseph Rykwert, "The Sitting Position—A Question of Method," in Jencks and Baird, eds., *Meaning in Architecture,* pp. 233–43.

28. For a fuller exploration of modern cultural tensions, see Fred Davis, *Fashion, Culture, and Identity,* especially p. 18.

29. Keegan, op. cit.

30. Verla Ubert, "Tilted Chairs and Desks Protect the Back," letter to the editor, *New York Times,* Nov. 3, 1991. The first person to demonstrate this was Jerome Keegan in 1953; Y. Yamaguchi and F. Umezewa have confirmed that compression forces are minimized with 135-degree hip angles, and added specific information about knee angles reducing compression at 45 degrees—"Development of a Chair to Minimize Disc Distortion in the Sitting Position." Cited in Etienne Grandjean, *Ergonomics of the Home* (London: Taylor & Francis, 1976).

31. A. C. Mandal, *The Sitting Position, Its Anatomy and Problems* (Klampenborg, Denmark: Daphne Publishing, 1984). The English Alexander teacher Walter Carrington was the first to construct a wooden stucture called a horse to put a person's legs and spine into this riding position for teaching purposes.

32. Jerome Keegan, "Alternations of the Lumbar Curve Related to Posture and Seating," *Journal of Bone and Joint Surgery,* vol. 35A, no. 3 (3 July 1953), pp. 589–603; and A. C. Mandal, "Investigation of the Lumbar Flexion of the Seated Man," *International Journal of Industrial Ergonomics,* 8 (1991), pp. 75–87.

33. Mandal is not the only one to acknowledge the problem of having to tuck the feet and ankles behind the knee support. Based on a comparison of six typists and six terminal-using students who used the chair for two and a half hours, one research team could not recommend the kneeling chair "for either prolonged industrial seating or for jobs requiring frequent chair entry and egress"—C. J. Drury and M. Francher, "Evaluation of a Forward-Sloping Chair," *Applied Ergonomics,* vol. 10, no. 1 (1985). When I interviewed Peter Opsvik in Norway in 1997, even he advocated active use of feet to change one's center of gravity in order to stimulate spatial thinking, needed for geometry, map reading, sewing, building things, and differentiating one form from another.

34. The reflex component of body movement is a recurrent theme in contemporary professional writing about the Alexander Technique. See, for example, Kathleen J. Ballard, "A Short Paper Describing the Nature of the Alexander Technique and Its Particular Contribution to the Management of Low Back Pain," *STATNEWS* (September 1993), p. 3, and Mark Arnold, "Rethinking 2: Benchmarks," ibid., p. 9. Physiologist David Garlick describes the role of subcortical, reflex mechanisms in movement that is experienced as effortless in "The Garlick Report," *Direction: A Journal on the Alexander Technique,* vol. 1, no. 4 (n.d.), pp. 118–20.

35. This "super-adjustable . . . executive style orthopedic chair" was used by the attorneys and Judge Ito during the infamous O. J. Simpson trial. Simpson himself, despite his back pain, was not allowed "special treatment," so he had to stick with a Steelcase 451 like all other defendants in that courtroom—Amber Veverka, "Lawyers Rest Case on Seating: Attorneys in the Simpson Trial Replace Their Steelcase Chairs," *Grand Rapids Press,* March 17, 1995, p. A1.

36. Lyon Metal Products advertising fact sheet, Aurora, Illinois, 1994. Thanks to Todd Yeomans for bringing this to my attention.

37. American Ergonomics Corporation flyer, " 'Continuous-Balance' Seat Solves Seated Worker Dilemma," Sausalito, California, 1990. Thanks to Christopher Jones for bringing this to my attention.

38. Nina L. Diamond, "From Outer Space to You: Turning NASA Research into a Concave Chair," *Omni,* vol. 16, no. 6 (March 1994), p. 24.

39. Jane and Michael Stern, *The Encyclopedia of Bad Taste* (New York: HarperPerennial, 1991), pp. 261–63.

40. Edward Tenner, "How the Chair Conquered the World," *Wilson Quarterly* (Spring 1997), pp. 64–70.

41. Stern and Stern, op. cit., p. 263.

42. Hanks, op. cit., p. 104.

43. Wing chairs with their high backs offer that sort of support, too, but they do not have the other advantages of rocking.

44. Dyer and Fraser, op. cit., concur, p. 72.

45. Nora Richter Greer, "Furnishings," *Architecture* (March 1984), p. 189.

46. Of those inventors who have attempted to turn the chair around from a health hazard to a health booster, probably none is more flamboyant than the "Japanese Edison," Dr. Yoshiro NakaMats, holder of over three thousand patents, including one for his "cerebrex chair," which bombards the sitter with alpha waves to stimulate intelligence and promote deep rest.

CHAPTER 6: BEYOND INTERIOR DESIGN

1. One of the "patterns" in Christopher Alexander, *The Pattern Language* (New York: Oxford University Press, 1979) specifies that each chair around a table should be different to reflect each personality.

2. Fin Biering-Sørensen, "A One-Year Prospective Study of Low Back Trouble in a General Population," *Danish Medical Bulletin,* vol. 32, no. 5 (October 1984), p. 373.

3. As a sociology graduate student interested in design, I had tried, unsuccessfully, to explore the artistic idea of intersecting planes when designing a "living complex" for a studio apartment. I built a large desk over a bed. After that I ran into a dilemma because I could not build bookshelves over the desk without it either looking too pragmatic (thereby losing the idea of multiple dimensions coming together) or not pragmatic enough to reach the shelves. I have since watched others with greater technical skill struggle with similar ideas about self-contained, complexes-in-lieu-of-furniture. I learned that the achievements of Gray and Loos were no mean feat.

4. Gesell cited in Glenn Doman, *What to Do About Your Brain-Injured Child* (Garden City, NY: Doubleday, 1974), p. 48.

5. Cited in *East West Center Magazine, Meetings with Remarkable Men and Women: Interviews with Leading Thinkers on Health, Medicine, Ecology, Culture, Society and Spirit* (Brookline, MA: East West Health Books, 1989). Thanks to Professor Lee Rivlin of CUNY for bringing this to my attention.

6. Ashley Montagu, in *Touching: The Human Significance of the Skin* (New York: Harper & Row, 1971), offers a social science and biological perspective, while Randolph Stone, in *Health Building* (Sebastopol, CA: CRCS Publications, 1985), offers a polarity therapy perspective on the therapeutic effects of touch, not only of the skin but also of the energy fields that encompass the body.

7. My brother and I have conceived of a bathtub that allows a person's head to rest while the spine lengthens without being flexed and nearly floats on the water.

8. When squatting, the angle between spine and thigh is much less than 90 degrees. In other contexts, this is a source of strain. But when squatting the spine isn't under compression as it is on a seat, so it can lengthen and stretch in both directions, which is good for it.

9. The heels are planted firmly on the ground, the weight equally distributed between right and left legs, and the thigh bones carried at about a 135-degree relation to the spine. This posture allows one to send the knees forward as a way to bend over without incurring one of three common but harmful patterns: (1) lock the knees and jut the pelvis forward; (2) arch the small of the back; or (3) thrust the neck forward and down. (From a somatic view point, years of this unacceptable posture produces the dowager's hump.)

10. Ubert, "Tilted Chairs and Desks Protect the Back."

11. An Italian female designer, Gini Boeri, designed an armchair in 1964 that included an ottoman, a built-in telephone, a notepad, a light, and a slanted reading stand on a swivel—Cini Boeri, "A Design Approach," *Ottagono,* 101 (December 1991), pp. 32–41.

12. The following books, among others, describe and analyze the use of the home as a locus for status display: Joan Kron, *Home-Psych: The Social Psychology of Home and Decoration* (New York: Clarkson N. Potter, 1983); T. Veblen, *Theory of the Leisure Class* (New York: Mentor Books, 1953); Mihaly Csikszentmihaly and Eugene Rochberg-Halton, *The Meaning of Things: Domestic Symbols and the Self* (New York: Cambridge University Press, 1981); and F. S. Chapin, *Contemporary American Institutions* (New York: Harper & Brothers, 1935).

13. Mandal, "The Correct Height of School Furniture," pp. 258–59.

14. Alexander teachers, from Alexander himself on, have tried to teach the Alexander Technique in grade schools, but the results have been uneven. In South Africa, they were opposed by those who wanted to institute traditional gymnastics; in England, his school had to close because of World War II; occasionally schoolteachers will try to pass on some of the techniques they have read about or learned. In any case, the absolute number of certified teachers is so small (even though the number has increased from 1,000 to 1,500 worldwide in the last ten years) that only a minuscule number of students will get this kind of training.

15. Anthony Jones, "A New Breed of Learning Environment Consultants," in Phillip S. Sleeman and D. M. Rockwell, eds., *Designing Learning Environments* (New York: Longman, 1981), pp. 48, 66.

16. Donna Huse, "Restructuring and the Physical Context: Redesigning Learning Environments," *Children's Environments,* vol. 12, no. 3 (1995), pp. 290–310.

17. Hart, personal communication, 1989; a journal devoted to the subject is *Children's Environments.*

18. Bacon, personal conference with the author, Nov. 30, 1985.

19. Bacon, "The New Paradigm for Teaching Design," a talk given on the occasion of the installation of Robert M. Beckley as dean of the College of Architecture and Planning, University of Michigan, Feb. 19, 1987.

20. Bianca Lepori, "Freedom of Movement in Birth Places," *Children's Environments,* vol. 11, no. 2 (1994), p. 87.

21. Vernon Alg, manager of aircraft interior engineering at Continental Airlines, has been supervising the redesign of their business-class seats since 1992 to include leg support, adjustable lumbar support, headrest "ears," and breathable upholstery. But what I experienced as most important is that they replaced their previous leather business-class seats with firmer and more planar seats and back cushions. American and United, the nation's two largest carriers, have recently redesigned their business-class seats; Delta, the third largest, may do so, and Virgin is considering a way to travel lying down; but I cannot confirm from experience that these redesigns use firmer and flatter seats and backs. The important change in seat configuration does not have to take up more space between the seats front to back (does not have to change the "pitch"), so I am waiting for improvements in coach class in any carrier. See David Cay Johnston, "Two Airlines Installing More Comfortable Seats," *New York Times,* Nov. 9, 1997.

22. Phyllis C. Richman, "For Want of a Chair; the Diner Was Lost: The Often Sad State of Restaurant Seating," *The Washington Post,* March 30, 1988, final edition. I would find it convenient to use the Berkeley Faculty Club room more often but for its captain chairs, with their backward-sloped seats and characteristically horseshoe-shaped backrests.

23. Cited in Joel Makower, "Designs for Working," *Review* (June 1983), p. 132.

24. See Edward T. Hall, *The Dance of Life: The Other Dimension of Time* (Garden City, NY: Anchor Press/Doubleday, 1983).

25. Takahashi, "Office Chair Encourages 'Active Sitting,' " *Wall Street Journal,* July 21, 1997, p. B1.

26. Grieco, "Sitting Posture: An Old Problem and a New One," p. 351. B. McPhee, "Deficiencies in the Ergonomic Design of Key-Board Work and Upper Limb and Neck Disorders in Operators," *Journal of Human Ergology,* 11 (1982), pp. 31–36.

27. Frank B. Gilbreth, "A Museum of Devices for the Elimination of Unnecessary Fatigue in the Industries," *Scientific American,* vol. 61, no. 20, Nov. 14, 1914, p. 411.

28. Mays, "The Ultimate Office Chair," p. 103.

29. Wolf Von Eckhardt, "A Chair with All the Angles," *Time,* Aug. 20, 1984, p. 97.

30. In the early 1980s, business analysts found that personal computers required the addition of 3.5 feet of desktop space per workstation. Without such additional space, they found, workers felt crowded, work was encumbered, and productivity dropped. So some planners advised adding 10 to 15 percent more space when computers were added. Other managers recommended, instead, redesigning the job to take into account the word processing or other computer work that will now be accomplished at the workstation. In that case, they found, individual computers could be accommodated in the same space used for non-computer functions, or even in a slightly smaller space. They warned, however, that integrating technology requires adequate training. But from our viewpoint what is interesting is that they are looking at the whole person–place–equipment complex—Armstrong, "CRT Impact in Office Design and Management," *Interiors* (August 1992).

31. Without this perception, lists of possible changes will be in vain. One of those do-and-don't lists is a guide to the homemade ergonomic office. Rather than asking their clients to spend a lot of money on specialized product solutions, Back Designs, Inc., in Berkeley, California, offers low-cost alternatives. An example of homemade ergonomic solutions: for an angled desk or copy-holder, prop a clipboard at an angle against a thick book. Taping the bottom edge of the clipboard to the desk makes it possible to slip the book back and forth to adjust the angle.

32. See Edward T. Hall, *The Silent Language* and *The Hidden Dimension* (both Garden City, NY: Doubleday, 1966). Social scientists have commented that lifeways are difficult to change because each feature is interconnected to all other features; some have described this as inertia, others as "lash up."

33. In terms of communication theory, commonplace furnishings like the chair have become so banal that they no longer convey a message. Their banality means that their primary denotative meaning has been assimilated and lost; but this frees them to take on new secondary meanings, usually connoting taste and status, as we saw in Part I— Martha Ourey, Larry Swartwood, and Allen Wallis, "Transformation in the Meaning of Objects," *Environmental Design Research Association Conference Proceedings,* Vol. 12 (1981), pp. 84–90.

34. Bob Baker and Martha Groves, "Judge Overturns SF's Landmark VDT Safety Law," *Los Angeles Times,* Feb. 14, 1992, p. D7; Bob Baker, "Sentencing Considers Law on VDT Safety," *Los Angeles Times,* Oct. 3, 1990, p. A3; Martha Groves, "VDT Safety Rules Backed by SF Board," *Los Angeles Times,* Dec. 11, 1990, p. A3.

35. Cranz, "The Chair Is Where the Body Meets the Environment," in Sontag, ed., *Curiosity Recaptured,* pp. 3–19.

36. Sebastian DeGrazia, *Of Time, Work and Leisure* (New York: Twentieth Century Fund, 1962).

37. As agents of social change, scholars vary in their directness. Provoking his readers to change was presumably the motivation behind Rudofsky's indignation that we do not realize that things could be different. One of the only other scholars in the specialty of human environment studies to have paid attention to chairs and their effects on culture is Amos Rapaport, an environmental design researcher with an anthropological background. In *House Form and Culture,* he described how the way people sit affects the form of houses. The introduction of the chair revolutionized living habits: by sitting on chairs rather than mats, "the need to take off shoes . . . would disappear, hence, also, the special covered space—porch or veranda—where they are taken off and left; the need for shoes which are easily taken off would be eliminated, and also the need for special floors. . . . The chair would also affect the sitting height, hence changing the placement and type of windows and the type of garden." Despite his attention to the subject, his style of scholarship is not imbued with the will to reform as was Rudofsky's (or my own). Instead, his style represents the first stage of change:

making us aware of practices that have slipped into unconsciousness—Amos Rapaport, *House Form and Culture* (Englewood Cliffs, NJ: Prentice-Hall, 1969), p. 63.

38. One furniture historian, John F. Pile, explains the rise of furniture as a response to the "desire to seek improved comfort through the use of inventions *rather* than through bodily training" (emphasis added)—*Modern Furniture* (New York: John Wiley, 1979), p. 26.

39. Even after years of Alexander training I still cannot rely on my training about how to use my body to overcome a harmful environment. If anything, I have become more sensitive to the stresses imposed by the environment. Thus, especially after body education, I have come to seek enabling furniture and equipment—and even clothes.

40. Quoted in Stewart, "Modern Designers Still Can't Make the Perfect Chair," p. 104.

41. "Gor Ratt Pa Gympan," *Tydningen Om Studentidrott,* Aug. 4, 1989, pp. 22–24.

42. University courses do not usually study physical sensation as a part of thinking and emotion. An exception is Donald Levine's course on sociological conflict theory and aikido at the University of Chicago. He describes it in Featherstone, ed., op. cit. One body-conscious designer and educator is Edmund Bacon, the city planner, who has studied both the Alexander Technique and Feldenkrais. His Alexander lessons informed his perspective on how a city like Rome was designed for the pedestrian point of view. He says that it is an "unmitigated crime that no architectural school sees the daily classroom experience as a laboratory for direct experience of design"—Bacon, "Bringing Us Back to our Senses," an address to the University of Michigan College of Architecture and Urban Planning, 1987. Bacon believes all education should include awareness of posture: "I get so angry when I teach a sixth grade and see the students slouching deep into their chairs. If they thumbed their noses at me, it would be no further insult"—Bacon, personal letter to the author, Nov. 22, 1989.

Another colleague, Donlyn Lyndon at the University of California-Berkeley, wrote an article addressed to architects and urban designers, offering "Five Ways to People Places," *Architectural Record* (September 1975), pp. 89–94. His Yale colleagues, Kent Bloomer and Charles Moore, wrote *Body, Memory, and Architecture* (New Haven: Yale University Press, 1977), which has been translated into several languages. This school of thought first suggests simply imagining inhabitants in a space, and then using seats, stairs, and colonnades in a design because they relate directly to the human body and imply its actions.

More recently I met Natalija Subotincia, a young architect at Carlton University in Ottawa, at a 1992 conference on "The Body and Design" sponsored by the technology section of the American Collegiate Schools of Architecture. Her presentation on the footbridge designs students produced in her studio attracted praise. When I asked her what in her own background made her so appreciative of the kinesthetic basis of design, she revealed that she had been a gymnast.

43. Hewes, op. cit., p. 132.

44. Kates, op. cit., p. 48, and FitzGerald, op. cit., pp. 71–72.

45. The Japanese still use the mats that were laid on top of the Chinese *k'ang* and run shoeless households, like those of the early Chinese. But now, as Japan is Westernizing, Japanese people have chairs and tables. Still, they often sit on the floor on occasions when there is a psychological advantage to doing so—appearing more family-like or cozy. (Visitors invited to sit on the floor with them should feel honored, for they are being invited to the figurative hearth.)—Hiromichi Terakado, "Sitting on the Floor versus Sitting on a Chair," *Journal of Human Ergology,* vol. 2, no. 1 (September 1973), pp. 91–92.

46. Pollack, "In a Painful Situation . . .", p. A2.

47. Linden (op. cit.) has independently noted the same link between body awareness and ecological awareness.

48. Remember I am an academic; I teach, write, supervise student research, and sometimes have research assistants working for me. I consult with organizations and architects on parking, housing, public art, sustainability, and urban design issues. As a scholar, I need quiet, change, social connection through phone and conference, filing, books, and dictaphone. I also run an Alexander practice for which I need a space for a stool, a massage table, a mirror, a grid for photographs of pupils' posture and alignment, and a stand-up surface for record keeping.

49. Of course we change music occasionally to avoid boredom. Alfred A. Tomatis, *The Conscious Ear: My Life of Transformation Through Listening* (Barrytown, NY: Station Hill Press, 1991). See also Tim Gilmore, Paul Madaule, and Billie Thompson, eds., *About the Tomatis Method* (Toronto: Listening Centre Press, 1989).

Bibliography

GENERAL

Abercrombie, Stanley. *A Philosophy of Interior Design.* New York: Harper & Row, 1990.

Alexander, F. M. *Constructive Conscious Control of the Individual.* London: Methuen, 1923.

———. *Man's Supreme Inheritance.* New York: Dutton, 1910.

Ames, Kenneth L. *Death in the Dining Room.* Philadelphia: Temple University Press, 1992.

Andersen, Kurt. "Looking Good Is Not Enough." *Time,* March 24, 1986, p. 88.

Andry de Bois-Regard, Nicolas. *Orthopaedia, or, The Art of Correcting and Preventing Deformities in Children.* Classics of Medicine Library Special Edition. Birmingham, AL, 1980.

Arias, P. E. *A History of 1000 Years of Greek Vase Painting.* New York: Abrams, 1962.

Arnold, Sue. "Sitting Comfortably?" *Observer Magazine,* June 23, 1985, p. 9.

Aronson, Joseph. *Encyclopedia of Furniture.* New York: Crown, 1938.

Auslander, Leora. "Historian Studies Furniture to Examine Change in Gender Roles." *Division of the Social Sciences Reports, University of Chicago,* no. 10 (Spring 1990), pp. 10–11.

———. *Taste and Power: Furnishing Modern France,* Berkeley, CA: University of California Press, 1996.

Baker, Hollis S. *Furniture in the Ancient World*. New York: Macmillan, 1966.

Banham, Reyner. *Modern Chairs 1918–70*. London: Victoria and Albert Museum, 1970.

Barlow, Wilfred. "Psychosomatic Problems in Postural Re-education." *The Lancet*, Sept. 24, 1955, pp. 659–64.

Bartenieff, Irmgard, with Dori Lewis. *Body Movement: Coping with the Environment*. Langhorne, PA: Gordon & Breach, 1980.

Bates, Elizabeth Bidwell, and J.L. Fairbanks. *American Furniture: 1620 to the Present*. New York: Richard Marek, 1981.

Becker, Franklin, and F. Steele. "Making Space for Teamwork." *Facilities Design & Management* (July 1995), pp. 56–59.

Beckman, Ronald. "Humble Beginnings, The Early Furniture of Eero Saarinen and Charles Eames." *Innovation* (Spring 1991), pp. 23–26.

Behbehani, Mandy. "Chair and Chair Alike." *San Francisco Examiner*, Sept. 18, 1988, Image section, pp. 2–6.

Bers, Joanna Smith. "Study Finds Cushioned Carpet Ergonomically Superior." *Facilities Design & Management* (September 1994), p. 43.

Blake, Peter. "Knoll." *AIA Journal* (April 1983), pp. 72–77.

Blake, Peter, and Jane Thompson. "A Very Significant Chair." *Architecture Plus* (May 1973), pp. 73–79.

Blakeslee, Sandra. "Complex and Hidden Brain in the Gut Makes Cramps, Butterflies and Valium." *New York Times*, Jan. 23, 1996, pp. B5–B10.

Bloomer, Kent, and Charles Moore. *Body, Memory, and Architecture*. New Haven: Yale University Press, 1977.

Boardman, John, J. Griffin, and O. Murray. *The Oxford History of the Classical World*. New York: Oxford University Press, 1986.

Bourdieu, Pierre. *Distinction: A Social Critique of the Judgment of Taste*. Cambridge, MA: Harvard University Press, 1984.

Braudel, Fernand. *The Structures of Everyday Life*. New York: Harper & Row, 1981.

Brill, Michael. *Using Office Design to Increase Productivity*. Vols. 1 and 2. Buffalo, NY: Workplace Design and Productivity, 1984.

Brink, Susan. "Smart Moves." *U.S. News & World Report*, May 15, 1995, pp. 76–83.

Bronson, Po. *Bombardiers*. New York: Random House, 1995.

Brown, Linda, and Deyan Sudjic. *The Modern Chair*. London: Institute of Contemporary Arts, 1988.

Brownmiller, Susan. "Locked Knees, the Debutante Slouch, Hair Twisting: The Contrived Postures of Femininity." *Femininity*. New York: Simon & Schuster, 1984.

Brutton, Mark. "Comfort." *Design,* 323 (November 1975), pp. 30–35.

Burke, O. M. *Among the Dervishes*. New York: E. P. Dutton, 1975.

Business Week. "Levitz: The Hot Name in 'Instant' Furniture." Dec. 4, 1971, pp. 90–93.

———. "A Glow on Unfinished Furniture." Apr. 6, 1981, pp. 121–25.

Byrne, John A. "Sittin' and Rockin'." *Forbes,* Nov. 7, 1983, p. 124.

Canetti, Elias. *Crowds and Power*. New York: Viking, 1962.

Caplan, Ralph. "How Chairs Behave." *Psychology Today* 17, no. 2 (February 1983), pp. 46–52.

Carbonaro, Simonetta. "The Office Cries and Asks for Freedom." Interview with Barbara Tietze, *Ufficiostile* (1989), pp. 82–93.

———. "The Chair and Its Sedative Effects." Interview with Hajo Eickhoff, *Ufficiostile* (1990), pp. 51–57.

———. "New Ergonomics Disagreements Between Old and New Ergonomic Concepts. The 'Floor Office' and Its Ergonomic Chair." *Ufficiostile,* Office Furniture Supplement, 10/90 (1991).

Chambers Edinburgh Journal. "Indian Handicrafts." Vol. 15, no. 387 (May 1851), pp. 342–45.

Chermayeff, Serge. "Art and the Industrial Designer." *Magazine of Art* 48 (February 1945), pp. 50–53.

Coghill, George Eliot. "Appreciation." In *Universal Constant in Living,* by F. M. Alexander. Long Beach, CA: Centerline Press, 1986, pp. xxi–xxviii.

Colani, Luigi. *For a Brighter Tomorrow*. Huntington Beach, CA: Kaneko Enterprises, 1981.

Commission de la Santé et de la Securité du travail du Quebec. *Good Posture at Work*. Quebec, 1983.

Conroy, Sarah Booth. *The Chair: Art or Architecture?* Washington, DC: American Institute of Architects Foundation, 1981.

Constant, Caroline. "The Nonheroic Modernism of Eileen Gray." *Journal of the Society of Architectural Historians* 53 (September 1954), pp. 265–79.

Consumer Reports. "Make Yourself Comfortable." May 1996, pp. 9, 34–37.

Cotton, Bernard. *The Chair in the North East Midlands.* Grimsby, UK: Lincolnshire County Council Recreational Services-Museums County Offices, 1987.

Cox, J. Charles. *English Church Furniture.* New York: E. P. Dutton, 1907, 2nd ed. with Alfred Harvey, 1908.

Cranz, Galen. *A New look at the Person in Person-Environment Relations: Theoretical Assumptions About the Body.* Berkeley, CA: Working Papers from the Center for Environmental Design Research, 1990.

———. "The Chair Is Where the Body Meets the Environment." In *Curiosity Recaptured,* edited by Jerry Sontag, San Francisco: Mornum Time Press, 1996, pp. 3–19.

Danto, Arthur. *397 Chairs.* New York: Abrams, 1988.

Dedera, Don. "New Directions: Upstanding Citizens Make the Case for the Vertical Desk." *America West Airlines Magazine* (May 1990), pp. 94–97.

Deetz, James. *In Small Things Forgotten.* Garden City, NY: Anchor Books, 1977.

De Giorgi, Monolo. "Peter Opsvik 1983–1985." *Domus* 689 (December 1987), pp. 76–79.

Deitz, Paula. "Twenty-Three Best Chairs Designed Since 1725." *Connoisseur* 221 (May 1991), pp. 58–63.

Della Corte, Evelyn. "The Chaise Longue." *Interior Design* (September 1985), pp. 254–59.

Design Quarterly, "A Serious Chair." 126 (1984).

Diamond, Nina. "Style: From Outer Space to You." *Omni* (1994), p. 24.

Diffrient, Niels, Alvin R. Tilley, and Joan C. Bardagjy. *Humanscale 1/2/3.* Cambridge, MA: MIT Press, 1974.

Ditlea, Steve. "Ergonomics: Designing to Fit Human Needs." *Hemispheres* (December 1992), pp. 45–46.

Doman, Glenn. *What to Do About Your Brain-Injured Child.* New York: Doubleday, 1974.

Donkin, Scott W. *Sitting on the Job: How to Survive the Stresses of Sitting Down to Work—A Practical Handbook.* Boston: Houghton Mifflin, 1989.

Duffy, Francis, and John Worthington. "Organizational Design." *Journal of Architectural Research* 6, no. 1 (March 1977), pp. 4–9.

Duffy, Francis, Andrew Laing, and Vic Crisp. *The Responsible Workplace: The Redesign of Work and Offices.* Oxford and Boston: Butterworth Architecture in association with Estates Gazette, 1993.

Dullea, Georgia. "What Women Want: Their Own Recliners." *New York Times,* Jan. 24, 1991, p. B1.

Dyer, Walter A., and Esther S. Fraser. *The Rocking Chair: An American Institution.* New York: The Century Co., 1928.

Eckardt, Wolf Von. "A Chair with All the Angles." *Time,* Aug. 20, 1984, p. 97.

The Economist. "British Furniture: Too Well Padded." Nov. 10, 1984, p. 81.

Eickhoff, Hajo. *Himmelsthron Und Schaukelstuhl.* Munich: Carl Hanser Verlag, 1993.

———. *Sitzen.* Frankfurt am Main: Anabas-Veri, 1997.

Emery, Marc. *Furniture by Architects.* New York: Abrams, 1988.

Encyclopaedia Americana. "Middle Ages." Vol. 4 (1994), p. 59.

Encyclopedia Britannica. "Furniture." Vol. 11 (1911), pp. 363–65.

Evans, Nancy Goyne. "The Genesis of the Boston Rocking Chair." *Antique* (January 1983), pp. 246–53.

Farkas, David. "Please Be Seated Properly." *Modern Office Technology* (October 1984), pp. 130–36.

Featherstone, Mike, M. Hepworth, and B. Turner, eds. *The Body: Social Process and Cultural Theory.* London: Sage, 1991.

Fehr, Michel, ed. *Fragments for a History of the Humam Body: Part Three.* New York: Urzone, distributed by MIT Press, 1989.

Field, Arthur. "How Humans Sit." *American Way,* Apr. 15, 1988, pp. 28–29.

Fiell, Charlotte, and Peter Fiell. *Modern Furniture Classics Since 1945.* London: Thames and Hudson, 1991.

———. *Modern Chairs.* New York: Perimeter, 1993.

FitzGerald, C. P. *Barbarian Beds: The Origin of the Chair in China.* London: Cresset, 1965.

Flanagan, Barbara. "The Office That (Almost) Does the Work for You." *Working Woman* (October 1990), pp. 112–15.

Fong-Torres, Ben. "Inclined to Recline." *San Francisco Chronicle,* Jan. 1, 1992, p. 1 (Z5).

Forty, Adrian. *Objects of Desire: Design and Society from Wedgwood to IBM.* New York: Pantheon, 1986.

Furniture Industry Research Association. "Anthropometric Data: Limitations in Use." *The Architects' Journal Information Library* (Feb. 6, 1963), pp. 316–25.

Garchik, Leah. "Working Toward a World Without Status." *San Francisco Chronicle,* Aug. 25, 1996, p. 2.

Giblin, James C. *Be Seated: A Book About Chairs.* New York: HarperCollins, 1993.

Giedion, Siegfried. *Mechanization Takes Command.* London: Oxford University Press, 1948.

Gilliatt, Mary. *Designing Rooms For Children.* Canada: Little, Brown & Co., 1984.

Gilman, Naomi. "The Chair and the Contemporary Artist." In *American Chairs: Form, Function and Fantasy.* Sheboygan, WI: John Michael Kohler Arts Center of the Sheboygan Arts Foundation, 1978.

Gimbutas, Marija. *The Language of the Goddess.* New York: HarperCollins, 1989.

———. *The Civilization of the Goddess: The World of Old Europe.* New York: Harper-Collins, 1991.

Gloag, John. *Time, Taste and Furniture.* London: F. A. Stokes, 1955.

———. *The Englishman's Chair; Origins, Design and Social History of Seat Furniture in England.* London: Allen & Unwin, 1964.

———. *A Social History of Furniture Design: From B.C. 1300 to A.D. 1960.* New York: Crown, 1966.

Golin, Mark. "Working with Your 9-to-5 Chair." *Prevention* (April 1996), pp. 167–70.

Gordon, Glen. "Design a Chair That Fits like a Glove." *Fine Woodworking* (September/October 1992), pp. 88–93.

Graham, Claire. *Ceremonial and Commemorative Chairs in Great Britain.* London: Victoria & Albert Museum, 1994.

Grandjean, Etienne. *Fitting the Task to the Man.* London: Taylor & Francis, 1980.

Greenberg, Allan. "Design Paradigms in the Eighteenth and Twentieth Centuries." In *Ornament, Via III: The Journal of the Graduate School of Fine Arts,* University of Pennsylvania, 1977.

Grieco, A. "Sitting Posture: An Old Problem and a New One." *Ergonomics* 29, no. 3 (1986), pp. 345–62.

Grier, Katherine C. *Culture and Comfort: People, Parlors, and Upholstery, 1859–1930*. Rochester, NY: Strong Museum, 1988.

Hall, Edward T. "The Language of Space." *AIA Journal* (February 1961), pp. 71–74.

———. *The Hidden Dimension*. Garden City, NY: Doubleday, 1966.

———. *The Silent Language*. Garden City, NY: Doubleday, 1966.

Hanks, David A. *Innovative Furniture in America from 1800 to the Present*. New York: Horizon Press, 1981.

Hanna, Thomas. *The Body of Life*. New York: Knopf, 1980.

Harris, David A., et al. *Planning and Designing the Office Environment*. New York: Van Nostrand Reinhold, 1981.

Hewes, Gordon W. "The Anthropology of Posture." *Scientific American* 196, no. 2 (February 1957), pp. 122–32.

Hoffman, Marilyn. "Motion Furniture." *Christian Science Monitor,* June 21, 1981, p. 25.

———. "Comfortable, Luxurious Leather Furniture for the Home." *Christian Science Monitor,* Aug. 3, 1983, p. 17.

———. "KD: Knock-Down Furniture Delivers Simplicity and Practicality." *Christian Science Monitor,* Sept. 26, 1984, pp. 25–26.

———. "Scandinavia Goes International." *Christian Science Monitor,* May 23, 1986, pp. 27–28.

———. "Cast in Stone." *Christian Science Monitor,* June 6, 1986, p. 27.

Hogben, Carol. Introduction to *Modern Chairs 1918–1970*. London: Whitechapel Art Gallery, 1970.

Huse, Donna. "Restructuring and the Physical Context: Redesigning Learning Environments." *Children's Environment* 12, no. 3 (1995), pp. 290–310.

Hwang, Suein L. "Coffee, Tea—or Maybe Gatorade? Lufthansa Provides Aerobics Aloft." *Wall Street Journal,* April 7, 1992, p. B1.

Janjigan, Robert. *High Touch*. New York: Running Heads, 1987.

Jevnaker, Birgit Helene. "Make the World a Better Place to Sit In!" *Design Management Journal* (Fall 1991), pp. 48–54.

Johnson, Don. *The Body*. Boston: Beacon Press, 1983.

———. *Body: Recovering Our Sensual Wisdom*. Berkeley, CA: North Atlantic Books, 1992.

————, ed. *Groundworks: Narratives of Embodiment.* Berkeley, CA: North Atlantic Books, 1997.

Johnson, Peter. *The Phillips Guide to Chairs.* London: Merehurst Press, 1989.

Johnston, David Cay. "Two Airlines Installing More-Comfortable Seats." *New York Times,* Nov. 9, 1997, p. TR3.

Jones, Anthony S. "A New Breed of Learning Environment Consultants." In *Designing Learning Environments,* Phillip Sleeman and D. M. Rockwell, eds. New York: Longman, 1981.

The Journal of the Furniture History Society. "Seating." 1977, pp. 178–215.

Joyce, Marilyn. "Ergonomics Offers Solutions to Numerous Health Complaints." *Occupational Health & Safety* (April 1988), pp. 58–66.

Juhan, Deane. *Job's Body: A Handbook for Bodywork.* Barrytown, NY: Station Hill Press, 1987.

Kane, Patricia E. *300 Years of American Seating Furniture.* Boston: New York Graphic Society, 1976.

Kates, George N. *Chinese Household Furniture.* New York: Harper & Brothers, 1948.

Kira, Alexander. *The Bathroom.* New York: Viking, 1976.

Kirkby, Ron. "The Probable Reality Behind Structural Integration—How Gravity Supports the Body." Boulder, CO: The Rolf Institute of Structural Integration, ca. 1980.

Kita, Toshiyuki. *Movement as Concept.* Japan: Rikuyo-sha Pub., 1990.

Kjaer, Bodil. "Everyday Furniture of the People of China." *Mobilia,* no. 291 (1980), pp. 41–45.

Kleeman, Walter B. "The Future of the Office." *Environment and Behavior* 14, no. 5 (September 1982), pp. 593–610.

————. *The Challenge of Interior Design.* New York: Van Nostrand Reinhold, 1983.

Kleeman, Walter B., et al. *Interior Design of the Electronic Office.* New York: Van Nostrand Reinhold, 1991.

Knoebel, Lawrence. *Office Furniture: Twentieth Century Design,* New York: E. P. Dutton, 1987.

Konar, E., et al. "Status Demarcation in the Office." *Environment and Behavior* 14, no. 5 (September 1982), pp. 561–80.

Kotzsch, Ronald. "The Alexander Technique." *East West* (October 1990), pp. 34–42.

Kron, Joan. *Homepsych.* New York: Potter, 1983.

Larkin, Jack. *The Reshaping of Everyday Life, 1790–1840.* New York: Harper & Row, 1988.

Larmer, Brook. "Wizardry in WC." *Christian Science Monitor,* Sept. 6, 1985, pp. 18–19.

Lepori, Bianca. "Freedom of Movement in Birth Places." *Children's Environments* 11, no. 2 (1994), pp. 81–87.

Levitch, Gerald. "Sitting Ergonomically Pretty." *Toronto Globe and Mail,* April 13, 1995, p. D5.

Linden, Paul. "Somatic Literacy: Bringing Somatic Education into Physical Education." *Journal of Physical Education, Recreation and Dance* (September 1994), pp. 15–21.

———. *Compute in Comfort: Body Awareness Training: a Day-to-Day Guide to Pain-Free Computing.* New York: Prentice Hall, 1995.

Louie, Elaine. "The Many Lives of an Important and Very Common Chair." *New York Times,* Feb. 7, 1991, p. B5.

Lucie-Smith, Edward. *Furniture: a Concise History.* New York: Thames and Hudson, 1990.

Lupton, Ellen. *Mechanical Brides.* New York: Cooper Hewitt National Museum of Design, 1993.

Lupton, Ellen, and J. A. Miller. *The Bathroom, the Kitchen, and the Aesthetics of Waste— A Process of Elimination.* Cambridge, MA: MIT List Visual Arts Center, 1992.

Maisel, Edward. *The Alexander Technique: The Essential Writings of F. Matthias Alexander.* New York: Carol Publishing Group, 1990.

Makower, Joel. "Designs for Working." *Review* (June 1983), pp. 131–35.

Mandal, A. C. *The Seated Man (Homo Sedens).* Klampenborg, Denmark: Daphne Press, ca. 1984.

Margolies, Jane. "The Comfort of Home." *House Beautiful* (October 1992), pp. 40–44.

Mays, Vernon. "P/A Technics. The Ultimate Office Chair." *Progressive Architecture* (May 1988), pp. 98–103.

McCloud, Mary. "Furniture and Femininity." *Architectural Review* 181 (January 1987), pp. 43–47.

Metzger, Bruce M., and Michael D. Coogan, eds. "Furniture." In *Oxford Companion to the Bible.* New York: Oxford University Press, 1993.

Miller, Nory. "Machines à s'asseoir." *Progressive Architecture* (May 1980), pp. 126–31.

Montagu, Ashley. *Touching: The Human Significance of the Skin.* New York: Harper & Row, 1971.

Murphy, Michael. *The Future of the Body: Explorations into the Further Evolution of Human Nature.* Los Angeles: J. P. Tarcher, 1992.

Neuhart, John, Marilyn Neuhart, and Ray Eames. *Eames Design: The Work of the Office of Charles and Ray Eames.* New York: Abrams, 1989.

Oates, Phyllis B. *The Story of Western Furniture.* New York: Harper & Row, 1981.

Ostergard, Derek E. *Mackintosh to Mollino: Fifty Years of Chair Design.* New York: Barry Friedman, Ltd., 1984.

Oury, Mary Anne, et al. "Transformation in the Meaning of Objects." EDRA (Environmental Design Research Association Conference Proceedings) 12 (1981), pp. 84–90.

Overton, Sharon. "Recliners Roar out of the Den." *Baltimore Sun,* Mar. 26, 1995, pp. 1K, 3K.

Papathanasopoulos, G. *Neolithic and Cycladic Civilization.* Athens: National Archaeological Museum, 1981.

Patinkin, Mark. "It's My La-Z-Boy Recliner and It's Staying Put." *Providence Journal,* Sept. 22, 1994, Lifebeat section, p. 2F.

Pearson, Emily Lee. *Elizabethans at Home.* Stanford, CA: Stanford University Press, 1957.

Perreault, John. "The Art That Would Be Life." *Village Voice,* June 4, 1988, pp. 32–34.

Petroski, Henry. *The Evolution of Everyday Things.* New York: Knopf, 1992.

Pevsner, Nicholas. "The Evolution of the Easy Chair." *The Architectural Review* (March 1942), pp. 59–62.

Pfaff, Carolyn. "IKEA: The Supermarket of Furniture Stores." *Adweek,* May 5, 1986, p. M.M.26.

Pierson, John. "Sculpted Chairs Offer Solid Support." *Wall Street Journal,* Apr. 10, 1992, p. B1.

———. "Stand Up and Listen: Your Chair May Harm Your Health." *Wall Street Journal,* Sept. 12, 1995, pp. B1, B5.

Pile, John F. *Modern Furniture.* New York: John Wiley, 1979.

———. *Furniture, Modern + Postmodern, Design + Technology.* New York: John Wiley, 1990.

Pitt, Leonard. "The Grounding of America." *Somatics* 6, no. 2 (Spring/Summer 1987), pp. 5–9.

Pollack, Andrew. "In a Painful Situation, Japanese Choose Chairs." *New York Times,* Aug. 25, 1995, p. A2.

Prathpaditya, Pal, and Vidya Denejia. *From Merchants to Emperors: British Artists and India, 1757–1930.* Ithaca, NY: Cornell University Press, 1986.

Pye, David. *The Nature of Design.* New York: Reinhold Publishing, 1964.

Rapaport, Amos. *House Form and Culture.* Englewood Cliffs, NJ: Prentice-Hall, 1969.

Rebsjohn-Gibbings, T.H. *Goodbye, Mr. Chippendale.* New York: Knopf, 1944.

Roaf, Robert. "In Support of Good Posture." *Saturday Evening Post* (November 1982), pp. 14–15.

Roalman, Suzann. "Sitting Still, Not Exercise, Gives Us Pain." Letter to the editor, *New York Times,* Sept. 17, 1991, p. A20.

Rudofsky, Bernard. *Now I Lay Me Down to Eat.* New York: Anchor Books, 1980.

Rybczynski, Witold. *Home: The Short History of an Idea.* New York: Viking, 1986.

Rykwert, Joseph. "The Sitting Position—A Question of Method." In *Meaning in Architecture,* C. Jencks and G. Baird, eds. New York: George Braziller, 1969, pp. 233–43.

Saarinen, Aline B., ed. *Eero Saarinen on His Work.* New Haven and London: Yale University Press, 1962.

Saeks, Diane Dorrans. "Sitting Pretty." *San Francisco Chronicle,* June 26, 1996, pp. 1, 6 Z1.

Salonen, Armas. *Die Mobel des Alten Mesopotamien (The Furniture of Ancient Mesopotamians).* Helsinki: Suomalainen Tiedeakatemia, 1963.

Sarno, John. *Mind Over Back Pain.* New York: Berkeley Publishing Group, 1986.

Scarry, Elaine. *The Body in Pain: The Making and Unmaking of the World.* New York: Oxford University Press, 1985.

Schatzman, Morton. *Soul Murder: Persecution in the Family.* New York: Random House, 1973.

Scully, Vincent. *New World Visions of Household Gods and Sacred Places: American Art and the Metropolitan Museum, 1650–1914*. Boston: Little, Brown, 1988.

Sennett, Richard. *Flesh and Stone: The Body and the City in Western Civilization*. New York: W. W. Norton, 1994.

Shumake, Glynn. *Increasing Productivity and Profit in the Workplace*. New York: John Wiley, 1992.

Sieber, Roy. *African Furniture and Household Objects*. Bloomington, IN: Indiana University Press, 1980.

Sizer, Alvin V. "Of Course We Can Build a Better Wheelchair." *New Haven Register,* May 7, 1995, p. D2.

————. "Work Continues on a Better Wheelchair." *New Haven Register,* Sept. 22, 1996, p. D2.

Slavin, Maeve. "Retro-Perspectives." *Interiors* 143, no. 10 (May 1984), pp. 222–27.

Slesin, Susan. "Chairs With Flair: Bold European Shapes." *San Francisco Chronicle,* Oct. 1, 1984, p. C1.

Sloan's Architectural Review and Builders' Journal. "Chairs, Settles, Pews, Forms, Stools, and Seats Generally." July 1868, pp. 38–44.

Stedman, Nancy. "Getting Straight." *Health* (November 1985), pp. 65–67.

Stellman, Jeanne M. "Finding a Chair That Fits." *Occupational Health & Safety* (January 1981), pp. 43–44.

Stewart, Doug. "Modern Designers Still Can't Make the Perfect Chair." *Smithsonian* (April 1986), pp. 97–104.

————. "One Man's Private Cache Pays Off for the Rest of Us." *Smithsonian* 25, no.11 (February 1995), pp. 103–10.

Success. "Profiting from Pain." January/February 1996, p. 8.

Sudjic, Deyan. "A Survey of the 20th Century Chair." In *A Catalogue of Modern Chair Design: Chairs from the "Sit" Exhibition, 22–24 March 1982 and the People Who Sat on Them*. London: IBA Magazine, 1982.

Sundstrom, Eric D. *Work Places: the Psychology of the Physical Environment in Offices and Factories*. Cambridge and New York: Cambridge University Press, 1986.

Takahashi, Corey. "Office Chair Encourages 'Active Sitting.' " *Wall Street Journal,* July 21, 1997, pp. B1, B7.

Taylor, Anne. "How Schools Are Redesigning Their Space." *Educational Leadership* (September 1993), pp. 36–41.

Tenner, Edward. *Why Things Bite Back.* New York: Knopf, 1996.

———. "The Life of Chairs." *Harvard Magazine* 99, no. 3 (January/February 1997), pp. 46–53.

———. "How the Chair Conquered the World." *Wilson Quarterly* 21, no. 2 (Spring 1997), pp. 64–70.

———. "How the Chair Conquered the World." *Whole Earth* (Summer 1997), pp. 54–58.

Terakado, Hiromichi. "Sitting on the Floor vs. Sitting on a Chair." *Journal of Human Ergology* 2, no. 1 (September 1973), pp. 91–92.

Teyssot, George. "The Disease of the Domicile." *Assemblage* 6 (1988), pp. 73–97.

Thompson, Elspeth. "The Bottom Line." *The Guardian* (U. K.), Nov. 20, 1991, p. 37.

Tillim, Sidney. "Designer Go Home: 'High Styles' at the Whitney." *Art in America* (March 1986), pp. 17–25.

Time-Life Books. *Living Spaces for Children.* Alexandria, VA: 1988.

Tracy, Eleanor Johnson. "Shopping Swedish-Style Comes to the U.S." *Fortune,* Jan. 20, 1986, p. 63.

Trollope, Mrs. *Domestic Manners of the Americans,* vol. 2. London: Whitaker, Treacher & Co., 1832.

Veverka, Amber. "Lawyers Rest Case on Seating: Attorneys in the Simpson Trial Replace Their Steelcase Chairs." *Grand Rapids Press,* Mar. 17, 1995, p. A1.

Viaux, Jacqueline, and Hazel Paget. *French Furniture.* New York: G. P. Putnam, 1964.

Viladas, Pilar. "The Risk Factor." *Progressive Architecture* (May 1988), pp. 74–81.

Von Eckardt, Wolf. "A Chair With All the Angles." *Time,* Aug. 20, 1984, p. 97.

Ward, Gerald W. R. *Perspectives on American Furniture.* New York: W. W. Norton, 1988.

Whiteley, Nigel. "Semi-Works of Art (Consumerism, Youth Culture and Chair Design in the 1960's)." *Journal of the Furniture History Society* 23, Nov. 17, 1987, pp. 108–26.

Wilford, John Noble. "Skeletons Record the Burdens of Work." *New York Times,* Oct. 27, 1987, pp. C1, C9.

Wilmott, Elizabeth. "The Body as Constructed Art." *The Structurist* 23/24 (1983–84), pp. 64–66.

Winick, Charles, and Herbert Holt. "Seating Position as Nonverbal Communication in Group Analysis." *Psychiatry* 24, no. 2 (May 1961), pp. 171–82.

Yee, Roger. "Slouching Towards Barcelona." *Progressive Architecture* (May 1975), pp. 78–85.

Zeldin, Theodore. *An Intimate History of Humanity.* New York: HarperCollins, 1994.

Zelinsky, Marilyn. "Finally Stress Free: Reclining Office Seating." *Interiors* 150 (November 1991), p. 34.

Zike, Debbie. " 'The Chairs' Will Remain." *Rockridge News,* Dec. 16, 1995, p. 5.

SPECIALIZED WORKS ON ERGONOMICS

Akerblom, Bengt. *Standing and Sitting Posture with Special Reference to the Consideration of Chairs.* Stockholm: Karolinska Instituter, 1948.

———. "Chairs and Sitting." *Ergonomics Research Society Proceedings,* W. F. Floyd and A. T. Weford, eds., vol. 2: *Human Factors in Equipment Design.* London: H. K. Lewis & Co., 1954, pp. 29–35.

———. "Anatomische und Physiologische Grundlagen zur Gestaltung von Sitzen." *Ergonomics* 12, no. 2 (1969), pp. 120–31.

Alexander, Colin James. "Chair-Sitting and Varicose Veins." *The Lancet* 1, no. 7753, Apr. 15, 1972, pp. 822–24.

Andersson, G. B. J. "The Load on the Lumbar Spine in Sitting Postures." *Department of Orthopaedic Surgery, Sahlgren Hospital,* Goteborg, Sweden, 1980, pp. 231–39.

———. "Epidemiologic Aspects on Low Back Pain in Industry." *Spine* 6 (1981), pp. 53–60.

———. "Posture and Compressive Spine Loading: Intradiscal Pressures, Trunk Myoelectric Activities, Intra-abdominal Pressures, and Biochemical Analyses." *Ergonomics* 28, no. 1 (1985), pp. 91–93.

Andersen, G. B. J., et al. "Lumbar Disc Pressure and Myoelectric Back Muscle Activity During Sitting." *Scandanavian Journal of Rehabilitation Medicine* 6 (1974), pp. 104–14.

Andersson, G. B. J., R. Ortengren, and A. Nachemeson. "Disc Pressure Measurements

When Rising and Sitting Down on a Chair." *Engineering in Medicine* 11, no. 4 (1982), pp. 189–90.

Arborelius, Ulf P., et al. "The Effects of Armrests and High Seat Height on Lower-Limb Joint Load and Muscular Activity During Sitting and Rising." *Ergonomics* 35, no. 11 (1992), pp. 1377–91.

Armstrong, David L. "CRT Impact in Office Design and Management." *Interiors* (August 1982), p. 12.

Astrand, Per-Olof, and Kaare Rodahl. *Textbook of Work Physiology.* New York: McGraw-Hill, 1986.

Ayoub, M. M. "Work Place Design and Posture." *Human Factors* 15, no. 3 (1973), pp. 265–68.

Barkla, D. M. "The Estimation of Body Measurements of British Population in Relation to Seat Design." *Ergonomics* 4, no. 2 (1961), pp. 123–32.

———. "Chair Angles, Duration of Sitting and Comfort Ratings." *Ergonomics* 7, no. 3 (1964), pp. 297–304.

Barlow, Wilfred. "Psychosomatic Problems in Postural Re-education." *The Lancet,* Sept. 24, 1955, pp. 659–64.

Bendix, Tom. "An Evaluation of a Tiltable Office Chair with Respect to Seat Height, Backrest Position and Task." *European Journal of Applied Physiology* 55 (1986), pp. 30–36.

———. "Adjustment of the Seated Workplace—with Special Reference to Heights and Inclinations of Seat and Table." *Danish Medical Bulletin* 34, no. 3 (1987), pp. 125–37.

Bendix, Tom, et al. "What Does a Backrest Actually Do to the Lumbar Spine?" *Ergonomics* 39, no. 4 (1996), pp. 533–42.

Bendix, Tom, Jorgen Winkel, and Flemming Jessen. "Comparison of Office Chairs with Fixed Forwards or Backwards Inclining, or Tiltable Seats." *European Journal of Applied Physiology* 54 (1985), pp. 378–85.

Bennett, D. L., et al. "Comparison of Integrated Electromyographic Activity and Lumbar Curvature During Standing and During Sitting in Three Chairs." *Physical Therapy* 69, no. 11 (November 1989), pp. 902–13.

Berglund, Erik. *Sittmoblers Matt: The Dimensions of Seating Furniture.* Stockholm: Mobelinstitutet, 1988.

SPECIALIZED WORKS ON ERGONOMICS

Berquet, K. H., and H. W. Jurgens. "Basic Dimensions of School Furniture." *Das öffentliche Gesundheitswesen* 34 (1972), pp. 51–56.

Bex, F. H. A. "Desk heights." *Applied Ergonomics* 2, no. 3 (September 1971), pp. 138–40.

Biering-Sorensen, Fin. "A One-Year Prospective Study of Low Back Trouble in a General Population." *Danish Medical Bulletin* 31, no. 5 (October 1984), pp. 362–73.

Branton, P. "Behaviour, Body Mechanics, and Discomfort." *Ergonomics* 12, no. 2 (1969), pp. 316–27.

———. "Backshapes of Seated Persons: How Close Can the Interface Be Designed?" *Applied Ergonomics* 15, no. 2 (1984), pp. 105–7.

Bridger, Robert S. "Postural Adaptations to a Sloping Chair and Work Surface." *Human Factors* 30, no. 2 (1988), pp. 237–47.

Burandt, Ulrich, and Etienne Grandjean. "Sitting Habits of Office Employees." *Ergonomics* 6 (1963), pp. 217–28.

Cailliet, Rene. *Neck and Arm Pain,* 3rd ed. The Pain Series. Philadelphia: F. A. Davis Co., 1991.

Canter, David. "Office Size: An Example of Psychological Research in Architecture." *Architects' Journal Information Library* 24 (April 1968), pp. 881–88.

Cohen, Aaron, and Elaine Cohen. "Ergonomics and the Electronic Office." *Architectural Record* 170 (September 1982), pp. 45–46.

Cornell, Paul. *The Biomechanics of Sitting,* 2nd ed. Grand Rapids, MI: Steelcase, 1989.

Croney, John. *Anthropometrics for Designers.* New York: Van Nostrand Reinhold, 1971.

Damon, Albert, Howard W. Stoudt, and Ross A. McFarland. *The Human Body in Equipment Design.* Cambridge, MA: Harvard University Press, 1966.

Dehlin, O., and S. Berg. "Back Symptoms and the Psychology of Perception of Work." *Scandinavian Journal of Rehabilitation Medicine* 9 (1977), pp. 61–65.

De Wall, M., et al. "The Effect on Sitting Posture of a Desk with a 10 Degree Inclination for Reading and Writing." *Ergonomics* 34, no. 5 (1991), pp. 575–84.

Dhesi, J. K., and F. M. Firebaugh. "The Effects of Stages of Chapati Making and Angles of Body Position on Heart Rate." *Ergonomics* 16, no. 6 (1973), pp. 811–15.

Diebschlag, W., and W. Muller-Limmroth. "Physiological Requirements on Car Seats: Some Results of Experimental Studies." In *Human Factors in Transport Research,*

D. J. Oborne and J. A. Levis, eds., vol. 2: *User Factors: Comfort, the Environment and Behaviour.* New York: Academic Press, 1980, pp. 223–30.

Donkin, Scott W. *Sitting on the Job.* Boston: Houghton Mifflin, 1989.

Dossey, Larry. "Work and Health: Of Isolation, Sisyphus, and Barbarian Beds." *Alternative Therapies* 3, no. 1 (January 1997), pp. 8–14.

Drury, C. G., and M. Francher. "Evaluation of a Forward-Sloping Chair." *Applied Ergonomics* 10, no. 1 (1985), pp. 41–47.

Eastman, M. C., and E. Kamon. "Posture and Subjective Evaluation at Flat and Slanted Desks." *Human Factors* 18, no. 1 (1976), pp. 15–26.

Eklund, Jorgen. "Industrial Seating and Spinal Loading." Ph.D. thesis, University of Nottingham, Department of Production Engineering and Production Management, October 1986.

Elftman, Herbert. "Body Dynamics and Dynamic Anthropometry." *Annals of New York Academy of Sciences* 63 (November 1955), pp. 553–85.

Ericson, Mats O., and Ian Goldie. "Spinal Shrinkage with Three Different Types of Chair Whilst Performing Video Display Unit Work." *International Journal of Industrial Ergonomics* 3 (1989), pp. 177–83.

Farkas, David L. "Please Be Seated, Properly." *Modern Office Technology* (October 1984), pp. 130–36.

Felding, P., N. Tryding, and P. Hyltoft Petersen. "Effects of Posture on Concentrations of Blood Constituents in Healthy Adults: Practical Application of Blood Specimen Collection Procedures Recommended by the Scandinavian Committee on Reference Values." *Scandinavian Journal of Clinical Laboratory Investigation* 40 (1980), pp. 615–21.

Floyd, W. F. "Postural Factors in the Design of Motor Car Seats." *Proceedings of Royal Society of Medicine* 60 (October 1967), pp. 953–57.

Floyd, W. F., and D. F. Roberts. "Anatomical and Physiological Principles in Chair and Table Design." *Ergonomics* 2, no.1 (1958), pp. 1–16.

Floyd, W. F., and Joan S. Ward. "Posture of Schoolchildren and Office Workers." *Proceedings of the Second International Congress on Ergonomics, Dortmund.* London: Taylor & Francis, 1964, pp. 351–60.

—————. "Anthropometric and Physiological Considerations in School, Office and Factory Seating." *Ergonomics* 12, no. 2 (1969), pp. 132–39.

Garlick, David G. "General Outlook." *Direction* 1, no. 4 (1988), pp. 118–19.

Garrett, J. T., et al. "The Industrial Back Problem: Role of the Industrial Hygienist and Ergonomics." *American Industrial Hygiene Association Journal* 38 (October 1977), pp. 560–62.

Gilbreth, Frank B. "A Museum of Devices for the Elimination of Unnecessary Fatigue in the Industries." *Scientific American* 61, no. 20, Nov. 14, 1914, p. 411.

Gilula, Louis A. "Degenerative Disease and Injury of the Back." *Occupational Health and Safety* (January 1981), pp. 14–19.

Gorman, John. *The Cause of Lumbar Back Pain and the Solution.* Eversley, UK: John Gorman, 1983.

Grandjean, Etienne. "Body Posture." *Ergonomics Supplement: Proceedings of the Second International Congress on Ergonomics, Dortmund.* London: Taylor & Francis, 1964, pp. 283–94.

———. "Fatigue." *American Industrial Hygiene Association Journal* 3, no. 4 (1970), pp. 101–11.

———. "Fitting the Task to the Man: An Ergonomic Approach." London: Taylor & Francis, 1980.

———. "Sitting Posture of Car Drivers from the Point of View of Ergonomics." In *Human Factors in Transport Research,* D. J. Oborne and J. A. Levis, eds., vol. 2: *User Factors: Comfort, the Environment and Behaviour.* New York: Academic Press, 1980, pp. 205–13.

Grandjean, E., A. Boni, and H. Kretzschmar. "Development of a Rest Chair Profile for Healthy and Notalgic People." *Ergonomics* 12, no. 2 (1969), pp. 307–15.

Grandjean, Etienne, W. Hunting, G. Wotzka, and R. Scharer. "An Ergonomic Investigation of Multipurpose Chairs." *Human Factors* 15, no. 3 (1973), pp. 247–55.

Grieco, A. "Sitting Posture: An Old Problem and a New One." *Ergonomics* 29, no. 3 (1986), pp. 345–62.

Grimsrud, T. M. "Humans Were Not Created to Sit—and Why You Have to Refurnish Your Life." *Ergonomics* 33, no. 3 (1990), pp. 291–95.

Gross, George A. "Preventing Low Back Pain." In *Preventing Disease,* R. B. Goldbloom and R. S. Lawrence, eds. New York: Springer-Verlag, 1990.

Habsburg, S., and L. Middendorf. "Calibrating Comfort: Systematic Studies of Human Responses to Seating." In *Human Factors in Transport Research,* Oborne and Levis, eds., vol. 2: *User Factors: Comfort, the Environment and Behaviour.* New York: Academic Press, pp. 214–22.

Hansen, Jens Aagaard, and A. S. Paulsen. "A Comparative Study of Three Different Kinds of School Furniture." *Ergonomics* 38, no. 5 (1995), pp. 1025–35.

Harris, Gerald F., et al. "A Method for the Display of Balance Platform Center of Pressure Data." *Biomechanics* 15, no. 10 (1982), pp. 741–45.

Hertzberg, H. T. E. "Some Contributions of Applied Physical Anthropology to Human Engineering." *Annals of New York Academy of Sciences* 63 (November 1955), pp. 616–29.

———. "Dynamic Anthropometry of Working Positions." *Human Factors* 2 (August 1960), pp. 147–55.

———. "The Human Buttocks in Sitting: Pressures, Patterns, and Palliatives." *Society of Automotive Engineers Journal (Transactions)* 81, no. 720005 (1972), pp. 39–47.

Hertzberger, Herman. "Central Beheer Offices, Apeldorn, Holland." *Architects' Journal* 29 (October 1975), pp. 893–904.

Hettinger, T. "Occupational Hazards Associated With Diseases of the Skeletal System." *Ergonomics* 28, no. 1 (1985), pp. 69–75.

Hirsch, Jules, et al. "Heart Rate Variability as a Measure of Autonomic Function During Weight Change in Humans." *American Journal of Physiology: Regulatory, Integrative and Comparative Physiology* 30, no. 6 (December 1991), pp. R1418–23.

Hockenberry, Jack. "A Systems Approach to Long Term Task Seating Design." In *Anthropometry and Biomechanics, Theory and Applications,* Ronald Easterby, K. H. E. Kroemer, and Don B. Chaffin, eds. New York: Plenum Press, 1982.

Hosea, Timothy M., et al. "Myoelectric Analysis of the Paraspinal Musculature in Relation to Automobile Driving." *Spine* 11, no. 9 (1986), pp. 928–36.

Hunting, W., T. Laubli, and E. Grandjean. "Postural and Visual Loads at VDT Workplaces: I. Constrained Postures." *Ergonomics* 24, no. 12 (1981), pp. 917–31.

Jacobs, Martin D. "A Review of the Development of an Ergonomically Balanced Chair." *Journal of Manipulative and Physiological Therapeutics* 10, no. 6 (December 1987), pp. 335–36.

Japsen, Bruce. "Addressing Ergonomics: A Pain in the Neck, and Wrist, and Shoulder." *Ergonomics* (March 1995), pp. 33–36.

Jevnaker, B. H. "Make the World a Better Place to SIT IN." *Design Management Journal* (Fall 1991), pp. 48–54.

Johnson, Arthur T. *Biomechanics and Exercise Physiology.* New York: John Wiley, 1991.

Jones, J. C. "Anthropometric Data: Limitations in Use." *Architects' Journal Information Library* 6 (February 1963), pp. 316–25.

———. "Methods and Results of Seating Research." *Ergonomics* 12, no. 2 (1969), pp. 171–81.

Keegan, Jay J. "Alterations of the Lumbar Curve Related to Posture and Seating." *Journal of Bone and Joint Surgery* 35A, no. 3 (July 1953), pp. 589–603.

Kira, Alexander. *The Bathroom.* New York: Viking, 1976.

Kirk, N. S., et al. "Discrimination of Chair Seat Heights." *Ergonomics* 12, no. 3 (1969), pp. 403–13.

Kleeman, Walter, and Thomas Prunier. "Evaluation of Chairs Used by Air Traffic Controllers of the U.S. Federal Aviation Administration—Implications for Design." In *Anthropometry and Biomechanics, Theory and Applications,* Easterby, Kroemer, and Chaffin, eds. New York: Plenum Press, 1982, pp. 236–39.

Kroemer, K. H., Dr. Ing Eberhard, and Joan C. Robinette. "Ergonomics in the Design of Office Furniture: A Review of European Literature." Wright-Patterson Airforce Base, OH: Aerospace Medical Research Laboratories (July 1968), pp. 1–25.

Laubli, T., W. Hunting, and E. Grandjean. "Postural and Visual Loads at VDT Workplaces: II. Lighting Conditions and Visual Impairments." *Ergonomics* 24, no. 12 (1981), pp. 933–44.

Laville, A. "Postural Stress in High-Speed Precision Work." *Ergonomics* 28, no. 1 (1985), pp. 229–36.

Lay, W. E., and L. C. Fisher. "Riding Comfort and Cushions." *Society of Automotive Engineers Journal (Transactions)* 47, no. 5 (1940), pp. 482–96.

Learner, David B., and Robert A. Wachsler. "An Analysis of Some Factors Influencing Seat Comfort." *Ergonomics* 3, no. 1 (1960), pp. 315–20.

Le Carpentier, E. F. "Easy Chair Dimensions for Comfort: A Subjective Approach." *Proceedings of the Symposium on Sitting Posture.* London: Taylor & Francis, 1969, pp. 214–23.

Lewin, T. "Anthropometric Studies on Swedish Industrial Workers When Standing and Sitting." *Ergonomics* 12, no. 6 (1969), pp. 883–902.

Link, C. S., et al. "Lumbar Curvature in Standing and Sitting in Two Types of Chairs: Relationship of Hamstring and Hip Flexor Muscle Length." *Physical Therapy* 70, no. 10 (October 1970), pp. 611–18.

Lippert, Stanley. "Designing for Comfort in Aircraft Seats." *Aeronautical Engineering Review* 9, no. 2 (1950), pp. 39–41.

Love, William S., and Vincent P. Houser. "Brief Communication: A Simple Method for Measuring Spontaneous Motor Activity in Squirrel Monkeys During Chair Restraint." *Physiology and Behavior* 10 (1973), pp. 1115–17.

Lueder, Rani Karen. "Seat Comfort: A Review of the Construct in the Office Environment." *Human Factors* 25, no. 6 (December 1983), pp. 701–11.

———. *The Ergonomics Payoff.* Toronto: Holt, Rinehart & Winston, 1986.

Mandal, A. C. "The Seated Man (Homo Sedens), the Seated Work Position: Theory and Practice," *Applied Ergonomics* (March 1981), pp. 19–26.

———. "The Correct Height of School Furniture." *Human Factors* 24, no. 3 (June 1982), pp. 257–69.

———. *The Sitting Position, Its Anatomy and Problems.* Klampenborg, Denmark: Daphne Publishing, ca. 1984.

———. "Balanced Seating." *Interior Design* 58, no. 15 (December 1987), pp. 178–79.

———. "Investigation of the Lumbar Flexion of the Seated Man." *International Journal of Industrial Ergonomics* 8 (1991), pp. 75–87.

———. "Changing Standards for School Furniture." *Ergonomics in Design* 5, no. 2 (April 1997), pp. 28–31.

Marschall, M., A. C. Harrington, and J. R. Steele. "Effect of Work Station Design on Sitting Posture in Young Children." *Ergonomics* 38, no. 9 (1995), pp. 1932–40.

Maruyama, Magoroh. "Designing a Space Community." *The Futurist* (October 1976), pp. 273–81.

Mays, Vernon. "The Ultimate Office Chair." *Progressive Architecture* (May 1988), pp. 98–105.

McCormick, Ernest J. "Applied Anthropometry and Work Space." Chap. 10 in *Human Factors in Engineering and Design.* New York: McGraw-Hill, 1976.

Monod, Hugues. "Contractility of Muscle During Prolonged Static and Repetitive Dynamic Activity." *Ergonomics* 28, no. 1 (1985), pp. 81–85.

Munton, J. S. "An Overview of Research on Seating." *Engineering in Medicine* 11, no. 3 (1982), pp. 107–10.

Murrell, K. F. H. *Ergonomics: Man in his Working Environment.* London: Chapman & Hall, 1969.

Nachemson, Alf, and G. Elfstrom. "Intravital Dynamic Pressure Measurements in Lumbar Discs." *Scandinavian Journal of Rehabilitative Medicine,* supplement no. 1 (1970), pp. 1–40.

Nordby, Eugene J. "Epidemiology and Diagnosis in Low Back Pain Injury." *Occupational Health and Safety* (January 1981), pp. 38–42.

Oborne, D. J. *Ergonomics at Work.* New York: John Wiley, 1982.

Oborne, D. J., and Levis, J. A., eds. *Human Factors in Transport Research,* vol. 2: *User Factors: Comfort, the Environment and Behaviour.* New York: Academic Press, 1980.

Occupational Health and Safety. "Sitting Down on the Job: Not as Easy as It Sounds." October 1981, pp. 24–26.

Orenstein, Susan R., Peter F. Whitington, and David M. Orenstein. "The Infant Seat As Treatment for Gastroesphageal Reflux." *New England Journal of Medicine* 309, no. 13 (1983), pp. 760–63.

Overstall, P. W., et al. "Falls in the Elderly Related to Postural Imbalance." *British Medical Journal* 1 (1977), pp. 261–64.

Oxford, H. W. "Anthropometric Data for Educational Chairs." *Ergonomics* 12, no. 2 (1969), pp. 140–61.

Perini, Renza, et al. "Body Position Affects the Power Spectrum of Heart Rate Variability During Dynamic Exercise." *European Journal of Applied Physiology* 66 (1993), pp. 207–13.

Pheasant, Stephen. *Bodyspace: Anthropometry, Ergonomics and Design.* New York: Taylor & Francis, 1988.

Pope, M. H., et al. "The Relationship Between Anthropometric, Postural, Muscular, and Mobility Characteristics of Males Ages 18–55." *Spine* 10, no. 7 (1985), pp. 644–48.

Pottier, M., A. Dubreuil, and H. Mondo. "The Effects of Sitting Posture on the Volume of the Foot." *Ergonomics* 12, no. 5 (1969), pp. 753–58.

Progressive Architecture. "Panel Discussion." May 1982, pp. 190–95.

Rebiffe, R. "General Reflections on the Postural Comfort of the Driver and Passengers; Consequences on Seat Design." In *Human Factors in Transport Research,* Oborne and Levis, eds., vol. 2: *User Factors: Comfort, the Environment and Behaviour.* New York: Academic Press, 1980, pp. 240–48.

Reed, Matthew P., et al. "An Investigation of Driver Discomfort and Related Seat Design Factors in Extended-Duration Driving." *SAE International,* International Congress and Exposition, Detroit, MI (Feb. 25–March 1, 1991).

Reisbord, Lesley S., and Sander Greenland. "Factors Associated with Self-Reported Back-Pain Prevalence: A Population-Based Study." *Journal of Chronic Diseases* 38, no. 8 (1985), pp. 691–702.

Research Institute for Consumer Affairs. *The Disabled User.* London: National Fund for Research in Crippling Diseases, July 1970, pp. 1–9.

Roberts, D. F. "Industrial Applications of Body Measurements." *American Anthropologist* 58, no. 3 (1950), pp. 526–35.

Schoberth, Von H. "Die Wirbelsaule von Schulkindern-Orthopadisclie Forderungen an Scholsitze," *Ergonomics* 12, no. 2 (1969), pp. 212–25.

Seki, Kunihiro, and Maurice Hugon. "Fatigue Subjective et Degradations de Performance en Environnement Hyperbare a Saturation." *Ergonomics* 20, no. 2 (1977), pp. 103–19.

Shackel, B., K. D. Chidsey, and Pat Shipley. "The Assessment of Chair Comfort." *Ergonomics* 12, no. 2 (1969), pp. 269–306.

Sjoflot, L. "Means of Improving a Tractor Driver's Working Posture." *Ergonomics* 23, no. 8 (1980), pp. 751–61.

Snook, Stover H. "The Design of Manual Handling Tasks." *Ergonomics* 21, no. 12 (1978), pp. 963–85.

Starr, Steven J., et al. "Effects of Video Display Terminals on Telephone Operators." *Human Factors* 24, no. 6 (1982), pp. 699–711.

———. "Relating Posture to Discomfort in VDT Use." *Journal of Occupational Medicine* 27, no. 4 (April 1985), pp. 269–71.

Stewart, Peter, et al. "A Randomized Trial to Evaluate the Use of a Birth Chair for Delivery." *The Lancet,* June 11, 1983, pp. 1296–98.

Sundstrom, Eric, and Mary Grahl Sundstrom. *Work Places: The Psychology of the Physical Environment in Offices and Factories.* Cambridge, UK: Cambridge University Press, 1986.

Svenson, H. O. "Low Back Pain in 40–47 Year Olds: Retrospective Cross Sectional Study." *Scandinavian Journal of Rehabilitation Medicine* 14 (1982), pp. 55–60.

Thorstensson, Alf, and Ake Arvidson. "Trunk Muscle Strength and Low Back Pain." *Scandinavian Journal of Rehabilitation Medicine* 14 (1982), pp. 69–75.

Tichauer, E. R. *The Biomechanical Basis of Ergonomics: Anatomy Applied to the Design of Work Situations.* New York: John Wiley, 1978.

Troup, J. D. G., J. W. Martin, and D. Lloyd. "Back Pain in Industry: A Prospective Survey." *Spine* 6, no. 1 (1982), pp. 61–69.

Troussier, B., et al. "Back Pain in Schoolchildren: A Study among 1178 Pupils." *Scandinavian Journal of Rehabilitation Medicine* 20 (1988), pp. 175–79.

Ubert, Verla. "Tilted Chairs and Desks Protect the Back." Letter to the editor, *New York Times,* Nov. 3, 1991.

United States Department of Labor Occupational Safety and Health Administration. *Ergonomics: The Study of Work.* Washington, DC: U.S. Government Printing Office, 1991.

Viladas, Pilar. "The Risk Factor." *Progressive Architecture* (May 1988), pp. 74–81.

Vollowitz, Eileen. "Furniture Prescription for the Conservative Management of Low-Back Pain." *Topics in Acute Care Trauma Rehabilitation* 2, no. 4 (1988), pp. 18–37.

Vos, H. W. "Physical Workload in Different Body Postures, While Working Near to, or Below Ground Level." *Ergonomics* 16, no. 6 (1973), pp. 817–28.

Weddell, G., and H. D. Darcus. "Some Anatomical Problems in Naval Warfare." *British Journal of Industrial Medicine* 4, no. 2 (1947), pp. 77–83.

Wiesel, Sam W., Henry L. Feffer, and Richard H. Rothman. "The Development of a Cervical Spine Algorithm and Its Prospective Application to Industrial Patients." *Journal of Occupational Medicine* 27, no. 4 (1985), pp. 272–76.

Wineman, Jean D. "Office Design and Evaluation: An Overview." *Environment and Behaviour* 14, no. 3 (1982), pp. 271–98.

Winkel, Jorgen, and Tom Bendix. "Muscular Performance During Seated Work Evaluated by Two Different EMG Methods." *European Journal of Applied Physiology* 55 (1986), pp. 167–73.

Woodson, Wesley E. *Human Factors Design Handbook.* New York: McGraw-Hill, 1981.

Wotzka, G., et al. "Investigations for the Development of an Auditorium Seat." *Ergonomics* 12, no. 2 (1969), pp. 182–97.

Yeaple, Frank, ed. "Engineered Chair Shell Flexes Independently Down, Back and Sideways." *Design News,* Oct. 17, 1984, pp. 124–26.

Zacharkow, Dennis. *Posture: Sitting, Standing, Chair Design and Exercise.* Springfield, IL: Charles C. Thomas, 1988.

Zimmerman, C., T. Cook, and V. K. Goel. "Effects of Seated Posture on Erector Spinae EMG Activity During Whole Body Vibration." *Ergonomics* 36, no. 6 (1993), pp. 667–75.

Index

Page numbers in *italics* refer to illustrations.